Lot Auereturials

OP 15⁰⁰

The Life and Times

of

Frédérick Lemaître

FRÉDÉRIC LEMAÎTRE.

FRÉDÉRICK LEMAÎTRE
Lithograph by Léon Noël

The Life and Times

of

Frédérick Lemaître

BY

ROBERT BALDICK

1959

ESSENTIAL BOOKS

FAIR LAWN, NEW JERSEY

Essential Books is an imprint of
Oxford University Press, Inc.
© 1959 *by Robert Baldick*

PRINTED IN GREAT BRITAIN BY
WESTERN PRINTING SERVICES LTD BRISTOL

ACKNOWLEDGEMENTS

I HAVE to acknowledge the gracious permission of Her Majesty the Queen to use material from the Royal Library at Windsor Castle.

I must also thank Sir Owen Morshead, the Librarian at Windsor Castle, Mr. A. H. Scott Elliot, the Keeper of Prints and Drawings at Windsor Castle, M. Le Quenu, the Deputy Mayor of Le Havre, and the Librarians and staffs of the Bibliothèque Nationale, the Bibliothèque de l'Arsenal, the Paris Prefecture of Police, the Bodleian Library, and the Library of the Taylor Institution at Oxford, for the courteous assistance they have given me. I am especially grateful to Mlle Monval of the Fonds Rondel at the Arsenal, and M. Marcel Thomas of the Cabinet des Manuscrits at the Bibliothèque Nationale, for their indefatigable and friendly co-operation. I wish to record my gratitude to the Sir Ernest Cassel Trust for a grant in aid of my research. For advice, information, books and documents, I am indebted to Miss Phyllis Hartnoll, Miss Janet Seligman, M. Francis Ambrière, Mr. Maurice Willson Disher, M. Pierre Lambert, M. Henry Lefai, M. Roger Lhombreaud, M. Bernard Loliée, Mr. W. Macqueen-Pope, Mr. Philip John Stead and Mr. J. C. Trewin. My wife, as always, has given me valuable help and encouragement, for which I am deeply grateful.

My greatest debt of gratitude is to the late Henry Lecomte, whose monumental Life of Frédérick Lemaître, published seventy years ago, has been of inestimable help to me; to M. Pierre Brasseur, whose magnificent performance in the Carné film *Les Enfants du Paradis* first aroused my interest in Frédérick; and to Mme Jeanne Sully, the gracious and brilliant daughter of the great Mounet-Sully, who has so often granted me the privilege and pleasure of consulting her collection and discussing this biography with her in her home on the Ile Saint-Louis. To these three fellow admirers of a very great actor this book is humbly and gratefully dedicated.

Oxford   R.B.
June 1958

CONTENTS

		page
Acknowledgements		7
1.	THE YOUNG LION	13
2.	PANTOMIME AND TRAGEDY	23
3.	THE BOULEVARD DU CRIME	36
4.	MARIE DORVAL	48
5.	ROMANTIC VICTORY	62
6.	THE JULY REVOLUTION	75
7.	MADEMOISELLE GEORGE	85
8.	CARNIVAL, PLAGUE AND RIOT	98
9.	LUCRÈCE BORGIA	113
10.	ROBERT MACAIRE	129
11.	THE FRENCH KEAN	145
12.	RUY BLAS	161
13.	BALZAC	174
14.	TO ENGLAND	184
15.	ROMANTIC DECLINE	196
16.	DEATH OF THE BOULEVARD	210
17.	THE OLD LION	224
18.	LAST YEARS	234
	CONCLUSION	243
	Bibliography	249
	Notes	253
	Index	273

ILLUSTRATIONS

FRÉDÉRICK LEMAÎTRE   *frontispiece*
From the lithograph by Léon Noël in the Author's
Collection

                                                      facing page

MARIE DORVAL   128
From a lithograph

FRÉDÉRICK AS ROBERT MACAIRE   129
From the lithograph by Langlumé in the Author's
Collection

BALZAC, FRÉDÉRICK AND GAUTIER AT
PIERREFITTE   176
From the water-colour by Gautier

CLARISSE MIROY IN *La Grâce de Dieu*   177
From a lithograph in the Bibliothèque de l'Arsenal

FRÉDÉRICK IN 1846   208
From the bust by Bonnassieu in the Author's Collection

QUEEN VICTORIA'S PROGRAMME FOR
Ruy Blas   209
In the Royal Library, Windsor Castle

FRÉDÉRICK CARICATURED BY GILL   224
From a copy of 'La Lune' in the Author's Collection

FRÉDÉRICK IN OLD AGE   225
From a photograph taken at his home

CHAPTER ONE

THE YOUNG LION

FRÉDÉRICK LEMAÎTRE!

The name echoes grandly down the years, losing nothing of
its magic on the way, nothing of its glory, above all nothing of
its evocative power. It calls to mind a picture of a theatrical
giant rousing Parisian audiences to frenzy with rampageous,
volcanic performances that would have crippled a score of lesser
men, and holding them breathless with those awesome silences
that are the prerogative of the great actor. Or it summons up a
vision of an impressive figure swaggering a little unsteadily
along a sunlit boulevard in the eighteen-thirties, a cigar in his
mouth and a top-hat cocked rakishly on his head, tossing a
flower to some woman and a jest to some man, throwing a
beggar a handful of coins and shooting a stream of spittle at the
cup of liquorice-water a vendor teasingly offers him. This was
the Frédérick that the public saw on and off the stage; but the
flamboyant behaviour and the superb artistry concealed from
them a tragic figure whose tragedy was essentially that of his
age—a tragedy of blighted ideals, thwarted passions and disappointed hopes. The actor, the legend, the man and the epoch
are intimately and inextricably united.

Frédérick was a child of his century in fact as well as in spirit:
not only did he exemplify better than any other man the fire and
passion and heartbreak of the Romantic era, but unlike that self-
styled *enfant du siècle*, Alfred de Musset, he was actually born
with the nineteenth century, in 1800.

In June that year Bonaparte turned defeat into victory at

Marengo, in a decisive battle which consolidated his position as First Consul and ensured the collapse of the Second Coalition. It was in the midst of general jubilation over this victory and the brighter prospect of peace that Frédérick came into the world, at midday on 28 July, in his parents' home in the Rue de la Gaffe at Le Havre. The next day he was taken to the sixteenth-century church of Notre-Dame to be baptized, and on 30 July (or 11 Thermidor Year VIII of the French Republic) his birth was registered at the Town Hall. The ecclesiastical and civil records [1] differ in the form of dating, but they agree on one point: the child's name is given in both as Antoine-Louis-Prosper Lemaître. Only at the start of his acting career did he call himself Frédérick, taking the name from his maternal grandfather.

Little is known of this man, Frédérick-Charles Mehrscheidt, save that he was a native of Rudesheim and before the Revolution had progressed by way of various regimental bands to the post of music-master at the Royal Military College of Beaumont-en-Auge.[2] His younger daughter, Victor-Sophie, was married at the age of seventeen, in the autumn of 1794, to a twenty-six-year-old architect from Paris called Antoine-Marie Lemaître.[3] Within a few years her husband had established a solid reputation at Le Havre, where he had been appointed Principal of the free school of drawing and architecture. But the respectful awe in which he was held by his fellow-citizens was not entirely due to his official position: it owed much to his herculean frame and his violent temper. At home he exercised a patriarchal despotism, and it was with mingled irritation and satisfaction that he discovered in his son Prosper a fiery spirit similar to his own.

'Poulot is coming along nicely,' he told his brother-in-law[4] when the boy was three; 'but he has begun showing a stubborn streak and will have to be broken in. However, he continues to be a joy to us both, and that means a great deal to me.'

Prosper soon found that the best means of turning away his father's wrath was to offer to recite some verse.[5] Instantly mollified, M. Lemaître would then drape his son in a curtain or a napkin, put a paper crown on his head and a wooden dagger in his hand, and ask him to declaim a tirade from a favourite tragedy. The fervent passion the boy put into these performances delighted him, and he boasted of it to his friends—only to be asked by some pessimist what he would do if Prosper took a fancy to the theatre.

'I should put no obstacle in the way of his vocation', he replied. 'My late father always used to tell me that the third generation of our family would produce a great artist. Who knows? Perhaps one day Prosper will be a famous tragedian!'

His friends marvelled at such tolerance, failing to realize that Antoine Lemaître was talking of a hypothetical situation he felt sure would never arise. In fact, he intended his son to become an engineer; and if he had lived to see the boy hankering after the stage, he would almost certainly have placed every conceivable obstacle in his way.

Meanwhile, Prosper's childhood pursued its humdrum course, the passage of time marked only by an odd succession of private and public events. Thus in 1802 the First Consul paid an official visit to Le Havre, and there was great excitement in the Lemaître home, for the Principal of the School of Drawing was one of the officials presented to the great man. The next year Grandfather Mehrscheidt died, and his widow made arrangements to go to Paris, where she was to live with her elder daughter and her husband, a decorator called Coussin.[6] Prosper heard the grown-ups saying that war had broken out again, but everyone agreed that the First Consul—soon to crown himself Emperor—would find it a simple matter to defeat the treacherous English, and life in the meantime seemed to go on much as usual.

In 1804, however, the war was suddenly brought home to the people of Le Havre as never before. The port was being used as a temporary depot for vessels of Napoleon's invasion flotilla built inland and towed down the Seine before being convoyed to the great entrepôt at Boulogne. In July a British squadron

consisting chiefly of sloops and bombs, under the command of
Captain Robert Dudley Oliver in the 38-gun frigate *Melpomene*,
arrived off Le Havre to block and harass the port. On the 23rd
they bombarded the town, setting it on fire and forcing several
of the French boats to retire up the river, and on 1 August
another equally effective attack was made.[7] The mortars on
both occasions were trained on the spire of Notre-Dame, in
the centre of Le Havre, so that several bomb-shells fell in the
nearby Rue de la Gaffe. All his life, Frédérick Lemaître remembered how his father's pupils had fled from the house, and how
his mother had picked him up in her arms and carried him into
the vaults of the Eure citadel, where the townspeople had
waited for the tide to go out and take the British warships with
it.[8]

The war hit Le Havre again a year later, for the winter of
1805 brought the news that many local men had lost their lives
in the disastrous encounter with Nelson and Collingwood off
Cape Trafalgar. But the plaints of widows and orphans were
soon drowned by the sound of bellringing and Te Deums to celebrate a whole sequence of victories at the other end of Europe:
Ulm, Austerlitz, Jena, Auerstadt, Friedland.

Year by year the death-roll mounted, but Napoleon was now
the master of Europe, his armies appeared to be invincible, and
for a French boy whose family was unscathed by war these must
have been wonderfully exciting days. Prosper savoured this
excitement to the full, as well as more personal pleasures —
such as playing truant to go to the Michaelmas Fair, or climb-
ing the heights of Sainte-Adresse with his father to be shown the
glories of the sunset.[9]

Then, in 1809, Antoine Lemaître died — not at the enemy's
hands, but as the result of a grotesque accident. It seems that
he had some responsibility for the maintenance of the local
theatre, and that one morning he was inspecting the stage when
he stepped backwards and fell through an open trap-door. One
of his legs was badly hurt, and after a few days a tumour
appeared behind the knee. His doctor wanted to apply a blister

to the swelling, but Lemaître had a poor opinion of the medical profession and refused to undergo any sort of treatment. Whether the proposed remedy would have done any good is a matter of opinion; as it was, the recalcitrant patient died some weeks later, at six o'clock in the evening of 15 June 1809.[10]

His widow was left utterly destitute, and was forced to appeal for help to the Mayor of Le Havre, Guillaume-Antoine Sery.[11] In a pathetically misspelt letter she explained that she had had to pawn some of her most necessary belongings in order to give her husband decent burial. Sery, whom she described as 'the father of the unfortunate', had already given her some money, and she assured him that she would not trouble him again. True to her word, she left Le Havre shortly afterwards, taking her son to Paris to live with her mother, her sister and her long-suffering brother-in-law in their fourth-floor flat in the Rue Guénégaud.[12] The Coussins also helped to set her up in business as a furniture-dealer in the Rue du Caire, and one of her husband's friends, Admiral Hamelin, obtained a scholarship for Prosper as a day-boy at the Collège Sainte-Barbe.

Every morning the boy would tuck his arm through the handle of his little lunch-basket and set off for school with the very best of intentions. But the habit of truancy is one that is not easily broken, and Prosper found that Paris offered far more exciting distractions than the Michaelmas Fair at Le Havre. He and his mother had scarcely arrived in the capital before the whole city was celebrating the birth of a son to the Empress Marie-Louise, with bells, cannons, and free wine for all who cared to drink it. Even on ordinary days there were plenty of fascinating alternatives to schoolwork, and when Prosper and his friends were not frolicking in the streets they were visiting museums, playing billiards, or waiting outside the Tuileries to catch a glimpse of the Emperor, for whom they had an almost religious veneration.

Mme Lemaître did nothing to remedy this state of affairs for three years; but in 1814, losing patience with her truant son,

B

she took swift and sudden action to bring a little discipline into
his life. Admiral Hamelin was once more asked for help, this
time in a strictly professional capacity, with the result that
Prosper was packed off to Le Havre to join a slave-ship bound
for Guinea. When he left Paris he doubtless meant to go to
sea as instructed, just as he had always meant to go to school;
but in fact he got no further than Rouen. There he was so
impressed by a performance given by the actor Joanny, the so-
called 'Talma of the provinces', that he stayed to see more.
The problem of finance was solved when he won a considerable
sum of money at billiards, and he settled down to a pleasant
routine of theatre-going and café-crawling, spending his win-
nings with a carefree prodigality which would one day become
legendary. When at last his money ran out, he made his way
back to Paris by easy stages, arriving home on 20 March 1815,
the same day that Napoleon returned to his capital after his
escape from Elba.[13]

A great deal had happened in the past twelve months. Defeated in battle and abandoned by his Marshals, the Emperor
had been forced to abdicate his throne, and the Allies had
marched triumphantly into Paris. They were soon followed by
the fat, gouty Comte de Provence, or Louis XVIII as he styled
himself, who was foisted on to an apathetic people by the efforts
of Talleyrand. He was tolerant and intelligent, and he granted
his subjects a liberal-sounding Charter which did much to allay
fears of a revengeful reaction; but his followers, most of whom
had in truth 'forgotten nothing and learnt nothing', did not
inspire confidence. Small wonder then that, when news came of
the Emperor's return from exile, Louis fled to Ghent and Paris
began excitedly substituting Imperial bees for Royal lilies.

Prosper Lemaître shared in the general enthusiasm, and after
playing the prodigal son for no more than a single night he left
home again, this time to join the army. He was put on the
strength of the 2nd regiment of the line, then quartered at the
'Nouvelle-France' in the Faubourg Poissonnière, and given
two months' training. In the barracks he met several old soldiers

who had been prisoners of war in English hulks, and who spoke pessimistically of the Emperor's chances in the approaching campaign.[14] His own military ardour was rapidly cooling, and it was further chilled by the discovery that the campaign kit he was expected to carry across Europe on his back weighed over sixty pounds.

At last the day came when the regiment was given its marching orders. Bent under their heavy loads, Prosper and his comrades left the 'Nouvelle-France' early in the morning, with bands playing, drums beating, and the local citizens shouting: 'Vive l'Empereur!' As soon as they were outside Paris on the road to Saint-Denis they were allowed to march at ease—much to Prosper's relief, for his feet were already sore and bleeding. He eventually found himself limping along far behind the main body of troops, and when the ambulance waggons caught up with him he begged a lift from one of the drivers. At this point, however, an officer rode up and asked what he was doing. When Prosper showed him his feet and explained that he was in considerable pain, he snorted with contempt and ordered the boy to rejoin his platoon. In his unpublished memoirs Lemaître calls this officer a 'stupid brute', but he admits that the man may well have saved him from death on the battlefield at Waterloo—for the young soldier, outraged by this cruel lack of sympathy, decided that army life was not for him, hid in a ditch until the regiment was just a cloud of dust on the horizon, and then returned home under cover of darkness.

His mother was appalled by what he had done, and convinced that he would be arrested and shot as a deserter. He pointed out that he was only fifteen, and that in any event he was unlikely to be missed. However, to reassure her, he presented himself at the regimental barracks the following morning and explained to an incredulous sergeant-major that he had fainted from pain while resting by the roadside and had not recovered consciousness till late at night. He was promptly locked in a cell where he spent three weeks on a diet of black bread and water, with his jailer cheerfully prophesying a court-martial every day. At last he was taken before the sergeant-major, who slapped him on the back and apologized for not considering his case before; the army, he explained, had been routed at Waterloo, the defeated troops were straggling back to Paris, and in the general confusion he had completely forgotten about his prisoner.

'You could probably do with some fresh air', he added face-tiously. 'Look, there are some of our men working on the forti-fications of the Buttes-Chaumont. Go and take them their soup.'

Rejoicing in his unexpected freedom, Prosper balanced the pot of soup on his head and sallied forth. But before he had gone very far he discovered that the pot was leaking, and care-fully put it down. At once a delicious smell invaded his nostrils. He had had nothing but bread and water for three weeks, and the temptation was too strong for him: within a few minutes there were a dozen rations of soup inside him and the pot was empty. Then, foreseeing a further period of detention if he returned to barracks after this fresh offence, he threw away his uniform and went home to his mother.[15]

A week later his sometime regiment was disbanded and the Allies marched yet again into Paris. Prosper perched for hours on the wall of the Bonne-Nouvelle Cemetery, where the Théâtre du Gymnase stands today, watching them go by with bitterness in his heart.[16] Paris received them with silence, and there was little cheering when Louis XVIII followed ignominiously in their train. It was abundantly clear to everyone, and not least to the King, that Paris did not want him, that he ruled only by virtue of foreign arms, and that the Hundred Days had left his resentful, humiliated people more deeply divided than ever before.

The political upheavals of the past two years had been bad for business, and Mme Lemaître had been obliged to give up her furniture shop to become a humble concierge at No. 47 Rue du Faubourg Saint-Denis, where she now lived with her mother and her son. Prosper did all the heavy work, and also ran errands for a local notary. Finding this job tiring and un-profitable, he left it to work in a shop specializing in colonial produce. He threw up this job too, once he had obtained suffi-cient experience of the trade, and proceeded to set up in business on his own account, laying in a stock of dried fruit in his attic bedroom and selling them at a profit to local shopkeepers. This new enterprise proved extremely lucrative, the more so as Prosper insisted on prompt payment by his customers but showed a marked reluctance to settle his wholesalers' accounts. The inevitable result was that soon nobody in the dried-fruit trade would give him credit, and he was forced to look around for some other outlet for his talents.[17]

It was then that an acrobat with whom he had recently struck up acquaintance suggested that he should go on the stage. The idea appealed to him, recalling pleasant memories of his child-hood recitations and of Joanny's performances at Rouen, as well as opening up a prospect of fame and fortune. However, he sus-pected that his mother would not see the matter in quite the same light, and so he decided to keep his plans from her. There remained the problem of finding a theatre which would take him on. His first choice was modest and realistic, for he applied to the manager of the smallest theatre in Paris, the Variétés-Amusantes, an establishment on the Boulevard du Temple which in spite of its name preferred heroic pantomime to farce.[18]

The manager, a little old man with a keen eye for youthful talent, was obviously impressed by Prosper's physique and apparently undeterred by his lack of experience. He offered the boy a place in his company at thirty francs a month—an offer which was promptly accepted—and told him he would start work in two days' time.

'But what about my part?' asked Prosper.

'That won't be hard to learn', replied the manager. 'You look as if you've got a fine pair of lungs: let's hear what you can do with them. Bawl away!'

Anxious to make a good impression on his new employer, Prosper gave a stentorian bellow that made the windows rattle.

The manager beamed approval. That, he said, was just what the part required.

Two days later, the Variétés-Amusantes put on a dialogued pantomime for three characters entitled *Pyrame et Thisbé*. When the curtain went up only two characters were revealed, and these, the ill-starred lovers of the title, acted out the legendary romance, exchanging their vows in secret and promising to meet outside the city walls of Babylon. As in the legend, of course, they never met, for Thisbe, arriving first at the appointed place, was frightened away by a blood-curdling roar and the entry of the third character.

This was none other than Prosper Lemaître, perhaps the greatest actor of modern times, making his début on all fours, dressed as a lion.

CHAPTER TWO

PANTOMIME AND TRAGEDY

THE Boulevard du Temple, where Prosper was now employed and where he was to spend a good part of his life, owed its name to the Templars, who had been associated with the district until the suppression of their Order in the fourteenth century.[1] Planted with trees in the seventeenth century and paved a hundred years later, it gradually became a favourite resort of all classes of Parisian society. The crowds inevitably attracted street-hawkers of every kind, peddling cakes, cocoa and barley-sugar, as well as showmen looking for suitable sites. The first to set up a booth on the Boulevard was a certain Gaudon, and he was followed by an acrobat called Nicolet who established the first building in the district which merited the name of theatre. Like his great rival Audinot, the puppeteer, he eventually introduced actors into his troupe and dialogue into his shows, and this example was followed by other booth-keepers. When the theatres were given their freedom in 1791 a crop of new play-houses sprang up along the Boulevard du Temple, but many of these had only a brief life-span, and twenty-five of the survivors were swept away by the savage Imperial decree of 1807. The Restoration might be synonymous with reaction and stagnation in some walks of life, but to the Boulevard it brought fresh hope and new activity.

All the theatres and most of the cafés and booths were to be found on the left-hand side of the Boulevard, coming from the Porte Saint-Martin. Among the theatres which were active in 1816 were the Gaîté and the Ambigu-Comique, founded by

Nicolet and Audinot respectively; the little Variétés-Amusantes; the Funambules, set up in 1813 by two tradesmen called Bertrand and Fabien in place of a performing-dog show; and a café-theatre known as the Bosquet. This last establishment was run by the famous tight-rope dancer Mme Saqui, who had won Napoleon's applause and admiration, and who in 1861, at the age of seventy-five, would cross the Hippodrome of the Porte Dauphine on a cord more than forty feet from the ground.

Interspersed with the theatres were countless cafés and cabarets, notably the Café de l'Épi-Scié, a haunt of pimps and prostitutes, and the Café d'Apollon, where Mme Saqui was to install her troupe at the end of 1816 and henceforth compete or collaborate with her next-door neighbours, the Funambules, over a period of years. There was also a marionette show and no less than three waxwork exhibitions, of which the oldest and most popular was that established before the Revolution by the German Curtius. It was rumoured that out of laziness or ironic amusement he used the same wax figures all his life, changing only their costumes and labels as one régime gave place to another; whatever the truth of the matter, the public certainly showed greater loyalty to the effigies than they did to the originals, for they flocked to see the Curtius waxworks year after year, under monarchy, republic or empire, in peace, war or revolution.

On the opposite side of the Boulevard there were no theatres and only two cafés of note. The bigger and busier of the two was the Jardin Turc, which catered for the current vogue for things Oriental. A life-size figure of a Turk placidly smoking his pipe set the right note at the entrance, and in the spacious gardens the illusion was fostered by innumerable stained-glass kiosks, a promenade lined with sofas, and a little Chinese bridge. The young people of the district used to stroll up and down under the trees or flirt in the summer-houses, while their elders sat drinking and talking, and playing chess, draughts or back-gammon. Not far from the Jardin Turc a certain Bricard had set up a rival establishment with the no less Oriental name of

Paphos. But Paphos was never as attractive or as exclusive as the Jardin Turc, and one almanach[2] dismissed it with brutal frankness as 'a haunt of idle and criminal types, of depraved working-girls, and of women who are as ugly as they are importunate'.

The Boulevard was quiet and almost deserted in the morning, but soon after midday the crowds began to arrive and the booths opened up. Practically every known variety of fairground attraction was on view, from dwarfs and giants, strong men and wild women, to performing fleas, fire-eaters and tight-rope walkers. In the din created by trumpets, drums and raucous voices, pick-pockets went about their work among the innocents gaping in wonder at human skeletons, at men swallowing snakes, pebbles or forks, at children drinking boiling oil or walking on bars of red-hot iron. There were also showmen pandering to the craze for scientific novelties which had started in the eighteenth century, each with his electric machine, his telescope or his camera obscura. One little man, armed with a microscope, could always be heard offering, in return for a single sou, to make any insect, however small, look as big as his fist; un-fortunately for him, insects were more readily available in his audience than sous.

Soon after four o'clock the local bourgeois left their dinner-tables to install themselves on the raised terrace of the Café Turc, overlooking the whole Boulevard, where they would remain until eleven at night. Then crowds of people would begin to collect outside the theatres, shrieking, jostling, laugh-ing and fighting, with hawkers circling round them, ringing their hand-bells and shouting their wares, from lorgnettes to lemo-nade, from apple turnovers to cut-price tickets. At six o'clock the theatres opened their doors and the crowds disappeared, only to emerge at every interval, when they were greeted by the hawkers with more shouting and bell-ringing. And so it would go on until eleven o'clock or midnight, when the last theatre-goer and the last café-customer went home.

It need scarcely be said that the theatre audiences of the

Boulevard du Temple rarely included any representatives of the upper classes, who preferred to patronize the 'official' theatres: the Théâtre-Français on the Right Bank and the Odéon, or Second Théâtre-Français, on the other side of the Seine. These two theatres enjoyed much the same privileged position as London's Patent Houses—Drury Lane and Covent Garden in winter and the Haymarket in summer—in that they had a monopoly of legitimate drama. The other theatres were restricted to less exalted forms of entertainment, such as melodramas, ballets, pantomimes or equestrian acts, and detailed regulations laid down what type of show each theatre was authorized to present, how many people were allowed to be on the stage at a time, whether music or speech was permitted, and so on. Some of these regulations were absurd enough to have been devised by a present-day bureaucrat. Thus at the Funambules, which were licensed to present acrobatics and pantomime harlequinades, actors were required by law to do a somersault or walk a tight-rope when they made their entrances, while if the Théâtre Comte was allowed to stage spoken productions it was on condition that a gauze curtain obscured the audience's view. Managers were perpetually looking for ways of circumventing these regulations. Perhaps the most ingenious scheme was that operated at the Panorama Dramatique, where only two actors were permitted to appear on the stage; one of these changed his part and his costume every few minutes, while supernumerary characters were represented by life-size marionettes, whose lines were spoken from the wings.[3] The manager of another theatre appealed directly to the Comédie-Française against a ban on an advertised performance of Voltaire's *Zaire*, promising to make full reparation if two delegates appointed by the Théâtre-Français could recognize Voltaire's play as presented by his actors.[4] He won his point, but it was a hollow victory, and the Comédie-Française continued to watch for and guard against any possible infringement of their monopoly.

Strangely enough, it was to the Funambules, a theatre which, as we have seen, was more encumbered with restrictive regulations than most, that Prosper Lemaître migrated from the Variétés-Amusantes. At the latter theatre he had been given two human parts as well as his original animal role, and no acrobatics were required of him, but he was lured away by Bertrand's honeyed promises of fame and fifteen francs a week.[5]

The Funambules had another advantage over the Variétés-Amusantes in that they went to the trouble of billing the names of their actors outside the theatre. But this meant that Prosper had to chose a pseudonym, for he could not use the name Lemaître without the family's permission. Rejecting his own Christian name as too dull and pompous, he finally decided to call himself Frédérick, after his grandfather. It was a good choice for reasons of diplomacy as well as euphony, since it assured him of his grandmother's support if his theatrical activities should be discovered and criticized —as, in fact, they soon were.

One of the first parts which 'M. Frédérick' played at the Funambules was that of an apothecary in *La Naissance d'Arlequin*, a spectacular pantomime by Hapdé. To put the finishing touch to his costume, he secretly borrowed a pair of superb black silk stockings from his mother, who searched high and low for them without ever suspecting her son. But one day, as luck would have it, a friendly tenant gave Mme Mehrscheidt a complimentary ticket for the Funambules. There, to her astonishment, the old lady recognized her own grandson in one of the actors, and on his legs the missing stockings. It was too good a secret to keep, and so the next day she naïvely confided it to Mme Lemaître, with disastrous results.

Recalling the scene which followed his grandmother's revelation,[6] Frédérick told Henry Lecomte: 'That day, my mother cursed me.' This was scarcely a surprising reaction on her part, for social and religious prejudice against the theatrical profession was still very strong. Joanny had considered it necessary to adopt a stage-name to avoid bringing discredit on his bourgeois family; Talma had been forced to wait a year before his parish priest would marry him; and more recently, in January 1815, the curé of Saint-Roch had refused to allow the coffin of the actress Mlle Raucourt to enter his church.[7] Small wonder then that Mme Lemaître, who was a devout, respectable woman, was shocked to discover that her son had already entered on the same unholy career.

Luckily for Frédérick, he had a staunch ally in Widow Mehrscheidt, who doted on her grandson, approved of the pseudonym he had chosen, and regretted having been the unwitting cause of his present disgrace. She pleaded with her daughter on his behalf, and at last Mme Lemaître grudgingly gave her consent for Frédérick to remain on the stage.

That same year, 1816, the property boy at the Funambules told Bertrand that he had seen a troupe of acrobats training in the courtyard of a house in the Rue Saint-Maur, and that he considered them superior to Mme Saqui's. Without losing a moment, Bertrand hurried round to the Rue Saint-Maur, where he witnessed a magnificent display of tight-rope dancing and acrobatics given by the children of Philippe Deburau, an old soldier, showman and vagabond. Knowing that Mme Saqui would hire them if he did not, and appreciating the drawing-power of a foreign troupe—for if Philippe Deburau was French, most of the others had been born on Austrian soil—Bertrand engaged them over a couple of bottle of wine at the Cabinet des Gentilshommes. In his eagerness to obtain their services, he even took on the clumsiest member of the troupe, twenty-year-old Jean-Gaspard Deburau, 'into the bargain'. It was thus, almost as an afterthought, that the future mime entered the theatre he was to make famous, there to work beside a budding actor whose destiny would be very similar to his own.

For several months Jean-Gaspard was employed simply as a stage-hand, rolling out the carpet for his father's troupe, fixing the cross-bars, adjusting the tight-rope. Then, one evening, the chance of a lifetime came his way. Blanchard, one of the mimes, had been dismissed for misbehaving himself below-stage with

Mlle Virginie, Bertrand's niece; and his cronies had come to the Funambules in full force, to protest against the manager's action and to demand Blanchard's reinstatement. At first they carried the audience with them, but Fabien, Bertrand's associate, restored order by describing Blanchard's iniquities, and won the public over completely by announcing that a young artist in whom the management had the highest hopes was going to make his début as Pierrot. He gave this young artist, who was none other than Jean-Gaspard, the name of Baptiste, possibly out of a mischievous desire to confuse him in the public's mind with the mime Baptiste Lalanne, Mme Saqui's father. Blanchard's friends continued to call for their hero, but the rest of the audience wanted to see the new mime and eventually silenced them. Jean-Gaspard came on, a long-faced, long-legged figure, quite unlike any Pierrot the Funambules had seen before, and won instant success.[9]

So the legend goes. Jean-Gaspard's latest biographer, however, is sceptical about this early, unexpected transformation of the stage-hand into the mime; he believes that Deburau did not play Pierrot at the Funambules until 1825, long after Frédérick had left the little theatre.[10] The fact remains that when Deburau's wife died in October 1819, after three months of married life, his Christian names were entered on the death-certificate as Jean-Baptiste-Gaspard.[11] Frédérick's testimony on this point, given in his old age, is of dubious value, for the memories of old men are notoriously unreliable; but it is perhaps worth recording that in the unpublished notes for his autobiography he treats his own triumphs at the Funambules and Deburau's as roughly contemporary.[12] 'I successfully created a host of parts,' he writes, 'and Deburau and I were worshipped by the public.'

He goes on: 'The part of Comte Adolphe in the *Le Faux Ermite* crowned my reputation, and the truth is that I looked very handsome in the role. Bets were laid as to my sex: some maintained that I had none, but others were convinced that Nature had adequately endowed me.'

Apart from arousing speculations of this sort, Frédérick's performance in *Le Faux Ermite*, a spectacular pantomime in three acts presented for the first time in December 1816, had two important consequences: a member of the audience recommended him to the veteran actor Théodore Michelot, who admitted him to his classes at the Conservatoire, while the Franconi brothers, Laurent and Henri, offered him eighty francs a month to appear at the Cirque-Olympique, starting as soon as his contract with the Funambules expired.[13]

Bertrand was sorry to see him go, for he had a high opinion of the young man, even though he later took all the credit for the actor's success to himself. 'I trained Frédérick Lemaître,' he was to boast in after years; 'and I would have made an even better actor of him if he had stayed with me longer.' Frédérick was naturally unwilling to concede this extravagant claim, but he readily admitted that his mastery of gesture and facial expression was acquired in the fourteen months he spent at the Funambules.[14] 'I learnt a great deal there,' he used to say; 'and it has always astonished me that the Conservatoire should have no classes in pantomime.'

The Cirque-Olympique, where he took up his engagement in January 1818, had been founded before the Revolution by the Englishman Philip Astley, whose London circus was immortalized by Dickens. Bought by Antonio Franconi during the Terror, and later handed down to his sons, the establishment had moved from one part of Paris to another, before returning in 1817 to the site of Astley's original circus in the Boulevard du Temple. In the meantime the shows put on by the Cirque-Olympique had changed in character: equestrian performances still formed the main attraction, but the horses were now joined by other animals such as the stag Coco, while the circus acts were themselves interspersed with melodramas.[15]

Acting in these plays, Frédérick gained new assurance and experience. Thus as the Duke of Moravia in *L'Ours et l'Enfant*, he played an old man for the first time, putting over the illusion with considerable success in view of his nineteen years. In

Le More de Venise, a somewhat crude adaptation of *Othello* by a M. Cuvelier, he made his first contact with Shakespeare, though admittedly at second hand and not in his own part—a gondolier called Mallorno invented by Cuvelier to support Iago. And in *La Mort de Kléber*, as a villainous Moslem, he gave the first recorded demonstration of his remarkable presence of mind: realizing that the right-hand side of his beard had come away, he raised his left hand in an emphatic gesture, snatched off the rest of the beard, and hid it in the folds of his burnous.[16]

Meanwhile he was diligently attending the classes at the Conservatoire, where Lafon, who had succeeded Michelot, claimed to have discovered in him a natural aptitude for tragic acting. The time to test it came at the end of 1819, when the Odéon invited applications from candidates for the honour of entering the Second Théâtre-Français. On Lafon's advice, Frédérick submitted himself for examination. Perhaps he chose his piece badly; more probably he recited it with greater gusto than finesse. In any event, the examiners turned down his application, only one of the nine members of the committee voting in his favour. But that one, significantly enough, was Talma.[17]

It was not really surprising that Napoleon's favourite tragedian should have cast his vote for the fiery nineteen-year-old, for they were essentially kindred spirits. Throughout his career François-Joseph Talma had been a theatrical revolutionary, tilting at tradition and convention in the interests of greater realism and stronger impact. He had persuaded his fellow actors to abandon the knee-breeches and powdered wigs they usually wore for Greek or Roman parts, in favour of historically accurate costumes. He had tried, with less success, to encourage a simpler delivery and a more natural stance in place of the pompous declamation and stiff attitudinizing which were current in the legitimate theatre. He had preached and practised the art of miming, vaunted the merits of Shakespeare's tragedies, and shown a marked preference for violent, passionate parts which offended against all the canons of theatrical good taste. In

Frédérick he may well have recognized an actor of similar temperament and beliefs, who was also young and vigorous enough to continue his work and put into effect the reforms he had instituted. The adverse vote certainly stung him into administering a sharp rebuke to his fellow examiners.

'You were wrong', he told them, 'to reject that young man, for he possesses qualities which cannot be acquired: beauty, intelligence, the sacred fire. . . . By spurning him, you are condemning him to fall back on melodrama and farce.'

Frédérick, however, was not so easily discouraged, and in June 1820 he appeared once more before the Odéon committee. This time, either because his delivery had improved or because Talma's words had borne fruit, he was accepted; and a contract was signed assuring him of 125 francs a month until the following April. He lost no time in telling Lafon and the elder Franconi of his success. Both men were sincerely pleased for his sake and warmly congratulated him; both added characteristic and prophetic comments.[18]

'Bravo, my boy!' said his old teacher. 'You have your foot in the stirrup now. Go ahead, and remember that there are no limits to what a pupil of Lafon's can achieve.'

'There is a great deal to be said for the popular theatres,' Franconi remarked; 'and one day, my dear Frédérick, you may be glad to come back to them.'

At the time this doubtless struck Frédérick as highly improbable. He had won a place in one of the most exclusive of theatres, and there seemed to be no reason why he should not aspire to a permanent position in the company.

Unfortunately for his ambitions, the Odéon management gave him little opportunity to display his talents.[19] Week after week he was allotted the smallest parts in the repertory, as a confidant, a guard or a valet, reciting a few lines of Racine, Molière, Voltaire, or some uninspiring contemporary author. As he stood stiffly before the small, unresponsive audience, delivering his trite little speeches in the approved monotone, he began to hanker after the movement and passion which were to be found on both sides of the footlights in the theatres of the Boulevard du Temple.

The Press, too, gave him little encouragement, for there was only one theatre critic of note in Paris, and he was anything but well disposed towards Frédérick. His name was Charles Maurice, and he concealed a mean, spiteful nature beneath a bland exterior and an unctuous manner. Tears came easily to his eyes, and callers generally found him dandling one of his children on his knee; but on his writing-table, displayed with suitably theatrical effect between his snuff-box and his wife's knitting, there was a foil with the button off.[20] The arrangement was symbolical. Any actor who neglected to subscribe to Maurice's periodical, the *Journal des Théâtres*, or to bestow presents on his wife, soon felt the sharp prick of his criticism. Frédérick was too poor, and later too independent, to buy his good will, so that almost every issue of Maurice's paper contained a laconic gibe at the young actor's dress or diction.

But if management and Press failed to appreciate him, he found favour with his colleagues. They saw that he was passionately devoted to the theatre, and they liked the way he always volunteered to take over a sick actor's part—even if they suspected that his motives were not entirely unselfish. When he himself went down with jaundice in May 1821 and had to stay at home for a month, Joanny, the idol of his youth, organized a collection for him at the Odéon.

His financial position at this time was not as good as he had expected. It was true that his salary had gone up when his contract was renewed, but only a little, and he had to bear the heavy expense of buying all his own costumes. To supplement his income, he used to try his luck in the gaming-rooms of the Palais-Royal. A surer source of money was provided by the pupils of the Conservatoire, who regularly put on shows in the outer suburbs of Paris and paid Frédérick 50 francs for every leading part he played.[21]

This was a profitable arrangement, and it flattered Frédérick's ego to be billed as a star, even though it was only in some little

C

country town. He had, in fact, already begun to develop something of the *panache* of the famous actor. One evening, crossing the Pont-Neuf after dinner, he stopped in front of a stall selling apple fritters.

'How much?' he asked, spearing one of the pancakes on the end of his stick.

'Two sous', stammered the stall-holder.

'That's too dear', said Frédérick. And dropping the soiled pancake back into its plate, he went calmly on his way, ignoring the indignant protests that followed him.[22]

By the time he was half-way through his third year at the Odéon, he felt convinced that he was not being given his due. Any change in salary or status had to be negotiated six months in advance, so in September 1822 he wrote to Gentil, the manager of the theatre, asking if he might begin to play juvenile leads, and occasionally leading parts, at twice his present salary of 2,000 francs.[23]

Gentil's reply reached him a week later.[24] It said simply that the Minister could not agree to his request, and that, as from the beginning of April 1823, he would cease to be a member of the Second Théâtre-Français.

Stunned by this unexpected blow, but unwilling to admit defeat, Frédérick made a gallant if naïve attempt to convince the authorities that there was some justification for his claim. Early in November he played the part of Achilles in Racine's *Iphigénie en Aulide*, at the theatre in the Rue Chantereine. It was a good performance, and it attracted favourable notice. But as far as the Minister of the Royal Household, the Intendant of the Royal Theatres, and the Manager of the Second Théâtre-Français were concerned, it might never have been given.

It was now that Frédérick remembered Franconi's parting words, and he decided to swallow his pride and go to the old circus-manager for advice. As it happened, he could not have chosen a better moment. Franconi had gained part-control of the Ambigu-Comique, and that theatre was looking for an actor to take the place of Fresnoy, who was due to retire in the spring.

It was agreed that he should submit himself to the judgment of the Boulevard public in March 1823. The test piece was the part of Vivaldi in *L'Homme à trois visages*, which Frédérick played to the satisfaction of management and audience. Even Charles Maurice, while prophesying that the young actor would be no better at the Ambigu than he had been at the Odéon, had to admit that 'in spite of everything, he won the noisy and honourable approval of a large troop in the gallery, who had the bad taste to cover him with ridicule by calling him back.' After an equally successful performance in another play, the owner-managers of the Ambigu, Audinot, Franconi and Senépart, engaged Frédérick for four years, at a starting salary of 2,500 francs.[26] Charles Maurice's only comment, when reporting the news to his readers, was: 'They could have done better.'

On 31 March 1823, with a small part in Racine's *Athalie*, Frédérick took leave of the Odéon public. His departure went almost unnoticed.

CHAPTER THREE

THE BOULEVARD DU CRIME

THE *Almanach des Spectacles* of 1823, commenting on a proposal to rename the Boulevard du Temple the Boulevard du Crime, remarked that there was ample justification for the change.

'We have counted up', it said, 'the crimes that have been committed on the Boulevard in the last twenty years. This is what we discovered: Tautin has been stabbed 16,302 times, Marty has suffered poisoning of one sort or another 11,000 times, Fresnoy has been done to death in various ways 27,000 times, Mlle Adèle Dupuis has in her innocence been seduced, abducted or drowned 75,000 times, 6,400 capital charges have tested Mlle Levesque's virtue, while Mlle Olivier, who has only recently embarked on her career, has already drunk 16,000 times from the cup of crime and vengeance. Unless we are mistaken, that makes 151,702 crimes to be shared between six individuals who none the less appear to enjoy excellent health and widespread esteem.'

The vast majority of these crimes had been committed on the stage of the Ambigu-Comique, which despite its name had a more sinister reputation than any other theatre save the similarly miscalled Gaîté.[1] It specialized in bloodcurdling melodramas, which often came from the pen of René-Charles Guilbert de Pixérécourt, the father of the genre, and which matched the Gothic style of the auditorium with their Gothic characters and settings, their brigands, forests and dungeons. These plays were eminently moral—vice was always punished in them and virtue rewarded—but very badly written. They were, in fact,

just as pompous and long-winded as the new neo-classical
tragedies put on at the Odéon, while the actors who appeared in
them were expected to conform to conventions no less rigid and
absurd than those taught at the Conservatoire and observed at
the Théâtre-Français. It is scarcely surprising that Frédérick,
faced, like Talma, with inferior plays and stifling conventions,
should, like Talma, have rebelled.

His first three parts at the Ambigu were just tolerable; the
fourth, as he realized as soon as he read it, was not. The play,
L'Auberge des Adrets, was a new work by three authors, Antier,
Saint-Amand and Polyanthe, who between them had accumulated in the space of three acts almost every cliché known to
melodrama. The action, set in an inn on the road from Grenoble
to Chambéry, centred on a villainous bandit called Robert
Macaire, who at the end of the play, stricken with remorse and
fatally wounded by his accomplice Bertrand, confessed to his
latest murder and thus cleared the name of his virtuous, wrongly-
suspected wife. Frédérick, who had been given the part of
Macaire, shuddered at the threadbare plot, the tearful recognition scenes, the stilted dialogue and the unconvincing ending.

Then he had a sudden inspiration: instead of playing Macaire
straight, as a sinister villain, he would turn him into a gay,
cynical rascal, quipping as he killed. There remained only the
problem of devising a costume to fit the part. Frédérick was
still hunting for something suitable when one day, looking down
from the terrace of the Café Turc, he saw an astonishing figure
standing outside a confectioner's shop. It was a man dressed in a
greasy green coat, patched trousers and a dirty white waistcoat, with a grey felt hat tilted to one side of his head and a
pair of high-heeled women's shoes on his feet. After daintily
demolishing a piece of pastry, the apparition took a bundle of
rags out of its pocket, wiped its hands, dusted itself down, and
sauntered away down the Boulevard. That, Frédérick decided,
was Robert Macaire to the life.[2]

The same evening he told the actor Firmin, who had been
cast as Bertrand, that he intended to guy the part of Macaire,

and Firmin readily agreed to follow his example. They kept their plans from the other members of the company, whose first inkling of what was afoot came at the final rehearsal. Instead of tiptoeing on to the stage as villains of melodrama always did, with their arms raised to hide their faces, Frédérick and Firmin walked on naturally, like the traditional lover or heavy father. Their colleagues tried to persuade them to go through the customary pantomime but met with a point-blank refusal. The two rebels had decided to keep their main effects for the first night, 2 July, but their behaviour at rehearsal was enough to cause the authors and the other actors serious disquiet.

Meanwhile Frédérick had found the various items of his costume in the old-clothes shops of the Temple, while Firmin had provided himself with a long grey box-coat with enormous pockets sewn on behind. They were still chuckling over their finds on the first night, and they could scarcely contain themselves when they overheard Saint-Amand telling some friends of his in the green-room:

'We are counting on a tearful success!'

Thanks to the two bandits, *L'Auberge des Adrets* was a hilarious success instead. Saint-Amand, however, was the first to congratulate Frédérick on what he had done for the play. The second of the three authors, Benjamin Antier, had had to stay in bed with a twisted ankle, but had sent his maid to the theatre to report on the audience's reaction. She came home almost breathless with laughing.

'Ah, Monsieur,' she gasped, 'what a wonderful play! And so funny! I've never laughed so much in all my life!'

Antier was furious at first, but when he was able to go to the theatre he laughed as much as anybody, and willingly forgave the two actors for making a travesty of the original work. Only Polyanthe, who was a doctor by profession and therefore touchier than his professional collaborators, continued to harbour a grievance; and even he relented to the extent of lithographing the portraits of Frédérick and Firmin which appeared in the published version of the *Auberge*.

The play meanwhile went from strength to strength, playing to packed houses for the rest of the year. Every night Frédérick and Firmin would add new witticisms which delighted the audience as a whole but sometimes shocked the odd theatre-goer. Thus one evening when Frédérick answered the young hero's accusation of murder with the comment: 'What do you expect, my son? We all have our little faults', Charles Maurice complained that he was going too far.

'Be careful, Frédérick', said Franconi next day; 'the Press is watching us.'

'Bah!' retorted the actor. 'You know perfectly well that, stripped of our jokes and by-play, the *Auberge* would be impossible.'

'Perhaps.'

'Will you let us put it to the test, by playing it seriously tonight?'

Franconi raised no objections, and so, for the first and last time, *L'Auberge des Adrets* was acted in earnest, as its authors had intended. This solemn performance—the seventieth—had to be abandoned half-way through. From then on, Frédérick had *carte blanche* to do what he liked with the play, and now only the actors cast in the serious parts complained of the liberties he took. Baron, who played the heavy father at the Ambigu, was particularly aggrieved at having his thunder stolen night after night, and he would sometimes lash out furiously at Frédérick once the curtain had gone down. Frédérick invariably returned his blows with interest.

After eighty-five performances a ban was imposed on the *Auberge*, on the flimsiest of grounds. The wife of the Prefect of Police had come to see the play everyone was talking about, and was so moved at the end by Robert Macaire's death-agony that she burst into tears. But then Frédérick, instead of taking his written confession from his breast-pocket, as he usually did, extracted it with infinite care from one of his shoes. The Prefect's wife started from her seat with a shriek of indignation.

'The wicked man!' she cried. 'He's making fun of my tears!
It's too bad!'

The Prefect, to whom she reported this affront to her sensibility, could scarcely be expected to disregard a complaint from
such a reliable and influential source. The very next day, 3
April 1824, the managers of the Ambigu were informed that no
further performances of the *Auberge* would be allowed.

Over forty years later, Benjamin Antier, whom old age had
made forgetful or presumptuous, was to assert that *L'Auberge
des Adrets* had been conceived by its authors as a comic work,
and that Frédérick had done nothing more than carry out their
intentions. Asked to comment on this somewhat belated claim,
the actor merely observed ironically that he was 'not the fourth
collaborator of these gentlemen, and had always considered
himself sufficiently fortunate to have been the chief interpreter
of their fine drama'. In fact, as everyone knew, it was not as a
collaborator but as a creator that he had won fame in the
Auberge, for he had created the part of Robert Macaire in much
more than the usual sense of that theatrical term. What he had
not suspected, though, when he light-heartedly decided to
parody the part, was that Macaire would grow into a kind of
Frankenstein monster from whose clutches he would never
really break free, or that in a sequel to *L'Auberge des Adrets*,
written and performed eleven years after the original play,
the cynical bandit would emerge as one of the great comic
figures of the century and a symbol of his age.

For the moment, the only result of Frédérick's inspired
travesty was to discourage dramatists from setting their plays
in wayside inns or choosing bandits as villains. It was too much
to hope that they should stop writing third-rate melodramas
altogether or that theatres such as the Ambigu should stop
accepting them; and Frédérick was obliged to perform, with as
good a grace as he could muster, in a variety of improbable
pieces. By the summer of 1824 he had played no fewer than
fourteen major parts at the Ambigu, drawing large and appreciative audiences, but his financial position had not improved.

Indeed, if anything, it had grown worse, for during the run of
the *Auberge* Frédérick had won in a lottery a prize of 8,000 francs,
and this had all been spent, leaving him with expensive tastes
which he could not afford to indulge.[3] This extravagance of his
was no doubt deplorable: it was also understandable. As
Hazlitt said[4] of Frédérick's English counterpart, Edmund Kean,
actors 'live from hand to mouth; they plunge from want into
luxury; they have no means of making money *breed*, and all
professions that do not live by turning money into money or
have not the certainty of accumulating it in the end by parsi-
mony, spend it.'

In July 1824 Frédérick decided the time had come for him to
apply to the managers of the Ambigu for an increase in salary.
But first, in order to feel the ground, he asked them to interrupt the run of a popular cloak-and-dagger piece called *Cardillac* in which he had been appearing since May.[5] When they
refused, pointing out that a break in the run would cause them
serious financial loss, and expressing surprise that so zealous
and devoted an actor should make such a suggestion, he retorted that zeal and devotion did not imply disinterestedness,
and asked outright for an improvement in the terms of his contract. To this request the management made no answer, and
their silence incited Frédérick to commit a foolhardy action
which damaged his reputation and might have ruined the career
of a lesser actor.

One night, in the green-room at the Ambigu, someone was
telling how Philippe, one of the leading actors of the Porte-
Saint-Martin, had once come on the stage carrying an open
umbrella, without provoking any reaction from the audience.

'I'm willing to bet', said Frédérick, 'that I can go on tonight
in *Cardillac* with a lighted cigar in my mouth, that I can offer
a pinch of snuff to the prompter, and that I can take my wig
off, wipe my forehead with it and hang it on the knob of my
walking stick for several minutes, without anyone in the
audience objecting.'

'I'll bet a hundred francs you can't', somebody said.

'You've lost your hundred', Frédérick replied. 'Go out in front and you'll see.'

Cardillac's entry always took place in darkness. Frédérick came on holding a lantern on a level with his face; this hid the light of his cigar, which he threw away after a few steps. Later in the play he came down-stage until he was close to the foot-lights; he then took out his handkerchief and his snuff-box, dropped the handkerchief, and while picking it up held out the open snuff-box to the prompter. As for the third condition of the bet, that was carried out while the public's attention was occupied by a ballet being performed on the stage.

Frédérick had been so dexterous that his odd behaviour went unnoticed—or, if it was noticed, was ignored. Unfortunately, the loser of the bet thought fit to tell the story to Charles Maurice, who gleefully seized the opportunity to berate the actor for his arrogance. Other journalists took up the cry, with the result that Frédérick was banned from appearing at the Ambigu for a fortnight.

Audiences of that day, in France as in England, held decided views on the responsibilities of an actor to his public, and they were quick to take offence at the least sign of insubordination. There were therefore many people who regarded Frédérick's innocent mischief in *Cardillac* as a deliberate insult. When he returned to the Ambigu, early in August, he was greeted with a storm of catcalls, and had to make a humble apology from the footlights before the play could begin. Even then, some of the audience were not satisfied, and one man went so far as to shout: 'Down on your knees!' But at this Frédérick only shrugged his shoulders, a police officer called for silence, and the incident was closed.

In November that year, Frédérick had another brush with Charles Maurice. A paper called the *Corsaire* was conducting a campaign against the venal critic, and several writers and actors had promised their support. Frédérick's contribution was a public appeal to Maurice to stop sending him free copies of his periodical (now the *Courrier des Théâtres*), a practice which he described as 'a novel method of persecution'. The journalist riposted by alleging that Frédérick had given him such a harrowing account of his poverty that he sent the actor his *Courrier* free of charge out of sheer charity. This drew from Frédérick a withering letter[6] in which he accused Maurice of blackmail and called on his fellow actors to follow his example in shunning both the man and his paper. Few in fact responded to this call, and the only effect the encounter between *Corsaire* and *Courrier* had on Maurice was to intensify his prejudice against Frédérick Lemaître.

The latter's protestations of poverty were well-founded, if we are to believe the will and testament which he drew up soon afterwards, in the course of his initiation as a freemason.[7] This document reads as follows:

> The layman Antoine-Louis-Prosper Lemaître, known as Frédérick, aged 24, born 28 July 1800 at Le Havre (Seine-Inférieure), living at 60 Rue de Bondy, Paris, by profession an actor, has replied to the following questions:
> What does man owe God?—Gratitude.
> What does he owe himself?—Respect.
> What does he owe his fellows?—Help and protection.

> ### TESTAMENT
> Having nothing but debts, I bequeath them to those who led me into contracting them; but my last wishes before I die are for the happiness of my mother, to whom I owe everything, and whose maternal tenderness is unsurpassed.
> I have nothing on my conscience save youthful follies.
> This being so, whoever loves me will mourn for me.
> Signed: Lemaître
> Paris, 9 January 1825.

Brother Lemaître was to add but few stones to the masonic fabric, and it may be that he joined the fraternity merely out of curiosity. But in at least one play, *Trente ans*, he incorporated the masonic greeting in his stage business, and he never failed to put the three dots of the initiate after his name.

That name gained fresh glory later in the year, when Frédérick appeared in a new melodrama called *Cagliostro*.

Playing the title part, he enjoyed a tremendous success, and the *Pandore*[8] was expressing the general opinion when it stated: 'Frédérick is gifted with stage-sense of a high order, and has none of the bombast of the old actors of melodrama. He is not only the best player on the boulevards, but one of the leading actors of Paris.' Certain tragic scenes in *Cagliostro* even led the critics to compare Frédérick with Talma, whom he seemed to have taken as his model, and it was now that the papers began calling him 'the Talma of the boulevards'. Nor were the critics the only profession to pay tribute to his acting, for in August that year, after his performance as the cab-driver 'Roule-Paris' in *Le Cocher de fiacre*, the cab-drivers' guild gave a banquet in his honour as a token of their admiration.[9]

At the same time as Frédérick was infusing new life into the stock characters of melodrama, his old comrade Deburau, only a few yards further down the Boulevard du Temple, was completely transforming the traditional role of Pierrot.[10] He had recently taken over the part at the Funambules from Félix Chiarigny, who had deserted to Mme Saqui's troupe, and had already succeeded in making his pathetic, childlike Pierrot the most important of pantomime characters, relegating even Harlequin to the background. He had also given Pierrot a new look, discarding the hat and ruff which Chiarigny and others had always worn, on the grounds that they sometimes masked the mime's all-important features, and rejecting his predecessor's white head-scarf in favour of a black handkerchief which contrasted effectively with his blanched face. But although enthusiastic audiences packing the Funambules every night testified to Deburau's popularity, Bertrand had no intention of paying him the salary due to a star performer. When mime and manager entered into a contract which was to come into effect in 1828, all that Deburau could look forward to receiving at that distant date was a paltry 35 francs a week.

Frédérick was more fortunate. In September 1825 he was given a contract by Merle and Serres, the managers of the Porte-Saint-Martin, who engaged him to appear in the leading parts of comedies, vaudevilles, melodramas and pantomimes for three years, starting in April 1827, at a salary of 500 francs a month.[11]

Luckily for Frédérick, this contract was signed two months before the *Pandore* published an anonymous letter accusing him of ruining a recent melodrama with the same sort of prank he had played in *Cardillac*.[12] The melodrama in question was a clumsy imitation of Lessing's *Emilia Galotti* which the public had howled down, and the letter-writer was Jules Dulong, one of its three authors. As soon as he discovered who was responsible for the libellous letter, Frédérick challenged him to a duel, which was fought with swords on 26 November. Both men were wounded, and Frédérick, who left the duelling-ground unassisted, fainted on the stairs when he reached home. The actor Bouffé, his next-door neighbour, called a doctor. The wound, which was turning blue, was cut open, leeches were applied, and Frédérick was pronounced out of danger. 'I can still see him,' Bouffé wrote in later life, 'stretched out on his bed, his chest bared, his hair a mass of curls, and in his marble-white face a pair of fine great eyes whose expression, accompanied by an imperceptible smile, seemed to say: "I am not dead yet." He looked truly magnificent.'

Within a few weeks Frédérick was back at the Ambigu, and by February he was well enough to pay his first visit to London. The object of this visit remains obscure, and the only record of it which we have been able to discover is a letter he wrote from London to a M. de Coisy in Paris, upbraiding his correspondent for not sending him a promised Lyonnais sausage, and boasting of his linguistic attainments.[13] 'I can read English perfectly,' he claimed, 'and soon I shall be able to speak it fluently.' Writing it, alas, was a different matter, and his address in London was given as the 'Prince of Walles Hotel'.

Among the plays in which he appeared on his return to France were a comedy and a melodrama, entitled respectively *Le Prisonnier amateur* and *Le Vieil Artiste, ou la Séduction*, which were given out to be his own work.[14] The archives of the Société des Auteurs et Compositeurs Dramatiques tell a different tale, however, for in each case royalties were paid to three professional authors. Doubtless Frédérick played some part in the writing or devising of these rather nondescript plays, but why he should have claimed sole authorship remains a mystery. It may have been simply to excite the curiosity and admiration of the public; it may have been to appease the literary ambitions which obsessed him all his life; or again, it may have been to impress Sophie Hallignier, the woman who was to become his wife. This last hypothesis seems the most probable; certainly Frédérick's children were led to believe that he had written *Le Vieil Artiste* for their mother.[15]

Sophie Hallignier, his partner in this and other melodramas, had met Frédérick at the Odéon, where they were under contract at the same time. She was a pale, dark-haired beauty with features set in an expression of haughty disdain. She was not much liked by the Boulevard public, for her cold, inhibited acting was more suited to the Odéon than the Ambigu. Indeed, how she succeeded in winning the love of someone as passionate and tempestuous as Frédérick Lemaître is difficult to explain, except by the attraction of opposites. From the brief acount of their romance given by Henry Lecomte, the actor's friend and biographer, it seems that Frédérick himself later held Sophie's sister responsible.[16] Julie Hallignier, a gay young singer at the Opéra-Comique, wanted others to share the happiness she had found in marriage to a M. Boulanger, and she decided that Sophie and Frédérick were ideal match-making material. 'Hearing it repeated on all sides that he was in love with Sophie,' writes Lecomte, 'Frédérick finally did fall in love, proposed to her and was accepted.'

The marriage was arranged to take place at the church of the Petits-Pères on 19 October 1826, and a host of actors and actresses from the Boulevard theatres were invited to the wedding. Sending Sophie her wedding-dress,[17] her impatient fiancé wrote that 'the day it embellishes your charms will be for me the source of eternal happiness'.

In point of fact, Frédérick's married life could not have

begun less auspiciously. Sophie had been trained at the Conservatoire, and there had been rumours linking her name with that of the composer Auber. 'These rumours', writes Lecomte,[18] 'which Frédérick had at first treated with contempt, came back to his mind at the moment of the decisive *tête-à-tête*. He spent part of the night weighing them up and wondering whether or not he had been a fool to marry, until at last love got the better of jealousy.'

This was not the only cloud to darken his wedding-day. Earlier in the evening, news had arrived[19] which had shocked the guests into silence and led Frédérick to cancel the festivities he had arranged.

Talma was dead.

CHAPTER FOUR

MARIE DORVAL

TALMA's death dealt a crippling blow to classical and neo-classical tragedy in France. No other member of the Comédie-Française could still fill the Théâtre-Français when a tragedy was billed: if the leading player was Joanny, Lafon, Firmin or Michelot, there was only a sprinkling of spectators in the house. True, Talma was said to have a penchant towards the bastard genre of drama, and the Romantics later maintained that if he had lived he would have imposed their work on the public. But in fact, though his reforms might foreshadow Romantic theory and practice, he remained above all tragedy's greatest exponent and best defence. Small wonder, then, that the devotees of the Rue de Richelieu listened anxiously to the bulletins on his health which in his last illness were read out before every performance at the Théâtre-Français, or that they heard the news of his death with grim foreboding.[1]

They had every reason to feel dismay, for there was a new revolutionary spirit in the air. 'It must be difficult', Gautier wrote in later life,[2] 'for the present generation to imagine the effervescence of men's minds at that time. A movement was taking place similar to that of the Renaissance. The sap of a new life was flowing impetuously. Everything was sprouting, everything was budding, everything was blossoming at once. The air was like wine, and men were drunk with lyricism and art.'

An impatience with the forms and traditions of the past, and an enthusiasm for novel techniques, violent emotion and vivid expression, had already become apparent in all the arts. In painting, Géricault had shown the way with his immensely colourful and harrowing *Radeau de la Méduse*, and Delacroix had followed with his exciting *Massacre de Scio*, a picture consecrated by an outraged protest from that Vicomte Sosthène de la Rochefoucauld who won immortal fame by lengthening the skirts of the dancers at the Opéra. In music, the cognoscenti had begun to extol what Gratry called 'the prodigious harmonies of the late Beethoven'.[3] The same spirit was evident among the young writers of the day, who were no longer satisfied with the lush lyricism and turgid melancholy of Chateaubriand's *René* or the sweet sadness of Lamartine's more recent *Méditations*. There seemed to be nothing in contemporary French literature that answered their requirements, and the writers they most admired were foreign: Scott for his picturesque historical novels, Byron for his rebellious attitudes and pale heroes dogged by fate, and now, in 1827, Shakespeare.

For the ordinary people of Paris, 1827 was the year of the Giraffe, a present from the Pasha of Egypt which caused such a sensation when it arrived from Marseilles that a street was named after it. But for the writers and artists of the capital, this was the year that Shakespeare was played in his native tongue by English actors and actresses at the Odéon. Till then, the nearest most of them had come to seeing Shakespeare on the stage had been at performances of Ducis's emasculated translations. An English company had, it is true, appeared at the Porte-Saint-Martin in 1822,[4] but only to be driven off by eggs and apples and cries of: 'Down with Shakespeare— he's an aide-de-camp of Wellington!' In 1827, however, circumstances were much more favourable. For one thing, the war had receded further into the past; then in 1823 Stendhal had published his pamphlet *Racine et Shakespeare*, expounding the latter's virtues to 'those misguided young men who thought they were influenced by motives of patriotism and national honour in hissing Shakespeare because he was an Englishman';[5] and finally there was a new admiration for things English which was to grow to such proportions that two years later a certain Lady Morgan

D

complained of being offered things like roast beef in Paris which she had left England to escape.[6]

The English season, which lasted from the autumn of 1827 into the summer of 1828, was an overwhelming success. On the first Shakespeare night, Tuesday, 11 September, Charles Kemble and Harriet Smithson appeared in *Hamlet* before an audience which included Victor Hugo, Alfred de Vigny, Alexandre Dumas, Gérard de Nerval, Hector Berlioz and Eugène Delacroix. To these young men it was a revelation. 'This was the first time', Dumas wrote,[7] 'that I saw in the theatre real passions felt by men and women of real flesh and blood.' Berlioz, 'thunderstruck' by Shakespeare and in love with Miss Smithson, whom he later married, spent the night walking the streets in delirium.[8] Hugo went home to write the Preface to *Cromwell*.[9] They all returned again and again, to see Macready after Kemble and Kean after Macready, and to gloat at the sight of Mlle Mars, the leading member of the Comédie-Française, sitting in one of the boxes. 'The most obstinate Classicists are weakening', crowed Delacroix.[10] 'Our actors have gone back to school and are staring their eyes out.'

The audiences at the Odéon certainly used their eyes more than their ears during the English season. Few of the young Romantics understood the language, and this led them into some curious errors. In the first place, they tended to misjudge the players, taking pretty Harriet Smithson for a great actress, when the London public knew her to be merely competent.[11] Similarly, and this was more serious, they misjudged the plays. Ignoring the beauty of the verse, which they could not appreciate, and fastening instead on the more sensational pieces of stage business, such as Miss Smithson's grimaces, Kean's convulsions and Kemble's sardonic laughter, they saw little more in Shakespeare than a combination of picturesque costumes, crude contrasts and violent action.

This, of course, was the traditional recipe for melodrama, and if violence was a novelty at the Odéon it was a commonplace on the Boulevard du Crime. When Hugo wrote his Preface to

Cromwell, calling for a fusion of tragedy and comedy, and the abandonment of the unities of time and place, Pixérécourt might well have retorted that melodrama had long ago anticipated his demands. Indeed, as long ago as 1804 the critic Geoffroy had recognized the freedom and vigour of the popular genre, and the danger it represented for tragedy.[12]

'Woe betide the French theatre', he wrote three years later,[13] 'if an author of talent, with some knowledge of scenic effects, should ever take it into his head to write melodramas! It is true that he would also need actors capable of performing them. So there is no need for alarm: for melodrama to exercise its evil influence to the extent of paralysing tragedy, it needs two bagatelles, authors and actors.'

In 1827 Geoffroy's 'authors of talent', Dumas, Hugo and Vigny, had still to write their superior melodramas. But the actors were already there to perform them. That same year, the two greatest Boulevard players, Frédérick Lemaître and Marie Dorval, had come together at the Porte-Saint-Martin.

Marie Dorval was a true child of the theatre.[14] She had been born in a sordid hotel in Lorient in January 1798, the bastard daughter of a pair of itinerant players, Marie Bourdais and Joseph-Charles Delaunay. Put on the stage as soon as she could walk, she suffered years of hardship and fatigue in ramshackle theatres and squalid lodging-houses, first with her parents and later with Allan Dorval, the young actor she married at the age of fifteen. Like Frédérick Lemaître, she studied for a while at the Conservatoire under Lafon, who saw her as a comic actress and tried unsuccessfully to make a soubrette out of her. Escaping from the Conservatoire before Lafon had time to force her natural talents into the strait-jacket of tradition, she made her début in 1818 at the Porte-Saint-Martin. The future looked brighter, but in 1820 Allan Dorval died at Smolensk, on his way to fulfil an engagement at St. Petersburg, leaving Marie with two daughters, Gabrielle and Louise, to whom Alexandre Piccini, the lovable but fickle conductor of the Porte-Saint-Martin orchestra, soon added a third, Caroline.

She was not easily daunted, however, and went on working and living with unabated ardour. 'Everything was passion with her,' wrote George Sand later,[15] 'whether it was motherhood, art, friendship, love or religion; and as she could not and would not practise moderation or restraint, her life was filled to over-flowing and agitated beyond the limits of human endurance.' The Boulevard public certainly loved the fire and favour of her personality. She did not measure up to the conventional idea of beauty—'I am not pretty, but worse', she used to say—and her voice was rough and husky. But when she was in the grip of emotion, her anguished features and tremulous voice stirred the least responsive audience to tears—and emotion dominated her acting as it did her life. 'Marie Dorval's talent', wrote Gautier after her death,[16] 'was of a passionate nature; not that she neglected art, but art came to her from inspiration; she did not calculate her stage-play gesture by gesture, or mark out her entrances and exits with chalk on the boards; she put her-self in the position of the character she was playing and became that character.' She was, in short, the perfect partner for Frédérick Lemaître.

The first play in which they appeared together, and Frédé-rick's first play at the Porte-Saint-Martin, was *Trente ans, ou la Vie d'un joueur*, a work which was to become the most popular melodrama of the period in France as well as a great favourite in England, where Milner turned it into *Thirty Years of a Gam-bler's Life* and Jerrold abbreviated it to *Fifteen Years of a Drunkard's Life*.[17] It was written by Prosper Goubaux, the founder and headmaster of the Saint-Victor boarding-school in the Rue Blanche where Frédérick was to send his sons to be educated. Goubaux had been talking about the theatre one day with some friends, one of whom had maintained that the unity of time was essential, since a play extending over a whole year would have no interest. He had retorted that a play might be spread over thirty years and still affect an audience more than one confined to the statutory twenty-four hours. Challenged by his friends to prove it, he had embarked on *Trente ans* with the aid of a banker friend called Beudin, submitting the finished work to the Porte-Saint-Martin under the pseudonym of Dinaux. Victor Ducange, the so-called 'Corneille of the Boulevard' and the greatest name in melodrama after Pixérécourt, was called in to make the play stage-worthy, which he did with great aplomb and complete disregard for the rules of grammar.[18] When the horrified pedagogue ventured to point out some of the errors of syntax he had committed, Ducange silenced him with the proud remark: 'My dear Monsieur, when I've done something, you can rest assured it's good!'

The first-night audience on 19 June 1827 gave little thought to the grammar and syntax of *Trente ans*, or even to the bold experiment in dramatic time represented by Goubaux's three widely separated acts. They were too deeply moved by Frédérick's performance as Georges de Germany, the gambler whose vice leads him to steal, cheat and finally murder, and by Dorval's acting in the part of his wife Amélie. She was brilliantly successful in rendering first the innocence of the sixteen-year-old girl, then the anguish of the young mother fighting to protect her son, and finally the heroic suffering of the middle-aged woman reduced to abject poverty; while Frédérick aged physically and disintegrated morally with equal skill.

Both players were particularly resourceful in inventing those suggestive details of stage business which today we should rightly attribute to the producer, but which in the early nineteenth century were the result of an actor's own thought and inspiration. To quote only one example, at the point where Amélie, after a bitter struggle, signs away her dowry to pay her husband's debts, Frédérick took a pinch of snuff—a dangerously trivial gesture which might well have reduced the scene to bathos, but in fact heightened the effect of tragedy.[19] But what most impressed the audience was the simplicity and realism of the leading actors' delivery. They spoke their lines naturally, without any of the bombast or affectation which normally characterized Boulevard acting.[20] Indeed, they obtained their greatest effects from the most banal questions and statements — Dorval with her innocent 'Is that you, Louise?' and Frédérick with his hoarse explanation of how he came by the murdered traveller's money: 'I found it!' Paying tribute to their achievement many years later,[21] the critic Jules Janin wrote:

> Between them, these two inspired players carried out a complete revolution in the art of drama. The audience, used to the shrill tones of melodrama with its din of words and voice, all looked at one another in astonishment, moved and charmed by such simplicity and grace. It should be added that Frédérick Lemaître was a handsome young man, admirably fitted for his art, tempestuous, passionate, violent and proud, while Mme Dorval, with her slightly bowed figure, had all that was required to command the liveliest compassion. She was frail, tearful, humble and trembling; she wept most movingly; she excelled in containing her feelings with a murmur of: 'Quiet, my heart!' One had only to see them joined together in the same dramatic action, those two children of an art which is forever ageing and changing all the while, to know that they were made, he to express all the transports of the human spirit, she to render all its sweet and intimate joys. Together they undoubtedly formed a bold, skilful and all-powerful combination, the one ready to break everything within reach and magnificent in his fury, the other gracious and humble, fearless, ingenious and sweetly tearful. He had strength, she had grace; he had violence, she had charm. . . . And the public, which had once booed them, hissed them and rejected them at the same time, now adopted them on the same day as the true representatives of its pity and passion.

When Frédérick had moved to the Porte-Saint-Martin, the *Figaro* had prophesied that the Ambigu public would follow him,[22] which it did with the success of *Trente ans*. Then in July, as if this were not enough, the actor unwittingly brought about the destruction of the theatre itself.

A play called *La Tabatière*, which he had written in collaboration with Théodore Maillard, had been accepted by the Ambigu before he left, and gone into rehearsal in June. One of the scenes included a display of fireworks, and it was decided to try them out after the evening performance on 13 July. The first few rockets, which were obviously designed for an outdoor display, set fire to the sky-pieces; the firemen who put out the blaze failed to make sure that everything was safe; and the stage-manager had scarcely left the theatre before it went up in flames.

Frédérick was still at the Porte-Saint-Martin when he heard of the fire. He threw a coat over the rags he was wearing and ran into the burning theatre to save some jewels and costumes in his wife's dressing-room. Meanwhile troops had been marched from the nearest barracks and stationed along the Boulevard from the Café Turc to the Château-d'Eau. Thinking that they could be more usefully employed, Frédérick, now a smoke-blackened scarecrow, suggested to their commanding officer that they should form a human chain to keep the firemen supplied with water. The Ambigu, a wood-and-plaster construction, was already doomed, but the actor's intervention probably saved the neighbouring buildings from destruction.

Later that week Frédérick starred in a benefit performance at the Porte-Saint-Martin in aid of his former colleagues. However, the management of the Ambigu harboured a grudge against the author of La Tabatière, and refused to put the play on when the theatre was rebuilt further down the Boulevard. Sued for breach of contract and condemned to produce the play or pay a heavy indemnity, they chose the latter course. The loss to drama was probably negligible.[23]

A son, christened Julien-Adolphe-Frédérick, was born to the Lemaîtres in the summer of 1827.[24] In the autumn Sophie was sufficiently recovered to go on tour in the provinces. Frédérick had to remain in Paris, where he was appearing in a new production, but he poured out his feelings in a succession of passionate letters to his wife. In the first of these[25] he wrote:

> You are afraid I may feel indifferent about you? Listen, my beloved, to what my life has been since I lost you. The day you left, I was like a drunken man. I could not eat my dinner. I played, or thought I played, my part, and then rushed home as if I were escaping from a fire. Calling you, thinking I heard you, kissing our sheets, helping you to food, crying, laughing, singing—what didn't I do? On top of all that, I felt utterly terrified. I put my pistols on my bedside table and my swords on my bed, and double-locked the door of my room—and even so sleep eluded me. Since then I have

been walking about without knowing where I am going, and I can't do anything right. And the women! Some of them are taking advantage of my position to flirt with me, and these wretches make me unhappier than ever. Don't think me a fool—women are devils for finding ways of getting their revenge. Everything is hateful to me, everything except the memory of you.

After a fortnight as a grass-widower, Frédérick could not bear her absence any longer, and wrote to her[26] at Boulogne:

On receipt of this letter, my Sophie, my lover, my God, who ought never to have left me, will take not the stage-coach but the post, and come home to me. I expect her on Saturday night. If she fails to appear, death will be welcome to me. I am mad, I know, but my excuse lies in my love. I adore, I adore my Sophie. . . .

It may be doubted whether these protestations of love, and others more ardent but less printable, ever elicited a comparable response from Sophie Lemaître. They would have been more suitably addressed to the warm-blooded Marie Dorval, and indeed Frédérick's contemporaries were forever hinting that Dorval would have made a better match for him than Sophie. 'She was Frédérick's real wife, just as Frédérick was her real husband', wrote Gautier,[27] hurriedly adding: 'on the stage, of course.' Other writers have stated emphatically that their partnership was not confined to the theatre, and that for a time Dorval was Frédérick's mistress. A letter she wrote to him some years later seems to bear this out, and it is tempting to think that two of the greatest stage lovers the French theatre has ever known should also have been lovers in actual life. But this is still not proven.[28]

After *Trente ans*, which ran for four months without a break, the next new play in which Frédérick and Dorval appeared together was *La Fiancée de Lamermoor*, in March 1828. In this stirring melodrama, adapted from Scott's novel by the indefatigable Ducange, Marie Dorval moved the audience to tears as Lucie, while Frédérick revealed unsuspected qualities in the heroic part of Edgard de Ravenswood, a very different character from Robert Macaire or Georges de Germany. 'There is real

poetry in the man', said the *Figaro*;[29] the *Globe*[30] ranked him
with Talma; and the *Annales*,[31] in a prophetic judgment, declared that he was surely destined to be 'one of the pillars of
Romantic drama'.

In spite of this and other successes, the finances of the Porte-
Saint-Martin were in a sorry condition. This state of affairs was
a legacy from the management of Merle, or *Monsieur* Merle
as he was usually called, the gentleman of letters, vaudevillist
and dramatic critic who had engaged Frédérick Lemaître and was
to marry Dorval. A great gourmet, with a cookery book always
within reach, Merle held open board at the Café de la Gaîté,
and if he was enjoying the company of one of his actors too
much to let him go, he simply cancelled the evening performance.
If, on the other hand, he had to mount a play in a hurry, he
divided the main part between two actors and announced at the
end of the third act that the leading player had fallen ill and that
his place would be taken by a colleague.[32] The Porte-Saint-
Martin had naturally suffered from these practices, and in 1826
control of the theatre had passed to the Baron de Montgenet.
The Baron, a wealthy cavalry officer and man of the world, was
a scarcely less eccentric manager than Merle, but his licence was
renewed in May 1828, on condition that repairs were carried
out to the ceiling of the theatre, which was showing signs of
collapse and 'greatly intimidating the public'. In June, therefore, the Porte-Saint-Martin closed for a few months.[33]

Towards the end of July, Frédérick and Marie Dorval left
together for Strasbourg, where Merle, undaunted by his experience in the capital, had taken over the management of the Grand
Théâtre. Sophie Lemaître, who was expecting her second child
in September, stayed behind in Paris, and occupied her time
writing plaintive letters to her husband. In his first reply[34]
Frédérick tried to console her with assurances of his love:

> Never, no never, has any woman been loved as you have. Absence
> does not make my heart any fonder—when I am beside you I adore
> you, but I conceal my happiness for fear of losing it, whereas when
> I am parted from you I must express my grief at having lost it. . . .

And when I think that soon you are going to give me another child, the fruit of our love! O my Sophie, you have made me a father, you have doubled, trebled my existence, and yet you regard me as a judge! May the day you come to fear me be the last of all our family! Besides, if you love me, and if your heart has nothing to reproach itself with, then fear should never enter it—remember that, Sophie.

Assurances and admonitions alike failed to satisfy Sophie, however, and she begged her husband to come home immediately. He replied[35] on 30 July:

My dear, I was going to leave today. The longing to kiss you again, to press you in my arms and to try by means of attentions and caresses to make you forget your pain as much as possible, as well as the anxiety your last letter caused me, all this made it my duty to hurry to your side. But I played here yesterday, and the effect I produced in the *Joueur* was such that, unless I wish to commit an unpardonable breach of good manners, I must give two more performances. Even so my leaving so soon puts Merle in an awkward position. So I shall set off on Monday. . . .

In a postscript intended to reconcile his wife to this delay, he reported 'an unparalleled success—according to these lumpish Alsatian beer-drinkers. They were as cold as death to begin with, but my miming and the end of the second act absolutely electrified them. I am being modest . . . as Lafon.'

After only a fortnight at home he left to fulfil an engagement at Calais. No pleas or recriminations followed him here, doubtless because this time he was not accompanied by Marie Dorval. In spite of a poor supporting cast, he scored a personal triumph at Calais, and was planning to move on to some other town when a lady arrived specially from London with a letter for him.[36] This offered him his fare and a large share of the profits if he would appear as Georges de Germany in a series of performances of *Trente ans* at the West London Theatre. 'The leading English tragedians', wrote the manager, 'have appeared in this part, and I am sure that the whole of London will want to see the man who created it.' He exaggerated, of course, but the three performances which Frédérick gave at the Tottenham Street theatre were greeted with remarkable enthusiasm. Back in Calais, where news reached him that he had a daughter, Caroline, he wrote on 10 September[37] 'that my success in London surpassed all expectations'.

He was now impatient to get home, but the manager of the Calais theatre persuaded him to give three more performances of *Trente ans*, to which he added a benefit in aid of a local charity. At last he set off for Paris,[38] preceded by a final triumphant bulletin:

> Baptiste, of Feydeau, was finishing when I arrived. He had made 700 francs with five performances, whereas I, with my old melodrama, will have collected 1,000 francs a night. Talma made more money here, because the price of the seats was raised, but he did not have any more people. My six performances will have brought me in 1,500 francs. I am leaving Calais with money, applause, esteem and regret—which is just how I like it!

On 29 September the Porte-Saint-Martin re-opened with a spectacular and much-publicized production.[39] This was *Faust*, a simplied version of Goethe's play by Antony Béraud, Merle and Charles Nodier, the erudite and charming writer whose drawing-room at the Arsenal, where he was librarian, had become the favourite meeting-place of the young Romantics. It was Nodier whom Alexandre Dumas had sat beside in 1823, at a performance at the Porte-Saint-Martin of an extravagant melodrama called *Le Vampire*; at the end of the third act the older man was expelled from the theatre for hissing the play, and only the next day did Dumas discover that he had written it.[40]

If no one hissed *Faust*, which was not a very much better work than *Le Vampire*, that was because of the acting of Frédérick as Mephistopheles and Dorval as Marguerite. All who went to see the play were particularly struck by Mephistopheles' terrifying laugh and captivating waltz. The laugh was the result of a lucky accident. Giving up hope of finding the right note, Frédérick had at one time decided to use a grimace instead, and he was pulling faces at himself in front of his bedroom mirror when he noticed his neighbours standing at their windows and staring at him in astonishment. He promptly pulled down the venetian blind—and realized that the shrill, creaking sound it made was exactly the effect he had been looking for. As for the waltz, he devised it with the help of the dancer Coraly to add warmth and movement to a role he considered too cold and monotonous. The dance in which Mephistopheles whirled his hypnotized partner around the stage proved in fact to be the most popular feature of a production rich in scenic effects.[41]

Piccini, who had composed the music for *Faust*, wrote to Frédérick after the first performance,[42] congratulating him on 'an inspired combination of mime, intonation, posture and facial expression', and declaring that 'Milton would be satisfied'. An even more eloquent tribute came from a party of deaf-mutes to whom Montgenet had given complimentary tickets.[43] They wrote to the manager:

> Allow us, Monsieur, to express here our admiration for the actor who played so well the part of Mephistopheles. His performance carried us away more than once. He is not an actor, but the black spirit himself, whose every movement chills the blood and evokes shudders of horror! We who follow every expression of the features and every movement of the heart, down to the finest nuance of feeling, also pay homage to Mme Dorval's intelligence. These two different talents are equal in their perfection.

News of Frédérick's triumph in *Faust* soon reached the ears of Baron Taylor, the Commissaire Royal of the Comédie-Française.[44] Isidore-Justin-Séverin Taylor was a naturalized Frenchman, born of British parents in Brussels in 1798, and ennobled by Charles X, who had appointed him to his present position in 1825. He was widely travelled—on one of his journeys he was to arrange for the transfer from Egypt of the obelisk which now stands in the Place de la Concorde—and his circle of friends was no less extensive. It included Vigny, with whom he had served in the same regiment, Hugo, whom he had known for some seven years, and Nodier, who had collaborated with him in translating the Rev. R. C. Mathurin's melodrama, *Bertram, or the Castle of St. Aldobrand*, into French. It may well have been Nodier who now urged him to secure Frédérick's services for the Comédie-Française.

Taylor had already done a great deal, in the three years he had ruled over the Théâtre-Français, to renovate both the company and the repertoire—much to the indignation of the more conservative actors, who suspected him of an excessive fondness for Shakespearian drama and insufficient respect for French classical tragedy. He had induced the Committee to accept first *Roméo et Juliette* by Vigny and Deschamps, then Dumas's *Christine*, and finally the same young author's *Henri III et sa Cour*; the first two plays had been shelved for different reasons, but the third was due to be put on early in 1829. Now, he decided, was the time to engage an actor who could interpret Shakespeare and the Romantics to the best advantage.

In October 1828 Frédérick was invited to become a *pensionnaire* of the Comédie-Française. He declined the invitation. Possibly he considered it humiliating to be offered the inferior rank of *pensionnaire*, in which he would have been patronized by the arrogant, all-powerful and often incompetent *sociétaires*, who according to a contemporary critic[45] 'had the right to sing without a voice, to dance without legs, to recite without a memory, and to take curtain-calls without being asked'. But the main reason for his refusal was no doubt the one he gave Taylor—that the stipend of a *pensionnaire* was not enough for a man with a mother, a wife and two children to support.

Frédérick was justified in refusing to accept anything less than the full *sociétariat*; Taylor was within his rights in refusing to offer him as much. But the net result was that the decisive battles of the Romantic theatre were fought without the greatest of Romantic actors. *Hamlet* was played without the Prince.

CHAPTER FIVE

ROMANTIC VICTORY

On 11 February 1829 something unusual happened at the Théâtre-Français: there was a full house. The occasion of this surprising event was the production of an historical drama entitled *Henri III et sa Cour*, the work of an author completely unknown to the public, Alexandre Dumas, a young man employed as a clerk in the secretariat of the Duc d'Orléans.

The public had been attracted to the Rue de Richelieu partly by the knowledge that Mlle Mars was to appear in the leading feminine role, but chiefly by rumours that the play was an astonishingly bold, flamboyant, vigorous piece to be performed in a theatrical mausoleum. Those rumours were well founded. The author of the play, after all, was no ordinary individual: a strapping, curly-headed quadroon of extraordinary vitality and charm, he was the son of one of Napoleon's bravest generals, and had as a boy proved his courage by smuggling pistols to two of his father's comrades when they were imprisoned in 1815. He knew, none better, that the young men of his generation felt bored and frustrated under the present régime and longed for the violence and excitement of the heroic days when they had been children and their fathers had fought for the Emperor. In *Henri III*, he gave them violence and excitement in good measure, with sword-fights, secret assignations, drugged potions, rope-ladders and hidden panels. These were the stock ingredients of melodrama, and of course Dumas's play, like most of the Romantic dramas which followed it, was little more than a superior melodrama. That it *was* superior to the average productions of the Boulevard du Crime cannot be denied. Where Hugo was to maintain the distinction between drama and melodrama by the use of verse, Dumas relied on a flair for dramatic construction, dialogue and movement second to none. In his *Memoirs*[1] he tells us proudly: 'I have written fifty dramas since *Henri III*, but not one of them is more cleverly constructed.'

It may seem strange at first sight that Dumas, not to mention Vigny and Hugo, should have wished his plays to be put on at the Théâtre-Français, whose company, if not uniformly hostile to Romantic drama, were ill-suited to it. For one thing, the leading players of the Comédie-Française were too old or infirm to give a convincing interpretation of the young and ardent characters created by the Romantic dramatists. Mlle Mars, though wonderfully preserved, was rising fifty, and placed a severe strain on the audience's credulity when she appeared in one of her favourite *ingénue* roles; Michelot was deaf and tended to miss his cues; Firmin had such a poor memory that an extra prompter was brought in when he was playing; Joanny was forever ailing.[2] What is more, they were all comic players, at their best in Molière and Marivaux; the paroxysms of passion required of them by Dumas and Hugo were neither to their taste nor within their capabilities. Yet in spite of these considerable drawbacks the fact remained that the Théâtre-Français was the first theatre in France, and that no playwright could be said to have 'arrived' until his work had received the official consecration of a performance on its stage.

Dumas 'arrived' that evening in February 1829, and with him, Romantic drama as a whole. The 'Battle of *Hernani*', which was waged in the same theatre a year later, has acquired greater fame for a variety of reasons: because it was more deliberately and ostentatiously organized, because it was a rowdier and more picturesque affair, because it found an even better publicist than Dumas in the person of Théophile Gautier, and because the play itself had greater literary if not dramatic merits than *Henri III*. But the honour of making the first serious breach in the classical defences belonged to Dumas, and he was well aware of it. There is a story[3] that Hugo met Dumas one day in later years and told him indignantly of a journalist who claimed that Vigny had invented the historical drama. 'The fool!' replied Dumas; 'as though everyone didn't know that it was I!'

As well as being an important theatrical event, the first night of *Henri III* was a brilliant social occasion. This was because Dumas, whose official salary had been suspended on account of his extra-bureaucratic activities, had appealed to the Duc d'Orléans to do him the honour and justice of seeing his play. The Duke brought with him a party of twenty to thirty princes and princesses he had been entertaining to dinner, the men plastered with decorations, the women sparkling with diamonds.

The play itself was a triumphant success. The most daring and violent scene, where the Duc de Guise seizes his wife's arm with his iron gauntlet and forces her to summon her lover to an ambush, evoked cries of horror but at the same time peals of applause. Hugo and Vigny, whom Dumas met for the first time that night, were enthusiastic; the great singer Garcia Malibran leant right out of her box, holding on to a pillar to keep herself from falling; and when Firmin announced the name of the author at the end of the play, the whole house, including the Duc d'Orléans, rose to its feet, clapping wildly.[4]

The following day *Henri III* suffered a fate which was to overtake many a Romantic drama, when it was suspended by the Minister of the Interior, though in this case the ban was soon lifted. It so happened that the King had suspected the play of being treasonable propaganda. Charles X, who had succeeded his brother Louis in 1824, was convinced that the Duc d'Orléans was waiting and watching for an opportunity to seize the throne for the younger branch of the family; and in Dumas's play— written by one of the Duke's employees—he had been told that Henri III and the Duc de Guise represented himself and his cousin. But the Duke had reassured him.[5] 'Sire,' he said, 'you have been misinformed, for three very good reasons. In the first place, I do not beat my wife. In the second place, Madame la Duchesse d'Orléans does not cuckold me. And in the third place, Your Majesty has no more loyal subject than myself.'

Henri III met rather more determined opposition from the classical coterie, who were furious that the House of Molière should have been desecrated by a Romantic drama, and that Mars and Samson should have stooped to 'competing in lung-power and sobs with M. Frédérick and Mme Dorval'.[6] They were horrified too by sinister rumours that after the first performance a sabbatical dance had taken place before the bust of Racine, by the light of the dying fires in the green-room, with the dancers chanting the sacrilegious refrain: 'Racine is fallen!' When they discovered that their favourite actors had no intention of throwing up the offending play—for it was playing to packed houses—they turned in panic to the King. A petition was drawn up by seven of the authors who had hitherto reigned supreme at the Théâtre-Français, asking His Majesty in all seriousness to outlaw the new genre.[7] The King was equal to the occasion. 'Gentlemen,' he replied, 'I cannot do anything about the matter of which you complain; I only occupy one seat in the theatre, like any other Frenchman.'

The disappointed Classicists were roused to new fury when their idol Casimir Delavigne, the so-called national bard, told that his latest play, *Marino Faliero*, would have to wait until *Henri III* had finished its run, decided in a fit of pique to take it to the Porte-Saint-Martin. But his choice of theatre was not as odd or outrageous as it might appear. Delavigne was an expert at getting the best of both worlds, and *Marino Faliero*, half tragedy and half melodrama, was just as likely to appeal to a Boulevard audience, with its scenic changes, elaborate accessories and impassioned dialogue, as it was to a more conservative public on account of its traditional versification and tragic theme. As for the main part, that of the Doge of Venice, it was sufficiently dramatic to suit Frédérick Lemaître, and provided the latter with a splendid opportunity to prove his worth. The first rehearsals went well, and the author declared himself to be delighted with his leading actor. But then, one day, the Baron de

E

Montgenet came up to Frédérick while he was rehearsing, and told him in front of some fifty people that the part of the Doge had been taken from him and given to Ligier, an actor of the Comédie-Française.[8] Frédérick exploded with anger at this humiliating affront; but in fact he had only himself to blame for it.

Earlier in the year, the shareholders of the new Ambigu had entrusted the management of the theatre to a writer called Tournemine, who had promptly offered Frédérick the post of director of productions. It was a tempting proposition, all the more so since Frédérick knew that the Porte-Saint-Martin was heading towards bankruptcy. However, by the terms of his contract, he could not leave the Porte-Saint-Martin without paying a forfeit of thirty thousand francs. An extraordinary meeting of the Ambigu shareholders was called for 28 April to consider the question. Frédérick outlined the policy he would follow if he were given the chance, whereupon the shareholders unanimously elected him director of productions and promised to buy him his freedom when *Marino Faliero* had completed its run.[9] But Montgenet had heard what was afoot and swiftly took his revenge. On the first night of Delavigne's play, 30 May 1829, it was Ligier who created the part of the Doge of Venice.

Frédérick retaliated by taking the matter to court, and the case was heard three days later. As this was the very first time a French actor had sued his manager, the court-room was crowded with representatives of both professions, eager to discover what their rights were in the eyes of the law. The result was a managerial victory, the court ruling that Montgenet was at liberty to give parts and take them away as he thought fit.

But the Baron's triumph was short-lived, for soon afterwards he was obliged to relinquish control of the Porte-Saint-Martin. The new manager, a certain Caruel-Marido, had little experience of the theatre, and his first few enterprises were resounding flops. He then had the idea of reviving *Marino Faliero*, with Frédérick playing the part created by Ligier. Since the time of his law-suit against Montgenet, Frédérick had been directing productions at the Ambigu, but he was still technically under contract to the Porte-Saint-Martin, as his forfeit had not yet been paid. However, he resented being treated as the plaything of successive managers, and flatly refused to attend rehearsals. Once again the matter was taken to court, and once again the management triumphed.[10] But this time, having made his protest, Frédérick submitted with a good grace. It was clearly in his interest to give of his best, in order to prove that Montgenet had been wrong to rob him of the part. As Caruel-Marido had foreseen, the public were intrigued by the unusual prospect of seeing a Boulevard actor in a role created by a member of the Comédie-Française. On 29 September, when Frédérick made his first appearance on the stage as the Doge of Venice, the Porte-Saint-Martin was packed to the doors. Ligier himself was in the audience.

Frédérick's performance began badly. A burst of applause greeted him as he came on, and for some reason this seemed to disconcert him. In the first two acts he was obviously ill-at-ease with the cold, solemn verse he had to declaim. But in the third act the dialogue became emotional, and he was able to get the measure of his character and of his audience too. The ovation they gave him at the final curtain left no doubt that they judged him superior to Ligier. When the latter went back-stage after the performance to offer his rival formal congratulations on his success, he received a monumental snub for his pains.[11]

'I thank you for your compliments, Monsieur Ligier,' said Frédérick, 'but the approval of the public was enough for me.'

After only thirteen performances of *Marino Faliero*, Frédérick paid half his forfeit-money to Caruel-Marido, who gave him his freedom on condition that he let a full month elapse before appearing at the Ambigu. The imposition of a delay proved to be a futile precaution, for the Porte-Saint-Martin was declared bankrupt and closed its doors on 5 January 1830, the very day that Frédérick opened in his first play at the new Ambigu.

This was a monstrous concoction entitled *Les Voleurs et les Comédiens*, in which the author Benjamin Antier, profiting from his experience with *L'Auberge des Adrets*, had written a portmanteau role designed to show off Frédérick's remarkable versatility. For three hours every night, the actor who had recently triumphed as the Doge of Venice sang, danced, recited and gave female impersonations in a non-stop series of scenes from farce, melodrama, tragedy and even opera. This grotesque entertainment ran for five weeks, leaving the public and the leading player exhausted.

The next production, a melodrama called *Peblo, ou le Jardinier de Valence*, was rather more worth while, and Frédérick was brilliantly partnered in it by Marie Dorval, who had joined him at the Ambigu on condition that she could leave if and when he left. But even *Peblo*, and the revivals of the *Auberge* and *Trente ans* which followed it, could not save the theatre from the same fate as the Porte-Saint-Martin. In May Frédérick resigned his post as direction of productions, in June Tournemine was dismissed, and in July the Ambigu went bankrupt.[12]

In the meantime, the victory which Dumas had won for Romantic drama with *Henri III* had been consolidated with the production of new works by Vigny, Hugo and Dumas himself.

The first of these to be staged was *Le More de Venise*, Vigny's adaptation of *Othello*, which was presented at the Théâtre-Français on 24 October 1829, with Joanny as the Moor and Mlle Mars as Desdemona. The Classicists, who had been taken off their guard by Dumas's play earlier in the year, were fully prepared to do battle on this occasion, and the play had a stormy reception. Derisive laughter greeted every mention of Desdemona's handkerchief, and there was an explosion of mirth at the lines:

> Demain soir, ou mardi matin, ou vers midi,
> Ou mardi soir, ou bien, au plus tard, mercredi . . .

But the Romantic battalions were there too in full force, and they gave their opponents shout for shout. In the end victory went to the new school, though the *Univers*[13] maintained that this was only because 'Mlle Mars-Desdemona was undressed on the stage, and everyone was interested to see how far the process would go'.

Le More de Venise was performed only sixteen times before it gave place to a play which promised to cause far greater controversy: Hugo's *Hernani*. An earlier work by the same author, *Marion de Lorme*, had been enthusiastically accepted by the Comédie-Française in July 1829, but it had been banned by the censor on the ground that Hugo's portrait of Louis XIII was likely to bring the monarchy into contempt. *Hernani*, on the other hand, was passed by the censor but aroused little enthusiasm in the Rue de Richelieu. If the Committee had accepted it without suggesting any cuts, that was because the author had brought some friends to the reading whose cries of admiration had cowed the actors into silence. It was a different matter at rehearsal, and there are many stories of the squabbles that took place between the author and his interpreters over their lines. Thus Mlle Mars boggled at saying: 'Vous êtes mon lion superbe et généreux', and though she appeared to submit when Hugo insisted that the line should stand, she said 'seigneur' instead of 'lion' on the first night.[14]

These quarrels became the talk of Paris, and excitement mounted as the first night drew near. Hugo refused the services of the official claque, thinking no doubt that his opponents might bribe them to turn against him, and asked his friends to recruit an amateur claque instead. Gérard de Nerval and Petrus Borel got together about a hundred students from the Latin Quarter, coached them in their duties, and issued them with blood-red passes romantically inscribed with the word: *Hierro*, from the war-cry of the Almogavares: *Hierro despierta te!* (Steel flash forth!).

The story of the first performance, on 25 February 1830, has been told a hundred times, and by now it is difficult to distinguish fact from fiction. As it stands, the legend of the Battle of *Hernani* is certainly unfair both to the actors and to the amateur claque. It tells how Hugo's supporters, unwashed and unkempt, were let into the theatre early in the afternoon and locked in for four hours; how they spent their time singing obscene ditties, drinking bottles of wine and eating food heavily flavoured with garlic; and how, being denied access to the cloak-rooms, they desecrated the temple of Melpomene in others ways, so that Mlle Mars remarked indignantly to Hugo: 'I've played to all sorts of audiences in my time, but never to one like this!' As for the actors, we are told that most of them were hostile to the play, and that Michelot for one did his best to spoil it by omitting lines or by openly guying his part.

The truth would seem to be that the claque were less uncouth and the company less hostile than we have been led to believe.[15] Gautier always maintained that the so-called 'pack of raga-muffins' who fought the Battle of *Hernani* for Hugo were in fact 'young men from good homes, educated and well-bred, painters and musicians, sculptors and architects, all mad on art and poetry'. As for 'desecrating the temple of Melpomene', he rebutted the charge that garlic was used to flavour their evening meal, for the very good reason that 'garlic is a classical food', and Armand de Pontmartin indignantly denied that any 'natural-istic offences' were committed. The clothes sported by the claque were probably enough in themselves to upset the staid *habitués* of the Théâtre-Français, for the young men were all flamboyantly dressed in picturesque costumes, the painter Eugène Devéria flaunting a Rubens hat and a Velasquez cloak, while Gautier was wearing pale-green trousers, a black jacket with velvet facings, a grey overcoat with a green satin lining, and the famous red doublet which he had had made specially for the occasion. No doubt the older members of the audience were also offended by the cheers and catcalls with which the claque greeted Hugo's supporters and opponents, and not a little alarmed when one young man, pointing to the row of bald heads lining the circle, shouted: 'To the guillotine with those bare knees!'

The actors themselves felt unhappy about the play, which was unlike anything they had performed before, and they felt even unhappier at the uproar it caused. But they played their parts conscientiously, if only because the box-office receipts mattered as much to them as to any company of actors. If Joanny mumbled when he said: 'Oui, de ta suite, ô Roi, de ta suite! j'en suis', and Michelot suppressed whole passages without the knowledge of the audience, that was to avoid the storm of protest which broke loose at every provocative line. The most that can be said against them is that they did not measure up to their parts. Firmin was disappointing as the rebel chief Hernani, a part which called for the fiery ardour of a Frédérick Lemaître, while however gamely Mlle Mars went through the motions of love and death, she lacked the passionate conviction of a Dorval.

The first night ended in victory for the Romantics, but their opponents maintained that this was simply because the theatre was packed with Hugo's friends and supporters. The fight continued at subsequent performances, and every night the amateur claque turned up to do battle for their hero against the reactionary forces of Classicism. The Press might be hostile and the actors weary, but the young Romantics gloried in the struggle. 'Happy days,' wrote a nostalgic Gautier towards the end of his life, 'when the things of the mind could rouse people to such excitement.'

Meanwhile, Dumas's verse-play *Christine* had been accepted at the Odéon, which was now under the management of Charles-Jean Harel, one of the most unscrupulous but engaging rogues in theatrical history.[16] Harel had been a sub-prefect under the Empire and the Prefect of Les Landes during the Hundred Days; after Waterloo he had been exiled to Belgium, but after five years he had come back to France and turned journalist and theatre-manager. He never had any ready money and was pursued everywhere by his creditors, even on to the stage, where he escaped from them several times by vanishing through a trap-door. Even if he was caught, he refused to admit defeat, and there is a story that once, when he was being taken to prison for debt, he persuaded the bailiff's man not only to let him go but also to lend him a thousand francs. The Press called him the 'Napoleon of managers', partly on account of the scope and brilliance of his theatrical enterprises, and partly because his mistress, Marguerite-Joséphine Weymer, whose stage-name was Mlle George, had also been Bonaparte's mistress for a while.[17] Stendhal calculated that she had slept with the First Consul no more than sixteen times, but even this brief liaison had been sufficient to bring about her expulsion from the Comédie-Française in 1817. Ever since then Mlle George had been looking for a way of taking her revenge, and her opportunity came when Harel obtained control of the Odéon and placed the Second Théâtre-Français at her disposal.

In 1830 Mlle George was generally admitted to be the supreme exponent of tragedy in France, as Mlle Mars was of comedy. The two great actresses were very different in character, however. 'George', said Dumas,[18] 'a good sport if ever there was one, in spite of her imperial airs, would allow any kind of joke to be told in her presence and roar with laughter, where Mlle Mars would usually give only a forced smile.' They differed in appearance too: Mlle Mars, at fifty, looked far younger than her years, while Mlle George, though still very beautiful at forty-three, was putting on weight. The gossip-writers never tired of poking fun at her figure, and Charles Maurice, who was one of her chief tormentors, assured his readers that Harel's stage-manager had been deputed to walk in front of her wherever she went, thumping the floor with his stick to make sure that it would bear her weight.[19]

George's ample proportions offered one advantage: they added to her air of queenly dignity. The Tsar was said to have told her that she wore a crown better than Catherine the Great, and certainly she excelled at playing tragic queens. The Romantics did their best to accommodate her, with a whole series of royal parts from Marguerite de Bourgogne to Mary Tudor. 'How many fat queens and outsize empresses have we not disinterred from history for her benefit!' wrote Gautier.[20] Dumas, as it happened, had not written *Christine* with George in mind, but she saw herself as the unhappy Queen of Sweden and insisted on having the play for the Odéon. Harel realized that it could not compare with *Henri III,* and would have liked Dumas to rewrite it in prose, but he was over-ruled by his mistress. The first performance was arranged for 30 March 1830.

Frédéric Soulié, who had written an unsuccessful play on the same subject, heard that the Classicists who had been demonstrating against *Hernani* at the Théâtre-Français were now planning to deliver a similar onslaught upon *Christine*, and he generously offered Dumas a claque of fifty workmen from a sawmill he owned. Their support proved extremely useful, for the first night was almost a repetition of the Battle of *Hernani*.[21]

The performance began at seven o'clock. The Prologue could not be heard for the din in the auditorium and had to be repeated. Then there was a quarrel about the chandelier, followed by noisy criticism of the play. Not until the fifth act did George as Christina and Lockroy as Monaldeschi conquer the audience. Monaldeschi's cowardice evoked shouts of rage, which turned to frantic cheers when he dragged himself, wounded and bleeding, to Christina's feet, only to hear her pronounce sentence of death upon him.

By now it was one o'clock in the morning, with the Epilogue still to come. The audience began to lose patience. When Christina asked her doctor how long she had to live, and he replied: 'You have another quarter of an hour', a student in the pit stood on his seat, took out his watch and observed that it was a quarter past one. 'If the play isn't over by half-past,' he said, 'we shall all go home.' In fact, it was two o'clock before the audience left, and no one knew for certain whether *Christine* was a success or a failure.

Afterwards Dumas invited some twenty-five friends to a supper-party in his rooms. He was worried about the play, for about a hundred lines had been marked down as in need of alteration, and this had to be done that night if the manuscript was to be amended and the changes rehearsed before the next performance. Hugo and Vigny told him to set his mind at rest. They shut themselves up in a little room, and while Dumas entertained his guests they worked at his play. When they came out at daybreak and found all their friends asleep, they propped the manuscript up on the mantelpiece, tiptoed out of the house, and went off arm in arm, like two brothers.

Though they could not know it, this was the last time the Romantic dramatists were to join together in a common purpose. In just over a year they had fought four battles and won them all—for even *Christine* turned out to be a success. But Hugo was too selfish, Vigny too proud and Dumas too independent to hold the alliance together, and after 1830 the three men would go their separate ways. For the Romantic theatre it was the end of the beginning and the beginning of the end.

CHAPTER SIX

THE JULY REVOLUTION

THE theatrical revolution of 1830 was followed within a few months by a political revolution which was initially just as successful and ultimately just as futile.

There had been trouble in the air ever since the accession of Charles X in 1824. His brother Louis XVIII, with the wisdom gained in exile during the Revolution and the Hundred Days, had shown a tolerant, conciliatory spirit towards the new France. Charles, on the other hand, had grown more inflexible in his pride and more bigoted in his piety over the years. He regarded the Charter which had been granted to the nation in 1814 as a monstrous concession to the mob, and he held the concept of constitutional monarchy in abomination. 'I would rather chop wood', he once declared, 'than reign after the fashion of the King of England.' Small wonder then that when he came to the throne the Liberals should have despaired and the reactionary Ultras rejoiced.

To begin with, however, he surprised both parties by abolishing the censorship and according an amnesty to certain political prisoners. But these were acts of inspired cunning or complacent generosity, and his true feelings soon became apparent. His revival of ancient titles, such as that of Dauphin for the Duc d'Angoulême, caused some disquiet, while the elaborate religious pomp of his coronation at Reims aroused fears that he meant to restore clerical influence as well as aristocratic privilege. Hugo, who was an ardent and interested Royalist at the time, might win a pension with an ode in praise of the occasion,

but popular acclaim (and nine months' honourable imprisonment) went to Béranger for his *Coronation of Charles the Simple*.
Unrest grew steadily with the introduction of various reactionary measures, such as the payment of an indemnity to the
émigrés for the lands they had lost in the Revolution, and a law
which made sacrilege a crime punishable by death. There were
several demonstrations of popular dissatisfaction, as when over
a hundred thousand people followed the funeral procession of the
Liberal General Foy, and when the King, reviewing the National
Guard in 1827, was greeted with cries of 'Down with the
Ministers!' and 'Down with the Jesuits!' Charles reacted
foolishly, disbanding the citizen militia, which after all had been
demonstrating against his Ministers and not himself, and thus
alienating the bourgeois and tradespeople who made up its
ranks. Elections held that same year returned an Opposition
majority to the Chamber, and the formation of a moderate
Ministry under the Vicomte de Martignac did something to
relieve tension. But a moderate Ministry was not to the King's
taste. In April 1829, he seized the first possible opportunity to
get rid of Martignac, and in his place chose the most reactionary
of all the Ultras, a former *émigré* who had refused to swear
obedience to the Charter, Prince Jules de Polignac.

The choice of such a man at such a time was generally inter-
preted as an act of deliberate provocation, and any doubt that
remained vanished when the names of the new Ministers were
published, for they included Bourmont, a general who had deserted Napoleon before Waterloo, and La Bourdonnais, who
had called for bloody vengeance on all Bonapartists after. The
new session of Parliament was not due to open until March
1830, but the Opposition Press launched into a violent attack on
the Government. At the spearhead of this attack was a new
Liberal paper called the *National*, whose moving spirits were
the aged Talleyrand and two young men, Armand Carrel and
Adolphe Thiers, historians respectively of the English and
French Revolutions. They chose this moment to devote a series
of articles to the Glorious Revolution of 1688, when one King

had been substituted for another without a drop of blood being shed. Even the least perceptive readers saw the parallel between James and William on the one hand and Charles X and the Duc d'Orléans on the other.

The soothsayers were busy, too, on 2 March, when Parliament met, for the King stumbled as he was mounting the steps of the throne, his cap fell to the floor, and the Duc d'Orléans stepped forward and picked it up. Faced with a hostile Chamber which refused to accept the Polignac Ministry, Charles first prorogued and then dissolved Parliament, fixing new elections for the end of June. He was confident that the Ultras would be victorious, but in fact the Opposition returned with a vastly increased majority. One last hope of rallying the country to the Government remained. For the past two years a French fleet had been blockading Algiers, after a diplomatic incident in which the Dey Hussein had struck the French Consul with his fly-whisk. A more serious provocation—the bombardment of the French flag-ship by Algerian shore-batteries—had given Polignac a pretext for mounting an expedition against the Dey, and in May 1830 a fleet of warships and merchant vessels had sailed from Toulon for Algiers. At last, in the afternoon of 9 July, news reached Paris that Algiers had capitulated. Guns were fired, public buildings were illuminated, fireworks were let off, and on Sunday the 11th the King attended a *Te Deum* at Notre-Dame in honour of the victory.[1] But the people of Paris remained unmoved. This African adventure meant little or nothing to them, and they were more interested in the struggle developing between Charles X and his Chamber. When the gilded coach which had been used for the Coronation drove by on its way to Notre-Dame, only a few voices shouted; 'Long live the King!'

Neither Charles nor Polignac paid any attention to these warning signs, for they had decided to stage a *coup d'état* which would muzzle the Opposition and bring the people back to a proper sense of loyalty and devotion to the Crown. Article XIV of the Charter empowered the King to 'issue such ordinances as were necessary for the safety of the State', and on Sunday 25 July Charles invoked this article to make four ordinances suppressing the freedom of the Press, dissolving the Chamber, limiting the franchise and fixing new elections for September. No special precautions were taken to make sure that this act of despotism was successful. The Deputy Minister of War was not even told that he might have an ugly situation on his hands, but was left to read the Ordinances in the *Moniteur* like everyone else. And the King himself, with serene self-confidence, went off to hunt at Rambouillet, taking care to see that his purse was filled with gold so that he could distribute largesse to any of his loyal subjects he might meet in the forest.[2]

In Paris there was tremendous indignation when the fateful issue of the *Moniteur* came out on the 26th. The *National* appeared too, despite a ban on unauthorized newspapers, and Thiers published a protest on behalf of his fellow journalists, declaring that 'the rule of law is at an end, and that of force has begun'. But the only advice the Liberal Press offered its readers was to stop paying taxes, which was scarcely an encouragement to violence. The streets were fairly quiet, and only in the evening did a few bands of printers and students gather together near the Palais Royal. They clamoured for the dismissal of the King's Ministers, but this was nothing new, and Polignac was unimpressed when he drove through the crowd.

The royal *coup d'état* might in fact have been successful if it had not been for the extraordinary complacency and ineptitude shown by Charles X and his Ministers. The supreme act of folly committed by the King was to appoint Marshal Marmont, Duke of Ragusa, to command the Paris garrison. Marmont, like Bourmont, had deserted Napoleon—indeed, in Parisian slang *raguser* meant to betray—and it would have been hard to make an appointment better calculated to antagonize the people.

On Tuesday the 27th the Prefect of Paris gave orders for the presses of the Opposition papers to be broken up. Public feeling was inflamed by this measure, especially when Baude, one of the editors of the *Temps*, invoked the law on burglary and defied the police in the presence of a couple of thousand people.[3] After two locksmiths had refused to open the newspaper offices, the street was cleared and a man called in whose job it was to rivet the fetters of convicts. But the moral victory remained with the Opposition.

During the day Marmont, who had only just received his orders, occupied the Boulevards, the Carrousel and the Pont-Neuf with troops. There was little resistance as yet; one man was killed in the Rue du Lycée and three others in the Rue Saint-Honoré, but the only barricade that was set up was forced by the Lancers before it was finished. In the evening, however, a decisive step was taken which plunged the capital into Revolution: the theatres of Paris entered the fight.

The man who was chiefly responsible for this development was Étienne Arago, the manager of the Vaudeville.[4] He was on his way to the theatre after dinner when he came across four or five carts and carriages waiting for a crowd in the Rue Saint-Honoré to disperse. One of the carts was loaded with rubble, and at Arago's suggestion it was tipped on its side and its contents piled up across the street to form a barricade. As soon as he reached the Vaudeville, he ordered the doors of the theatre to be shut, telling the disappointed playgoers: 'There shall be no laughter at the Vaudeville while Paris is in tears!' He then set about closing all the other theatres in the capital. Just before he arrived at the Nouveautés, the soldiers in the guard-house outside the Bourse opened fire on some rioters and killed a woman of thirty. Arago and his companions propped the corpse on the steps, where it could be seen by the audience as they poured out of the theatre. Then, turning to the men who were with him, the fiery little manager called out: 'To the Variétés, my friends! To close the theatres is to hoist the black flag over Paris!' And off they went, filling the streets with their cries of: 'Stop the play! Close the theatres! They are killing people in the streets of Paris!'

Deprived of their evening's amusement, angered by stories and evidence of bloodshed, and infuriated by the news that the hated Marmont was in command of the Royal troops, the people of Paris set to work raiding gunsmiths' shops, tearing up paving-stones and building barricades. Students, workers, actors and printers worked through the night side by side with bourgeois members of the National Guard, who had been allowed to keep their arms when they were disbanded in 1827 and now brought them out again. By dawn on the 28th, the second of what were later called the Three Glorious Days, the city was ready for battle.

Within a few hours the insurgents had captured the Hôtel de Ville and Notre-Dame and by nightfall nearly the whole of Paris was in their hands. The Royal troops, fighting in tropical heat without food or drink through a labyrinth of narrow streets, with the populace firing at them over the barricades or throwing furniture down on them from the windows, suffered heavy casualties and rapidly lost heart. The next day two regiments went over to the rebels, the Louvre was invaded, and the last of Marmont's soldiers fled in panic.

The theatres, which had played their part in bringing about the Revolution, were in the thick of the battle. One of them actually provided weapons for the insurgents, for Arago and his scene-shifters smuggled a load of rifles, swords and powder flasks out of the Vaudeville property stores under the noses of Marmont's men.[5] Some of the fiercest fighting—in which Frédérick Lemaître joined with his friend and neighbour, the young novelist Paul de Kock—took place in the very heart of theatre-land, at the Porte Saint-Martin, where from midday till eight at night on the 28th a handful of citizens held their own against a battalion of Royal grenadiers.[6]

But then there was something theatrical about the entire Revolution, and the heroes of the Three Glorious Days be-haved exactly as if they were modelling themselves on the heroes of Dumas and Ducange. For instance there was the cobbler who set a row of caps on pikes behind his deserted barricade and walked across to the Ministry of Foreign Affairs, calling out to his non-existent troops to avenge him if the sentry shot him, and thus taking the Ministry single-handed. There was the young National Guardsman called Boulet (cannon-ball) who captured a cannon and turned it against the Royal Guard, proclaiming to all and sundry 'that his name would be fatal to the enemy'. There was the little shopkeeper of the Rue des Cannettes who kissed the bullet a medical student had taken from his body, and gasped out with his dying breath: 'Take it to my wife!' And there was the boy of twelve who had brought down an officer of the Lancers and had been wounded himself, but who brushed aside congratulations on his courage with the words: 'Love of one's motherland turns a child into a man!' We may smile a little now at these grandiloquent words and gestures, but we should remember that they were typical of 1830. The flamboyant heroism of Romantic drama had been translated quite naturally from the stage to the barricades.[7]

All those who recorded their impressions of the July Revolution paid particular tribute to the insurgents' high idealism, which was of a kind rarely seen before or since in a popular movement. None of them would touch wine or brandy during the fighting, for fear they lost their self-control, and they drank nothing but liquorice-water. The rebels who removed the entire stock of a gunsmith in the Rue de l'Université paid for what they took or gave drafts which were scrupulously honoured. The man who seized a medieval battle-axe in the attack on the Louvre promised to return it when he had finished with it, and kept his word.[8] And when the Archbishopric of Paris was sacked and precious folios and vestments thrown into the Seine, any attempt at salvage was greeted with indignant cries of 'Into the water with it! Do you think we are thieves?'

There were some, of course, whose behaviour was not so disinterested and who were determined to turn the Revolution to their own account. Several shopkeepers, for example, took the opportunity to cut down the trees lining the boulevards, ostensibly to make barricades but really because they obstructed their shop windows. Thiers and his friends took no part in the fighting, and scuttled like frightened rabbits when they thought

F

the Royal Guard were going to interrupt one of their meetings; but while the people in their innocence were celebrating their victory with dancing and singing and illuminations, the Liberals posted placards on the walls exalting the merits of the Duc d'Orléans and invited him to come to Paris and take office as Lieutenant-General of the Kingdom. The Duke's sister, the ambitious Madame Adélaïde, declared that her brother had no pretensions to the throne, and then set to work making him a tricolour cockade while she waited for advice to come from Talleyrand. That arch-intriguer, who under the Revolution, the Empire and the Restoration had always managed to be on the winning side, who had served as Grand Chamberlain to Napoleon, Louis XVIII and Charles X and outlasted them all, was confident that this new Revolution which he had helped to foment would go as he had planned; but meanwhile, in case the people should remember that it was he who had helped to restore the Bourbons he was now helping to overthrow, he had the gilt letters spelling out his name taken down from the carriage entrance to his house. At last, deciding that the moment was ripe, he sent Madame Adélaïde the laconic message: 'Let him come.' And the Duc d'Orléans, after a last letter to Charles X protesting his eternal loyalty, crept into Paris by night in civilian clothes, and was taken the next day, sweating with fear and excitement, to be sworn in at the Hôtel de Ville.

There was a difficult moment here, for the people were still bewildered by the turn events had taken, and they were not satisfied with a proclamation by the new Lieutenant-General which merely declared that 'the Charter would henceforth be a reality'. But the Duc d'Orléans saved the situation with the help of the aged Lafayette, who had reluctantly accepted Thiers' assurances that a monarchy would prove to be the best of republics. Holding a tricolour in one hand, the Duke led the so-called 'hero of two worlds' to one of the windows of the Hôtel de Ville and publicly embraced him. It was a kiss of betrayal, but the crowds were not to know that. They were reassured by the sight of the tricolour and the knowledge that the liberty-loving Lafayette approved of their new ruler, and they quietly dispersed. The Revolution was over.

Charles X, who had moved from Saint-Cloud to Rambouillet, now nominated the Duc d'Orléans to the position he already held by the authority of the Chamber, sent him his own and his son's abdication, and instructed him to proclaim his grandson the Duc de Bordeaux King of France, with the title of Henri V. Orléans replied with hypocritical regret that he was powerless to do anything without the Chamber's approval, and urged his cousin to leave the country. Charles hesitated, but when he was told that an armed mob was on its way to Rambouillet he decided that the best service he could do his little grandson was to go into exile. With his family he travelled towards the coast in a dignified and unhurried progress, meeting with nothing but courtesy and respect on the way. Court protocol was strictly observed, even in the most difficult circumstances: in one château a round table was cut square so that Charles could sit at it. Finally, on 16 August, the four companies of the Garde du Corps which had escorted the royal party all the way from Saint-Cloud lined up at Cherbourg, facing the sea; bugles sounded a farewell; and the last King of France and Navarre set sail for England.

Meanwhile, without even waiting for Charles to leave the country, the Duc d'Orléans had accepted a crown of sorts from the Chamber. On 9 August, sitting on a makeshift throne draped with tricolour flags, he swore to observe the newly revised Charter and was formally acclaimed Louis-Philippe, King of the French. There could scarcely be a greater contrast than that presented by the gorgeous ceremony at Reims in 1824 and this travesty of a coronation, but Louis-Philippe's wealthy backers were fully satisfied. They had hoisted him to power to safeguard the interests of the bourgeoisie, and a plain civil contract was all that they required. Thiers found the most apt description for the new régime when he called it 'an administrative monarchy'.

It was only now that the people of Paris awoke to the realization that they had been the victims of a gigantic confidence-trick. Daumier put all the bitterness they felt into a brilliant cartoon which showed the dead of July lifting their tombstones and asking if they had died in vain. The Republican Cavaignac protested that the insurgents had been cheated of the fruits of victory by the bourgeoisie, and swore that they would never allow the same thing to happen again. For the moment, however, there was nothing to be done. The spirit of the July Revolution was not dead, but for many years to come it was to find expression only in spasmodic insurrections and in the theatre.

CHAPTER SEVEN

MADEMOISELLE GEORGE

A few days before the July Revolution Frédérick Lemaître was engaged by Harel to play at the Odéon for twenty months in tragedy, comedy, drama and vaudeville.[1] His partner in many of the Odéon productions was to be Mlle George, and it was not long before he was invited to pay his respects to the great actress at her house in the Rue Madame.

This was a curious establishment.[2] The attics were occupied by the young Jules Janin, who was beginning to make a name for himself as a novelist and dramatic critic. Then came Harel, the principal tenant, who lived on the second floor. And on the first and ground floors George herself was established, together with her sister and two boys who passed for her nephews.

The elder boy, Tom Harel, was ten years old in 1830, and ten he remained, for theatrical purposes, for five or six years running. His younger brother Paul, or Popol as he was called, was remarkable for his enormous head, which gave him a rather grotesque appearance, and his capacity for guzzling. One day it was discovered that he had managed to establish a credit account at a local shop and in three months had run through no less than three hundred francs' worth of confectionery.

If Popol was a glutton, his Uncle Harel's besetting sin was uncleanliness. He had all a small boy's loathing for water, and he used to declare that St. Anthony was the happiest of saints to have a pig as a companion. Indeed, he spoke so enviously of St. Anthony's good fortune that on his birthday George and Dumas gave him a young pig wearing a diamond crown and carrying a bouquet of roses. Harel was delighted with the present. He called the pig Piaff-Piaff, petted him, pampered him, even slept with him. Unfortunately Piaff-Piaff became conscious of his power and began abusing it, and when he bit off the head of a pet pheasant belonging to Tom, he was sentenced to death in his owner's absence. Harel arrived home unexpectedly to hear piercing shrieks coming from the room where Piaff-Piaff was suffering execution. He guessed at once what was happening.

'Poor animal!' he cried; 'they are cutting his throat!' Then, after a moment's pause, he added in suitably sorrowful tones: 'At least I hope you told the butcher to put plenty of onions in the black pudding—because I simply adore onions!'

George too had her faults, the chief of which was an incurable addiction to comfort and luxury. She enjoyed nothing better than to lie on a big couch, dressed in furred pelisses and cashmere shawls in the winter and batiste teagowns in the summer, with the heads of two or three greyhounds peeping out from under her skirts. On the other hand her love of cleanliness was proverbial and put Harel to shame. She used to wash thoroughly before taking a bath, so as not to soil the water in which she would remain for over an hour, receiving her male friends with unselfconscious charm. Dumas for one never forgot the sight of her 'fastening up her hair with golden pins from time to time when it came down, giving her the opportunity to lift a pair of splendid arms right out of the water and reveal a bosom that might have been carved in Parian marble'.

Frédérick took an intense dislike to her, and in the unpublished notes for his memoirs he refers to her contemptuously as 'the most frightful hack and whore imaginable'. However, he had to resign himself to working with her, particularly as Harel decided for some reason to try him out in tragedy, which was George's own special domain. Thus his first appearance, on 12 August, was in Casimir Delavigne's tragedy *Les Vêpres siciliennes*. Paris had not yet recovered from the turmoil of the Revolution and the theatres were going through a difficult period, but the prospect of seeing Frédérick again in a play by the

'national bard' attracted a large audience to the Odéon. The
critics were all full of praise for his performance. The *Figaro*[3] declared that in verse tragedy as in prose drama Frédérick had
shown himself to be 'an ardent actor with no desire to gain
applause the easy way', while the *Corsaire*[4] paid tribute to 'his
sombre declamation, his brusque gestures, the love of liberty
shining in his eyes, and above all his subtle revelation of a con-
spiratorial soul'. But in spite of these favourable notices, and
others which acclaimed his acting in the Ducis adaptations of
Hamlet and *Othello*, Frédérick was convinced that tragedy was
not his genre. A significant anecdote[5] tells how, at a rehearsal of
Jouy's *Sylla*, the author assured him that his interpretation of
the part was even finer than Talma's. Frédérick promptly called
the manager over.

'Harel,' he said, in a voice choked with emotion, 'Monsieur de
Jouy has just said something which has hurt me deeply. Cancel
the rehearsal. I refuse to have anything more to do with *Sylla*.'

It was probably this awareness of his limitations as a tragic
actor that led Frédérick, after a performance of Racine's *Iphigénie* in September, to abandon tragedy in favour of modern
drama. The wisdom of this decision was shown the very next
month, when he won a tremendous success in *La Mère et la Fille*,
a play by Empis and Mazères in which he played the part of a
deceived husband who accidentally discovers his wife's infide-
lity.[6] The authors had courageously broken with the tradition
that a cuckold was a figure of fun, but it was left to Frédérick
to win the audience over to their point of view. He succeeded
beyond all expectations. Dumas, who was present at the first
night, declared that he was 'sublime in his artless, poignant grief,
his restrained despair'. And the audience, who had expected an
evening's uproarious amusement, left the theatre in tears.

Frédérick's next play was a far inferior work called *L'Abbesse
des Ursulines*, in which he played Père Joseph and Mlle George
the nymphomaniac abbess of the title.[7] This was only one of
countless productions in which the theatres of Paris, free at last
of all censorship, took their revenge on the priest-ridden régime

of Charles X with plays about scheming Jesuits, depraved nuns and concupiscent curés. The most lurid of these anticlerical concoctions, alluringly entitled *Les Victimes cloîtrées*, with Marie Dorval as the principal victim, played to packed houses at the Porte-Saint-Martin, and Harel expected the combination of George and Frédérick in a similar work to draw huge crowds. But by the time he launched out into anticlericalism the public was beginning to tire of it. In October a production of his which subjected the clergy to vulgar abuse[8] fell flat, and *L'Abbesse des Ursulines* was no luckier. After four performances it was taken off.

Harel was likewise one of the last managers to exploit the current Napoleonic vogue, though in this case through no fault of his own. He had in fact been the first to think of the idea of putting on a play about the Emperor, and on the morning after the July Revolution he asked Dumas to write one for him.[9] But Dumas refused. The memory of the scurvy fashion in which Napoleon had treated his father, General Thomas Dumas, still rankled in his mind, and he also considered it impossible to write a drama of this kind without arousing dangerous passions. Harel, however, was not an easy man to put off, and he continued to pester the playwright for a *Napoléon*. In the meantime, to his intense annoyance, other managers awoke to the realization that they could now present the great man on the stage with complete impunity, not only because there was no censorship, but also because the Bonapartists had helped to put Louis-Philippe on the throne. Soon every theatre save the Odéon had its Bonaparte or its Napoleon—studying in the Brienne Academy at the Nouveautés, crossing the Alps at the Cirque Olympique, dying at St. Helena at the Porte-Saint-Martin, and entering Paradise at the Gaîté. As he watched his rivals making money out of an idea which he regarded as his by right, Harel felt his patience draining away, and he finally decided to try force where persuasion had failed. Dumas was invited to a supper party at George's house after the first performance of *La Mère et la Fille*, and asked to stay on after the other guests had left. Then he was shown into a handsomely furnished room and told that he would not be allowed to leave it until *Napoléon* was written. He protested violently at first, but when it was pointed out to him that his room communicated with George's, and that splendid creature urged him not to be in too much of a hurry to get away, he accepted the situation with a good grace. Within a week the play was finished.[10]

Perhaps 'play' is not the right word to apply to *Napoléon Bonaparte*, for with its nine thousand lines and nineteen scenes it was rather an immense historical pageant. To link the various episodes together, Dumas invented a mysterious spy whom Napoleon pardoned in the first scene and who followed him devotedly wherever he went, dying with him at St. Helena. Inasmuch as the spy never really came to life but remained just a convenient symbol of loyalty, this was a crude technical device, and the play itself was a shoddy piece of work. Dumas dismissed it as 'scissors and paste stuff', but he maintained that 'the title would ensure a popular success, while the part of the spy would be sufficient to secure literary success'.

There remained the problem of choosing an actor to play the title role. Among the innumerable Napoleons walking the boards at this time there were four—Gobert, his stand-in Prudent, Edmond and Cazot—who bore an astonishing resemblance to the Emperor. Even off the stage they looked and behaved just like the victor of Austerlitz, Gobert walking along with a scowl on his face and his hands behind his back, Edmond stroking his forelock and taking pinches of snuff from a leather-lined waistcoat pocket, and Cazot barking at his dresser as if he were on the parade-ground. It was a common occurrence in that autumn of 1830 for some old soldier taking the air on the Boulevard to turn pale and spring to attention as he saw his Emperor approaching him.[11] But Frédérick, whom Harel suggested for the part at the Odéon, was quite unlike Napoleon in appearance, and Dumas held that in this case a physical resemblance was essential.[12] He was over-ruled by George, who stood up for her partner with admirable loyalty.

'My dear fellow,' she told the author, 'a genius like Frédérick can play any part well.'

Dumas gave in, and Frédérick was cast as the Emperor, with Lockroy as the Spy. Rehearsals were something of a nightmare for everyone concerned. There were over a hundred different characters in the play, and this meant that forty or fifty actors were required, some of them taking two or three parts. The stage-manager, Jouslin de la Salle, grew quite haggard with worry. Harel emptied three snuff-boxes at every rehearsal. As for Frédérick, faced with the task of committing four thousand lines to memory, he resorted to his favourite practice when learning a difficult part. This was to hire a cab and have himself driven out of Paris and back, declaiming all the way. Passersby were surprised to hear the sole occupant of a cab bellowing angrily and shaking his fist at a non-existent companion, but the driver enjoyed the experience and the part was rapidly mastered.

Meanwhile Harel had launched a massive publicity campaign, announcing that the production was going to cost a hundred thousand francs. Every newspaper had some item of gossip to retail about the play. Even Charles Maurice helped[13] by maliciously suggesting that George's name should have appeared on the playbills, 'in view of the *intimate* details this actress has furnished concerning Napoleon Bonaparte'.

The first night, on 10 January 1831, was a triumph for both manager and actors.[14] The audience had been asked to wear their National Guard uniforms, and the orchestra played military marches in the intervals. Every time the curtain went up there was a burst of applause for the scenery, which had taken a good part of Harel's hundred thousand francs. Two spectacular episodes—the burning of Moscow and the crossing of the Beresina—were considered particularly impressive. The supporting actors gave of their best, and Delaistre, who played the part of Hudson Lowe, was so convincing that he had to be provided with an escort after the show to save him from being stoned on his way home. But the centre of attraction was of course the latest Little Corporal.

Ever since childhood Frédérick had felt a passionate adoration for Napoleon, and he had been overjoyed when Dumas had offered him the chance to represent his hero on the stage. Wishing to do full justice to the part, he had made a point of consulting as many people as possible who had known the Emperor personally. The Duc de Bassano in particular had given him some useful indications as to Napoleon's speech, dress and mannerisms. The result was that in spite of the difference in build and appearance, and although Frédérick avoided the more obvious Napoleonic characteristics as being too commonplace, he deceived even those who had served the Emperor into believing for a few hours that this was what the great man had looked like. Thus at one point in the play, the scene depicting the crossing of the Beresina, a former secretary of Napoleon's called Menneval cried out: 'That's just like him!'[15]

But Frédérick's performance in *Napoléon Bonaparte* was never anything more than a brilliant and daring imposture. Gobert had identified himself completely with the Emperor—so completely, indeed, that he could not rid himself of his model's tics of speech and gesture, and became incapable of playing any other part on the stage.[16] Even if Frédérick had been closer to Napoleon in appearance, his personality was too strong to be submerged like Gobert's in that of an historical character. On the other hand he was prevented from imposing his personality on the part, as he usually did, by the combined forces of history, legend and the author. The public might be moved to tears every night by his acting of Napoleon's death-agony at St. Helena,[17] and Dumas might inscribe his copy of the play with the dedication 'To the Romantic Talma',[18] but Frédérick's greatest creations were still to come.

In the meantime, Dumas had been having trouble with the Comédie-Française over *Antony*, the most personal and passionate of all his plays. Based largely on his affair with Mélanie Waldor, it concerned the love of a bastard and social rebel for a married woman, and was a brilliant representation of contemporary passion. But Firmin, who had been given the title

role, had nothing of the necessary Byronic quality, while Mlle
Mars was determined to reduce the character of the heroine,
Adèle d'Hervey, to the limits of her own narrow emotional
range. At last Dumas lost patience with his two principal
players and offered *Antony* to Crosnier, the then manager of the
Porte-Saint-Martin. It was staged there on 3 May, with Marie
Dorval as Adèle and Pierre Bocage as Antony. Dumas had proposed casting Frédérick as the hero, but Dorval had rightly
pointed out that her old partner was not sufficiently pallid and
melancholy to play a star-crossed lover. Bocage was an inferior
actor with a gangling figure and a nasal voice—someone[19]
called him 'one of Frédérick Lemaître's colds in the head'—but
with his pale face and sad eyes he made the perfect Antony.

The first night of *Antony* was one of the great moments of
Romantic drama. 'The audience', wrote Gautier in later years,[20]
'was delirious; people clapped, sobbed, wept and shouted. The
flaming passion of the play had set every heart on fire. The young
women were all hopelessly in love with Antony; the young men
would have blown their brains out for Adèle d'Hervey. Modern
love was admirably portrayed, with quite extraordinary inten-
sity, by Bocage and Mme Dorval: Bocage the man of destiny
and Mme Dorval the weak woman *par excellence.*' Frédérick,
who was there to give Dorval his support and Bocage his
critical attention, maintained for the rest of his life that the
fourth act of *Antony* as they played it was the finest thing he had
ever seen on the stage.[21] As for the astounding climax of the
play, where Antony stabs Adèle and flings the dagger at the
feet of her returning husband, saying: 'She resisted me, so I
killed her!' it sent the audience into a frenzy of enthusiasm, and
they mobbed the author after the show, tearing his green tail-
coat to shreds. Indeed, Antony's last line became the most celebrated curtain-line in France, and audiences who saw the play
in Paris and the provinces waited for it in expectant anguish.
At one performance in Rouen, the curtain was accidentally rung
down before Bocage had time to pronounce the famous last
words.[22] The disappointed audience threatened to break up the

benches, Bocage sulkily refused to return to the stage, and it was left to Dorval to save the situation. She had the curtain raised, and advancing to the footlights, treated her public to a delightful variation of the usual dénouement.

'Gentlemen,' she said, 'I resisted him, so he killed me.'

Antony was an influential play in several respects. In the first place it mirrored the youthful passions of the age so well that it inspired countless young men to ape their own reflection. Flaubert later recorded how his schoolfellows in Rouen took to wearing daggers and assuming melancholic expressions, while Eugène de Mirecourt[23] stated that 'the salons were suddenly filled with crowds of young men with pale faces, bushy eyebrows, bony frames, long black hair, and eyes veiled by tortoiseshell eye-glasses'. *Antony* also started off a whole series of plays, lasting down to the present day, concerned with the problem of passion and adultery in modern society. But in the history of Romantic drama its chief importance was that it marked the beginning of the move from the official theatre to the Boulevard, and of the close collaboration between authors and actors.

The first Romantic playwright to follow Dumas's example was Hugo, who took his *Marion de Lorme* to the Porte-Saint-Martin, where it was put on immediately after *Antony*, in August 1831.[24] Dorval was universally acclaimed for her performance in the title-role, which had in fact been largely rewritten to suit her frenzied, exclamatory style. Bocage, on the other hand, was unimpressive and monotonous, and the minor parts were poorly acted. *Marion* played to reasonably good houses for some weeks, but the public rated dramatic invention higher than poetic skill, and gave voice to its disapproval night after night.

It is said[25] that when Vigny, who had lately become Dorval's lover, complained to Hugo of the opposition she had to contend with, the author of *Marion de Lorme* retorted: 'What can I do about it, my dear fellow? It isn't given to everyone to have the calm of the desert at his theatre.' This was a wounding refer-

ence to Vigny's play *La Maréchale d'Ancre*, which had fallen
flat at the Odéon in spite of creditable performances by Frédérick
and Mlle George.[26] Other people had drawn similar contrasts
between the two plays, the two theatres and the two actresses —
among them George herself. Tired of the Odéon and envious of
Dorval's success, she told Harel that she wanted to move to one
of the Boulevard theatres, where she would have a better chance
of triumphing over her new rival in a Dumas or Hugo play than
if she remained in her present backwater. George's wish was
always Harel's command, and towards the end of the year he
bought the licence of the Porte-Saint-Martin from Crosnier for
the ruinous sum of 250,000 francs.[27] However, he was delighted
with his purchase, for with two theatres at his disposal he could
arrange exchanges of plays and actors, transferring the Odéon
company to the Right Bank for a while and vice versa.

For his opening production at the Porte-Saint-Martin Harel
chose *Richard Darlington*, the first of many dramas which Dumas
wrote in collaboration.[28] Prosper Goubaux and Jacques Beudin,
the authors of *Trente ans*, had brought him the unfinished draft
of a play based on Scott's novel *The Surgeon's Daughter*, about
an English politician who murdered his low-born wife for the
sake of a rich marriage, a vast fortune and a peerage. The hero
of this play was yet another bastard, this time the offspring of an
improbable union between an aristocratic lady and the public
executioner, but he was forceful and ambitious, with nothing of
Antony's melancholy. Dumas saw at once that this was a part
for Frédérick rather than Bocage, and he developed it with an
eye to his interpreter's special gifts. Pages of dialogue were
written or re-written to give full scope to Frédérick's thunderous
voice and vehement delivery, notably in a noisy election scene
and in a heated exchange of words between Darlington and the
King's Ministers. At last the play was put into rehearsal, complete except for one important detail: the authors were unable
to decide how Darlington's wife Jenny was to be killed. Then
one morning inspiration came to Dumas,[29] and when Goubaux
arrived to see him he stood on his bed in his night-shirt,

waving his arms excitedly and shouting: 'I chuck her out of the window! I chuck her out of the window!' This was a murder method which had never been used before on the French stage, and the authors were sure that it would have a sensational effect. So were the privileged people who were allowed to watch the final rehearsals. 'What they are saying about Richard Darlington', reported the Courrier des Théâtres.[30] 'is enough to make your hair stand on end.'

The audience at the first night, on 10 December 1831, had also been drawn to the Porte-Saint-Martin by the knowledge that Richard Darlington had a political side to it. Admittedly the play was set in England, but in their restive state the French public were quite prepared to get excited over a representation of English political life. Harel certainly did his best to give them every satisfaction. The election scene was like a Rowlandson drawing come to life, with practically the entire company on the stage, watching the voting, waving banners, tearing down posters, fighting, screaming and cursing.[31] The scene in the House of Commons was no less impressive, and called for so many actors that Harel co-opted little Popol to play the part of the Speaker.[32] The boy was placed in such a position as to appear the height of a grown man, with a bell at his right hand and a glass of sugared water at his left, and everyone admired the deliberate fashion in which he rang for silence or sipped his drink. Doligny, who played Richard's villainous accomplice Tompson, was also highly praised. So was the actor Delafosse, who when both his pistols missed fire kept his head and killed Tompson with an imaginary dagger. As for Louise Noblet, though Dumas would not admit that she could compare with Marie Dorval, she delighted the audience with her playing of the tender, loyal Jenny. But in the last analysis it was Frédérick who carried the play on his shoulders and made it the triumph it was.

'He had been excellent at the rehearsals', wrote Dumas;[33] 'at the actual performance he was stupendous. I do not know where he had studied that gambler on a grand scale we call a man of ambition: no doubt where every genius has to study what he cannot know except in dreams—in his own heart.'

Audience and actors alike were electrified by what one critic[34] called Frédérick's 'physical fascination, his animal magnetism'. When he advanced on Jenny to throw her over the precipice on which their house was perched, Louise Noblet fell so completely under his influence that she uttered screams of genuine terror. 'This last scene', says Dumas,[35] 'was one of the most frightening things I have ever seen on the stage. When Jenny asked Richard: "What are you going to do?" and he replied: "I don't know, but say your prayers!" a tremendous shudder went through the whole house, and a murmur of fear, escaping from every breast, turned into a terrified shriek.'

Not content with this, Frederick went on to petrify his audience with a characteristic piece of stage business he had devised. Recalling the first performance of *Richard Darlington* over fifty years later,[36] Ernest Legouvé wrote:

> Do you know what Frédérick did to make his reappearance on the balcony doubly frightful? First, he arranged for a ray of green light to shine on his face from the wings. Then, to complete the desired effect, he got the actress who played Jenny to drop her muslin veil as she fled from him on to the balcony. This veil was the first thing that met Frédérick's gaze as he came back on-stage. A lesser actor would have shuddered at the sight, for it was like Jenny's ghost. But Frédérick ran up to the veil, snatched it up and stuffed it into his pocket as if it had been a handkerchief. Then, with that insolent sang-froid that was his alone, he went to open the door to his prospective father-in-law with the end of the veil fluttering from his pocket. The effect was overwhelming.

It was too much for some members of the audience. Dumas came across Musset in the corridor, looking rather green about the gills.

'What's the matter, my dear poet?' he asked.

'What's the matter?' repeated Musset. 'Why, I'm suffocating, that's all.'

He could scarcely have paid a higher compliment to Frédérick's acting. Other tributes were more explicit. Edmond Got, for instance, remembering in later life the great actors he had seen in his youth, put Frédérick's performance in *Richard Darlington* on a level with Mlle Mars's Célimène in *Le Misanthrope*, Dorval's Kitty Bell in *Chatterton* and Rachel's Camille in *Horace*.[37] There was certainly no doubting the admiration the public felt for Dumas's interpreter. If, as even Charles Maurice had to admit,[38] *Richard Darlington* was 'not just a success, but a madness, a mania, a craving, a necessity', it was because Frédérick Lemaître had at last won general recognition as the first actor of France.

CHAPTER EIGHT

CARNIVAL, PLAGUE AND RIOT

THE Boulevard du Crime was a very different place in the eighteen-thirties from what it had been before the July Revolution. For one thing, the hey-day of melodrama was over. Pixérécourt might still hold sway at the Gaîté and the Ambigu, but the repertory of the other theatres had undergone a drastic change. The public had grown tired of the time-worn tales of villainy punished and virtue triumphant, and of the stereotyped characters, the familiar situations and the hackneyed words which had once moved them to tears. As a result melodrama had given place to the more literary Romantic drama, sentimentality to passion, hatchets to daggers, brigands and shepherdesses to poisoners, adulterers and politicians.

In appearance too the Boulevard had changed considerably.[1] The ditches had been filled in, pavements had been laid, the shacks and hovels adjoining the theatres had been pulled down and houses or cafés built in their place, and wooden barriers had been erected to make queuing for the play a more orderly business. The street was still crowded every night with actors, actresses, dancers, dressers, scene-shifters and theatre-goers, not to mention the scores of hawkers selling joke-books, almanachs, programmes and cut-price tickets. But the orange-girls were now installed under great red umbrellas which protected them from the sunshine and the rain, and the *marchands de coco* in their smart cocked hats now dispensed their liquorice-water from brightly coloured urns decorated with gilded genies or winged lions. Most important of all, the knockabout turns given outside the smaller theatres to attract an audience had been prohibited, and the open-air stalls and drinking-booths swept away. The Boulevard du Temple could not hope to compete in elegance with a worldly thoroughfare like the Boulevard des Italiens, but it had at least lost its old fairground appearance. Only once a year did it regain something of the riotous gaiety it had known in the eighteen-twenties, and that was at Carnival time. Then all the fever and violence seething under the surface of Parisian life would erupt in a vast bacchanalia that lasted for days on end. In later years the Carnival celebrations would be confined to the theatres and dance-halls, but as yet the new régime did not feel strong enough to introduce repressive measures which might easily spark off a revolution. So it was on the open Boulevard that Paris spent its energy each spring in a wild orgy of dancing and drinking.

Every afternoon in Carnival week the streets were filled with thousands of masked revellers in cheap fancy dress—harlequins and colombines, pierrots and pierrettes, shepherds and shepherdesses. Through the crowd moved every conceivable type of wheeled vehicle, from the vast carriages of the Faubourg Saint-Germain, manned by specially hired market porters to defend the occupants against the unfriendly attentions of the mob, down to the elegant tilburies in which frock-coated, top-hatted, yellow-gloved dandies sat with their diminutive grooms or 'tigers'. The best-known carriage of all made its appearance on the last Sunday before Lent. It was a large open *barouche* drawn by four horses and preceded by out-riders blowing great hunting horns that were wound round their bodies. About a dozen young men and women in fancy dress stood in it as it bowled along the boulevards, showering the crowds with confetti and flower-filled egg-shells and money. And as the mob scrambled for the coins in the gutter they yelled: 'Vive Lord Seymour! Vive Milord l'Arsouille!'

Lord Henry Seymour was a hearty young sportsman who made horse-racing fashionable in France and became the first president of the French Jockey Club, from which he resigned in disgust when he discovered that his fellow members preferred gambling to physical exercise.[2] He was a misanthropic individual with a taste for cruel practical jokes and humiliating remarks. Thus he enjoyed nothing better than making an unsuspecting guest drink an emetic or bribing a cab-driver to knock people down in the street; and he was reputed to have said to one of his mistresses: 'Please put my boots outside the door. They will return the compliment one of these days.' His mania for sport, his sadistic humour and his splenetic temperament were all regarded as typically English. In fact, however, he never set foot in England and was not of English birth, being the illegitimate son of the Comte Casimir de Montrond and the Marchioness of Hertford. Nor was he the 'Milord l'Arsouille' of the Paris Carnival, for while he thoroughly deserved the name of 'rake', he was scarcely the man to scatter largesse among the people. The real 'Milord l'Arsouille' was a certain Charles de La Battut, who in spite of his French name was more of an Englishman than Seymour, for he was the illegitimate son of a rich English chemist.[3] Having bought his name from a Breton aristocrat, he now wanted to buy notoriety from the people of Paris, and he squandered his fortune recklessly in a desperate attempt to attain popular recognition. But it was all in vain. Either because they could not tell the difference between the two eccentrics, or out of a desire to punish the upstart La Battut for his pretentiousness, the Paris mob persisted in identifying him with Seymour. At last, furious at being greeted wherever he went with cries of 'Vive Lord Seymour! Vive Milord l'Arsouille!' he gave up the struggle and retired to Naples, where he died before the age of thirty, broken in mind and body.

We do not know if he and Seymour ever came together, but they may well have met at the climax of the Carnival, during the notorious 'Descent from La Courtille'. At dawn on Ash Wednesday tens of thousands of people would gather outside the drinking-dens and dance-halls in this high-lying suburb and then sweep down upon Paris in a fearsome human avalanche. Originally this annual invasion of the capital had been a plebeian affair, but in recent years the carriage classes had taken part after dancing all night at the masked balls in the city. So for four hours rich and poor joined together in this extra-ordinary rout, tramps and beggars in filthy rags rubbing shoulders with dishevelled revellers in fancy dress, the whole motley mob dancing and singing and fighting and reeling in and out of the roadside taverns until at last, about ten in the morning, they reached the Boulevard du Temple and dispersed.

The Carnival celebrations of 1832 were unusually hectic, even for these tumultuous times. This was because a great cholera epidemic had spread from India across Russia and Poland to reach London during February, and it was only a matter of time before it would cross the Channel. In a desperate attempt to forget the threat that hung over them, the people of Paris danced with feverish abandon, and nowhere more wildly than at the Théâtre des Variétés. The masked balls there were already the gayest and most popular of the Carnival festivities, but never before had they known the success they obtained this year. They owed this enormous vogue to La Battut and his friends, who invaded the theatre on the last Monday in Lent, linked arms at the head of the temporary staircase from the grand circle to the orchestra stalls and hurled themselves down upon the merry-makers. Then, snatching partners from the crowd, they proceeded to dance the *cancan*, which had been introduced to France from Algeria the previous year but had never been seen before except in low suburban taverns. The police promptly expelled La Battut and his companions from the theatre, but ten minutes later they were back to delight the crowd with another display of the exciting new dance. The next morning Armand Dartois, the manager of the Variétés, called on La Battut to assure him that the police would not interfere again and begged him to return to the theatre that night and dance the *cancan* once more.

Soon it was all the rage in Paris, intoxicating the young and scandalizing the old. 'When one sees', wrote one observer,[4] 'with what gestures and movements of the body the masked men approach the masked women, press close to them, and actually throw them backwards and forwards between themselves to the accompaniment of continual cries and laughter and ribald jokes, one can only be filled with disgust, nay more, with horror and revulsion at this mass depravity, this flouting of all morality and shame.'

The musical director at the Variétés was just the man to exploit the new vogue. Napoléon Musard, the so-called Emperor of the Carnival, was a seemingly insignificant creature, always dressed in black, with a yellow pock-marked face. But as soon as he picked up his baton he was seized with a demoniacal frenzy, and this communicated itself to the orchestra and the dancers. At the height of the excitement he would suddenly smash a chair or fire off a pistol, and then utter pandemonium would break loose. An onlooker[5] has described how at this point one could see 'masked women, like ecstatic mænads, with flushed cheeks, breathlessly heaving breasts, parched lips, and half-undone flying hair, careering round the room, less on their feet than being dragged along bodily, until with the last chord they collapsed breathlessly on the nearest seat'. Small wonder that the little man in black who conducted these orgies was popularly supposed to be in league with the Devil.

The two favourite diversions during this tense waiting period were dancing the *cancan* at the Variétés and going to see Frédérick at the Porte-Saint-Martin. *Richard Darlington* had been taken off at the end of January, and Harel had decided to follow it with a revival of *L'Auberge des Adrets*. But first he had had to fight a legal battle in the courts with Couder, the manager of the Ambigu, who maintained[6] that 'the *moral ownership*, the *poem* of the costumes worn by Macaire and Bertrand belonged to him, seeing that it was his tailor who had *composed* or *created* them'. Couder had lost his case, the magistrates refusing to see anything poetic in a bundle of rags worth 1 franc 20 centimes, and on 28 January the *Auberge* had opened with an actor called Serres playing Bertrand to Frédérick's Macaire.[7]

It was a brilliant partnership, and all Paris flocked to the

Porte-Saint-Martin to see the two bandits. Anne-Gabrielle de Cisternes de Coutiras, Vicomtesse de Poilloüe de Saint-Mars, better known by her laconic pen-name of the Comtesse Dash, recorded that 'Frédérick Lemaître and Serres were splendid. Frédérick had found certain gestures and intonations which I feel sure the bitterest grief would have been powerless to resist. Whether you liked it or not you had to laugh.' No one performance of the *Auberge* was quite like the next, for every night Frédérick and Serres improvised new topical references and hilarious situations. The novelty which found most favour with the public, though not with the authorities, was a scene in which Frédérick pursued a gendarme into one of the boxes, shot him, and tossed the corpse on to the stage. One night when there was a rather thin house, he had the curtain raised during an interval, bowed to the audience, and asked leave to make an announcement.

'Gentlemen,' he said, 'we regret that we are unable to murder a gendarme this evening, as the actor who plays that part is indisposed. But tomorrow we shall kill two.'

And the next night the house was packed.

At last, however, the febrile gaiety of the capital was suddenly stilled, for on 26 March the plague arrived.[8] The weather at this time was magnificent, the air was filled with the scent of almond blossom, and Paris was noisily celebrating the middle of Lent with another carnival. Then a harlequin at one of the public balls snatched off his mask and it was seen that his face had turned blue. Other dancers collapsed and were taken to the central hospital, the Hôtel-Dieu, where most of them died within a few hours. They were buried with frantic haste, still wearing their fancy dress, and their places were quickly taken by fresh victims. Day by day the death-roll mounted; in one day alone over eight hundred people were reported to have died. There were not enough hearses to cope with the situation, so farm carts were brought into service, and then huge removal vans draped in black and crammed with coffins. No relatives or friends followed these common funerals to the common grave, and often the dead were simply wrapped in sheets and left on the doorstep to be collected by some passing cart.

Reactions to the plague varied enormously. The poorer classes suspected that the cholera was an official invention and that the authorities were really trying to poison the common people; when the Prefect of Police took the trouble to issue a denial, suspicion turned to certainty, and several innocent citizens were lynched because they bent over wells or lingered outside food-shops. Those who could afford to leave the capital fled to the country, but the Royal Family stayed at the Tuileries; the young Duc d'Orléans even visited the hospitals with the Président du Conseil, Casimir Périer, who died of cholera shortly afterwards. Writers such as Fontaney and Merimée also toured the wards, but only to indulge their taste for the macabre. Hugo gave a party at his house in the Place Royale, at which Liszt gave a haunting rendering of the Funeral March from Beethoven's piano sonata. As for Dumas, he occupied his time between entertaining friends and counting the hearses that passed his window by dashing off a little comedy for a benefit performance. 'If the cholera calls,' he told his maid, 'don't open the door, Catherine.' But the cholera slipped in despite this prohibition, and the playwright was obliged to take to his bed, where he was anæsthetized and possibly cured by a glass of ether which the distracted Catherine gave him to drink. The relevant chapter in his memoirs is proudly if untruthfully entitled: 'I invent etherization.'

One of the few people who seemed to be entirely unaffected by the plague was Harel.[9] He regarded it as a myth, and a medieval superstition, and put a bit of paper in his snuff-box to remind himself that he was in nineteenth-century Paris. A confirmed Voltairian, he was deeply shocked one day to come across one of his own nephews, Popol, on his knees, praying for divine protection.

'O Lord,' he heard the boy say, 'take my Aunt George, take my Uncle Harel, take my brother Tom, take mama Bébelle, take my friend Provost, but leave little Popol and the cook!'

This remarkable prayer went unanswered, for Popol was carried off by the plague a few hours later. Uncle Harel was not noticeably grief-stricken; he was too concerned about falling box-office receipts to care about the death of a little nephew. Other managers had given up the struggle and closed their doors, but not Harel. First, showing a lack of scruples which amazed even those who knew him of old, he put a paragraph in all the newspapers to the effect that not a single case of cholera had occurred in a theatre, and blandly 'presented this incontestable fact for scientific investigation'. Then he set about looking for a play that would bring the public flocking to the Porte-Saint-Martin as soon as the epidemic showed some sign of abating.

He found it in *La Tour de Nesle*, a play by a young provincial called Frédéric Gaillardet. Set in Paris at the beginning of the fourteenth century, it showed the Queen of France, Marguerite de Bourgogne, and her two sisters indulging every night in adulterous orgies with strangers who were lured to the lonely Tour de Nesle for the purpose and thrown into the river the next morning. One of these young men, Captain Buridan, had been Marguerite's lover some years before, and he escaped to blackmail the Queen into having him appointed First Minister. Together, Queen and Minister embarked on further crimes, until at last, in a dramatic conclusion, they were brought to justice as a pair of common murderers.

This, as Harel saw at once, was just the play to shake the public out of its apathy—provided it was written with sufficient skill and zest to conceal the improbability of the plot. But young Frédéric Gaillardet had no experience of writing for the theatre, and Jules Janin, who was summoned from his attic to doctor the play, abandoned the attempt in disgust. So once again Harel turned to Dumas for help, laying siege to him in his sick-room, sending in his card to the playwright every day, and finally persuading him to re-write *La Tour de Nesle* while he was still convalescent.

Dumas was delighted with Gaillardet's story, which had all the violence and excitement he saw in his own times and put into his own works. But the play lacked what he considered the essential element of conflict. 'The real crux of the drama', he wrote, 'seemed to me to be the struggle between Buridan and Marguerite de Bourgogne, between an adventurer and a queen, the one armed with all the resources of his genius, the other with the powerful weapons of her rank.' He therefore altered the play in such a way as to highlight this struggle, moulding the part of Marguerite de Bourgogne to fit the queenly George and that of Buridan to suit the tempestuous, swashbuckling Frédérick. As fast as he completed an act it was delivered to Harel, copied out and put into rehearsal.

Harel's worries, however, were not yet over. Gaillardet was indignant to learn that his play had been tampered with, and challenged his enforced collaborator to a duel as soon as he arrived in Paris. Eventually he agreed to a compromise: that both authors should be entitled to include the play in their collected works, but that it should be billed as by 'Messieurs Gaillardet and * * *'. Dumas was quite happy to remain anonymous, as he had done in the case of *Richard Darlington* and was to do again, but Harel wanted the public to know that he was responsible for the new play. As usual, the wily little manager had his way in the end. The authors of *La Tour de Nesle* were stated on the bills to be 'Messieurs * * * and Gaillardet', the younger man brought an action to put the asterisks in their proper place—and Harel got all the publicity he wanted.

In the meantime the play had run into casting trouble. Dumas, who described Frédérick[10] as 'the French Kean, a man of a capricious nature, violent and passionate—and therefore very natural in passionate, violent and capricious parts', states in his memoirs that the actor 'was afraid of the cholera, stayed in the country, and in spite of all the rehearsal notices that were sent to him gave no sign of life'. The *Souvenirs de Frédérick Lemaître*, based on the actor's verbal reminiscences, tell a rather different story.[11] Here Frédérick is reported as saying:

One evening, as I was leaving the theatre, I was struck down by the cholera with such violence that for five days I lay between life

and death. As soon as Poulletier and the theatre doctors felt that I
was out of danger they urged me to go and spend my convalescence
in the country. Not wanting to go far from Paris, where I hoped to
resume my rehearsals of *La Tour de Nesle* any day, I rented a little
house at Saint-Mandé. There I installed my wife and my mother, together with the children, whom I was happy to put out of reach
of the plague, which I had been afraid to see striking them down in
their turn.

But Harel and George, far from waiting for my convalescence to
come to an end, eagerly seized on the opportunity that presented
itself to take my part away from me. Did George imagine that
her popularity with the Boulevard public was enough in itself to
ensure the success of the play? Or had the triumphant run of
Richard Darlington annoyed her? Whatever the truth of the matter,
the upshot was that a few days later Bocage was engaged instead of
me to create the part of Buridan.

When he heard what had happened, Frédérick rushed to Paris
to protest. 'I have never seen anybody', write Dumas, 'in such
a state of vexation as he was. A great actor, an artist of talent
and feeling, Frédérick was hurt in both respects.' Dumas himself was annoyed that a part he had written specially for
Frédérick should have been transferred without his knowledge
to a lesser actor of very different gifts, and he promised to do
his best to restore the original arrangement.[12] 'It is absolutely
in my interests', he wrote,[13] 'that you should play Buridan and
Bocage l'Échelle.' But Bocage refused to abandon his part unless
Harel paid him the forfeit of 4,000 francs stipulated in his
contract.[14] With no hope of finding this sum, Frédérick had to
give way. 'Your grief was a fine sight, Frédérick,' declared
Dumas, 'and I shall never forget it.'

As it happened, the initial success of *La Tour de Nesle*, which
opened on 29 May with George and Bocage in the leading
parts, was extremely short-lived, for a week later rioting broke
out in Paris and all the theatres were closed.

The occasion of this fresh insurrection was the funeral on 5
June of General Lamarque, a Liberal deputy who had fought
under Napoleon and who had won the people's respect in the
July Revolution.[15] The weather that day was hot and oppressive,

black clouds rolled across the sky, and the atmosphere was electric. The funeral procession had all the appearance of a huge anti-monarchical demonstration. Led by the Republican gunners of the National Guard, students, foreign refugees, workers and members of the powerful secret societies, some fifty thousand people advanced across Paris to the sound of muffled drums, giving voice from time to time to a vast cry of: 'Honour to General Lamarque!' When one man, terrified by the mood of the crowd, asked: 'Where are they leading us?' a voice replied: 'To the Republic, and we invite you to sup with us tonight in the Tuileries!' At the Pont d'Austerlitz the *Marseillaise*, which had been forbidden for over a year, was sung with frantic enthusiasm; and Étienne Arago, who had played an important part in the July Revolution, sparked off a new revolt with a great cry of: 'Vive la République!' Within a matter of hours, fighting was going on all over Paris.

This time, however, the insurrection took a very different course from that of 1830. For one thing, the King was in Paris at the time, and behaved with remarkable courage, riding down the boulevards while the revolt was still raging. Then the authorities, after a few hours of complete confusion, began moving troops in from Saint-Cloud and Versailles, and rapidly broke down the barricades. As for the National Guard, who apart from the gunners were bourgeois satisfied with their bourgeois monarch, they had been thoroughly scared by the sight of a red flag at General Lamarque's funeral, so that this time they ranged themselves against the insurgents. But perhaps the most significant change was in the attitude of the women of Paris, who were tired of bloodshed and longed for peace. When Dumas saw a young mother administer a hiding to her child for throwing a stone at a cavalryman, he remarked sadly: 'The women are not with us this time. We are lost!'

As was usual in a Paris insurrection, the revolt was concentrated in the Saint-Martin district, around the theatres. Dumas was shot at by regular troops as he was entering the Porte-Saint-Martin, where he found Harel in despair at the closing of his theatre and George half-dead with fright. Minutes later a party of insurgents broke in and refused to leave until they had been loaned a score of rifles from Crosnier's production of *Napoléon at Schœnbrunn*. A few yards down the Boulevard Saint-Martin, in his fourth-floor flat at No. 8, Frédérick was sitting down to dinner with his fellow-actors Provost and Serres when they heard the sound of galloping hoofs.[16] Leaning out of the window, the three friends saw, first a squadron of lancers charging towards the Porte Saint-Denis, and then a detachment of the National Guard shooting two youths against a wall. Years later Frédérick declared:

> I can still see the younger of the two, a boy of about fifteen, bareheaded and pale-faced, his white shirt torn open so that his chest was exposed. He had gone down on his knees and was holding his hands out as if to ask for mercy. He fell the first.
>
> Without knowing or caring about the rights and wrongs of the affair, we wished we could have gone to the rescue of those two poor devils slaughtered by a score of men. Seeing the brutes leave their victims and go staggering off, more under the influence of drink than gunpowder, I could not help thinking of the savagery of the bourgeois shop-keeper who turns soldier without anything warlike in his temperament, who tries to hide his fear under a pretence of courage that rapidly degenerates into ferocity, and who appoints himself judge and executioner with the fixed idea of doing his killing and getting safely home as quickly as possible.

These reflections were interrupted by the sound of breaking glass, as some of the National Guardsmen about whom Frédérick had been musing opened fire on the three actors, shattering a mirror at the back of the room. He hurriedly shut the window and they went back to their meal. After dinner Provost left for home, but Frédérick and Serres stayed up all night in the dining-room, going into the sitting-room from time to time to see what was happening on the Boulevard.

When morning came, Frédérick took Serres into the adjoining flat, which he had only just taken over to provide extra accommodation for his growing family. While he was explaining what alterations he intended making, he noticed a cupboard concealed in the wainscoting. It was locked, but he forced it open—and discovered to his horror that it contained a miniature arsenal complete with powder, lead, bullets, bullet moulds and cartridges. The previous tenant had obviously been an insurgent who had not had time to remove all his belongings, but who would believe that? Firing was still going on in the street, and soldiers or National Guardsmen could be seen going in and out of other houses. If any loyal troops broke into Frédérick's flat and found this stock of explosives, then Robert Macaire and Bertrand could look forward to being put against a wall and shot like the two youths the night before. Looking round in desperation for some means of getting rid of the incriminating ammunition, Frédérick hit upon the idea of throwing it all down the lavatory. But he had scarcely dropped the first handful of bullets into space than there was a tremendous explosion five floors down, in Paul de Kock's basement flat. The terrified novelist rushed into the courtyard yelling for help, and Frédérick got downstairs only just in time to stop the concierge from calling in the National Guard. When he explained what had happened, it was agreed that it was in everybody's interests to dispose of the remaining munitions, but in a rather more orthodox fashion; and in the end they were buried in the cellar of No. 8.

By now the insurrection had been reduced to a small pocket of resistance around the Cloître Saint-Merry. Here about sixty insurgents went on fighting under the leadership of a man called Jeanne, a veteran of the July Days, making bullets out of the lead gutter-pipes and cartridge-wads out of posters torn from the walls. At Laffitte's house, which had become the Opposition headquarters as in 1830, someone observed that everything was over.

'No it isn't', said a working-man who had overheard the remark. And in a dramatic phrase typical of the times he explained: 'They are still ringing the tocsin of Saint-Merry, and as long as you can hear a sick man's death-rattle he is alive.'

But in the afternoon of the 6th the sound of the bell was

drowned by a dull explosion as a cannon was brought to bear on the Cloître. The last rebel defences were breached and the troops poured into the Saint-Merry stronghold, wreaking the same savage vengeance that Frédérick had witnessed that morning. The defeated insurgents were shot, bayoneted or clubbed to death, and their wounded hurled out of upper-storey windows. By four o'clock Paris was quiet again.

The suppression of the Republican insurrection in Paris was followed by good news for Louis-Philippe from Schœnbrunn in Austria. There, on 22 July, the young Duc de Reichstadt, formerly King of Rome, died in his bed. The death of the Emperor's son, whom loyal Bonapartists had always regarded as Napoleon II, removed from the scene a figure who inspired dangerous enthusiasm even if he was not dangerous in himself. True, there was an heir to the Imperial title in Prince Louis-Napoleon Bonaparte, the son of the late King of Holland and Hortense de Beauharnais. But he was generally considered to be a foolish young man who could never become a rallying-point for Bonapartist loyalties and intrigues. Louis-Philippe felt that he could breathe more freely.

There remained the problem of the Legitimists, which had now reached an acute stage. In May the Duchesse de Berry had raised the flag of revolt in the Vendée, calling for the overthrow of her Uncle Louis-Philippe, and proclaiming her son, the Duc de Bordeaux, Henri V of France. But the people of the Vendée had lost most of their old ardour for the Legitimist cause, and the revolt was a miserable fiasco. Hunted by Government troops, the Duchess finally took refuge in a house in Nantes, where in October she was literally smoked out of her hiding-place behind an attic chimney-piece. For a time it seemed as if she might prove more dangerous in captivity than at large, for the romantic plight of a princess imprisoned in a gloomy fortress touched the hearts of the public. But then it was discovered that she was pregnant, and she confessed to having secretly married an Italian nobleman. The laughter that greeted this news dealt a deadly blow to Legitimist hopes. Even the most devoted supporters of the Regent of France could summon up little enthusiasm for the Countess Lucchesi-Palli. After the birth of her supposedly Italian offspring, the Government felt quite safe in releasing her.

The seal was set on Louis-Philippe's triumph in November 1832, ironically enough by an attempt on his life. He was riding across the Pont Royal one day when a shot rang out. With his usual presence of mind he bent down over the saddle, and then waved to the crowd, who cheered his courage. This unsuccessful coup aroused widespread indignation, and had the effect of discrediting the Opposition and consolidating the monarchy. There was a general reaction against the idea of violence, and a longing for peace and tranquillity. The reign of the bourgeois had begun in earnest.

CHAPTER NINE

LUCRÈCE BORGIA

AFTER the *Tour de Nesle* dispute, Frédérick's friends fully expected him to break with Harel and leave the Porte-Saint-Martin. In fact, however, he stayed at the theatre, acted in several revivals and a nondescript novelty called *Le Barbier du roi d'Aragon*,[1] and was finally rewarded with the principal male part in Dumas's next play, *Le Fils de l'émigré*.

Dumas had written this work in collaboration with a certain Anicet-Bourgeois, turning out the last two acts during 7 and 8 June, in the aftermath of the Lamarque insurrection.[2] On the 9th he read in a newspaper that he had been taken with arms on him in the Cloître Saint-Merry, court-martialled during the night, and shot at three in the morning. Charles Nodier, always a model of tact, wrote to inquire whether his execution would prevent him from dining the next day at the Arsenal, adding that he would be 'delighted at the opportunity to ask you for news of the other world'. But Dumas's friends at court told him that the possibility of his arrest had been seriously discussed, and advised him to leave the country for a few months. The consequence was that Dumas was in Switzerland, industriously gathering material for a book of travel impressions, when *Le Fils de l'émigré* was launched upon Paris, on 28 August.

It was an utter fiasco.[3] The theme of the play—the diabolical hatred of an *émigré* nobleman for the common people—was crude enough, but the development of the theme was cruder still. The dramatic critic of the *Constitutionnel* described the work, not unjustly, as 'an incredible chaos of iniquities and absurdities' set

H

in 'a den of slavery, murder and prostitution', and assured his readers that at first he took it to be a parody in which the two authors had 'piled up crudity upon crudity, mountain upon mountain, crime upon crime, obscenity upon obscenity, to bring the more shame upon our licentious dramatists'. The discovery that *Le Fils de l'émigré* was meant as serious drama filled him, so he said, with 'ennui and disgust'.

Two scenes struck audience and critics as particularly shocking. One was in the Prologue, when a curtain at the back of the stage was raised to show the heroine on her bed of labour, having just given birth to the nobleman's bastard son. The other was in the last act, when the hero, if such he could be called, was marched off to the guillotine with his head shaved and his hands tied behind his back. 'At this point,' reported the *Constitutionnel*, 'the public rose in a body and would not see or hear any more; they felt sick with disgust; the women turned away or averted their eyes to avoid seeing the head that was about to be cut off; they hissed, they shouted down these shameful things, and justice was done.'

Doing justice to the play appears to have involved hurling seats at the actors. It was the noisiest performance Frédérick had ever known. Mlle George, who had been eager to play a woman of the people as a change from her usual queens and empresses, began to wish she had never asked Dumas to write her a 'common' part. Dumas himself, when he returned to Paris, found that several of his acquaintances 'had become shortsighted during my absence and failed to recognize me'. Even the notorious Dr. Véron, who used to boast that he had drunk champagne every day of his life and possessed every woman he wanted, felt entitled to give him a stern lecture on his immorality.

The odd thing was that, while *Le Fils de l'émigré* had to be taken off after nine riotous nights, *La Tour de Nesle*, with the same author, the same actors and the same basic ingredients of sex and violence, continued to enjoy tremendous popularity. Bocage went on leave in the autumn, and Harel promptly offered

Frédérick the part of Buridan which Dumas had written for him in the first place.[4] On 15 September Frédérick gave the public his interpretation of the Captain: tempestuous where Bocage had been tender, angry where Bocage had been sad. It was generally agreed that he made better sense of the role than his rival. 'The figure of Buridan', remarked Charles Maurice,[5] 'took on a new character, or rather it acquired a character, and the play gained considerably as a result. Frédérick's acting was quite remarkable.' The box-office takings went from strength to strength. In October the Queen herself honoured the theatre with a visit.[6] Harel was beside himself with joy.

Frédérick's engagement with the Porte-Saint-Martin was now nearing its end. Harel had no desire to lose the best actor in his company, so in December he offered him a fresh contract.[7] This guaranteed Frédérick twenty performances a month, at 60 francs a performance; and in return the actor undertook to play 'at any time, at any hour, and at any place the manager thinks fit, even in two theatres on the same day if need be, leading parts in tragedy and drama, without the right to refuse any such parts under any pretext whatever'. As soon as Frédérick had put his name to this agreement, Harel hurried to the Place Royale and begged Hugo to give him a new play.

He could scarcely have chosen a better time, for Hugo was still smarting from the failure of his latest play at the Théâtre-Français.[8] The first theatre in France had made an astonishing recovery from the chaos into which the 1830 Revolution had plunged it. The auditorium had been modernized, the company strengthened, and plays by authors such as Casimir Delavigne staged with considerable success. Hugo had therefore been tempted to return to the scene of his first theatrical triumph, and he had offered the Comédie-Française his verse-drama *Le Roi s'amuse*, which Verdi was to use twenty years later for the opera *Rigoletto*. The play's first performance, on 22 November, had been an unmitigated disaster. Only Frédérick could have done justice to the physically and emotionally exhausting part of Triboulet, the deformed jester, and Ligier, who had created the role, always described it as the nightmare of his career. To make matters worse, certain daring situations and provocative lines — notably 'Vos mères à des laquais se sont prostituées'—had aroused a storm of indignation, while the scarcely veiled attack on the monarchy had offended an audience impressed by Louis-Philippe's courage in the recent attempt on his life. The next day the Government had banned all further performances of the play, allegedly because of its immorality but really on account of its political bias. Hugo had appealed against the ban, pointing out that the censorship had been abolished in the July Revolution—but all in vain. The *première* of *Le Roi s'amuse* had also been its *dernière* for a good many years.

The playwright was accordingly delighted when Harel put the Porte-Saint-Martin at his disposal. He knew, of course, that the 'Napoleon of managers' was turning into something of a circus proprietor: before leaving the Odéon he had scandalized the staider patrons of the Second Théâtre-Français with a production called *Dik-Rajah* starring the famous elephant Kiouny, and more recently he had put on a play whose chief character was a performing monkey.[9] On the other hand, the two official theatres were now closed to Hugo as a result of *Le Roi s'amuse*, and at the Porte-Saint-Martin he would at least have the services of the best dramatic actors in Paris. He therefore offered Harel a prose drama he had written in July 1832 called *Le Souper à Ferrare*.[10] Mlle George, who had to be consulted on such an important matter, waxed enthusiastic about the principal role of Lucrezia Borgia, and Harel himself had only two points to raise with the author. First he asked Hugo whether he might use music to mark the entries and exits of the characters and highlight certain situations. Though this would formally classify the play as a melodrama—which in fact it was—Hugo gave his permission. Then Harel suggested a change of title.

'The play is too beautiful', he said, 'to be called *Le Souper à Ferrare*. The title is neither sufficiently grand nor sufficiently solemn. If I were you, I should call it simply *Lucrèce Borgia*.'

Hugo saw at once that the little manager wanted to please

Mlle George by having the play named after her part. But
Harel's advice was good even if it was not entirely disinterested,
and the author took it.

Lucrèce Borgia was inspired partly by an anecdote Hugo had
read in Marchangy's Gaule poétique, but largely by Dumas's
Tour de Nesle: Lucrezia and Gennaro, her son by an incestuous
union with her brother Giovanni, were obviously modelled,
consciously or unconsciously, on Marguerite de Bourgogne
and Buridan.[11] The result was that, since La Tour de Nesle had
been tailor-made for Mlle George and Frédérick, Hugo's play
was a perfect fit as well. The last act in particular might have
been calculated to bring out, not only the actor's special talents,
but also the manager's flair for scenic effect. It opens with a
supper-party arranged by Lucrezia for five of her enemies, who
have brought along their friend Gennaro. Their merriment is
suddenly interrupted by the entry of a file of monks in black-
and-white robes, holding torches and singing the De Profundis.
Then Lucrezia appears, to inform the revellers that their wine
was poisoned and they have less than an hour to live. She shows
them five coffins draped in black which are waiting to receive
their bodies, and at this point Gennaro, who has been standing
in the background, steps forward and remarks that a sixth will
be necessary. Horrified to discover that she has poisoned her
son, Lucrezia urges him to drink the antidote. But there is only
enough for one person, and Gennaro declares his intention of
dying with his friends after killing Lucrezia. She begs for mercy,
telling him that he is her brother's child, and he is on the point
of yielding when he hears his best friend calling for vengeance.
Answering Lucrezia's pleas with an implacable 'No!' he stabs
her to death, and the play ends with her last words: 'Ah! You
have killed me! . . . Gennaro, I am your mother!'

After the preliminary reading at Mlle George's house, Hugo
read the play again to his actors in the green-room at the Porte-
Saint-Martin. On this occasion he noticed one of the actresses,
a young dark-eyed woman he had seen before at a ball, looking
at him with passionate admiration. 'That day', he told her later,

'when your eyes met mine for the first time, a ray of light struck from your heart on mine, like the radiance of dawn striking on a ruin.' She was a small-time player possessed of great beauty but little talent, who had snatched at the minor role of the Princess Negroni when it was offered to her, telling Harel: 'There is no such thing as a minor role in a play by Monsieur Victor Hugo.' During rehearsals she was to pursue the author with her attentions, with the result that they became lovers soon after the first night of *Lucrèce Borgia*, at the height of the Carnival; and she remained devoted to Hugo for the rest of his life. Her name was Juliette Drouet.

According to Adèle Hugo, her husband offered Frédérick the choice between two parts, those of Alphonse d'Este and Gennaro. This was probably just a matter of courtesy, for if Gennaro was the shorter of the two roles it was undoubtedly the more effective and the better suited to Frédérick's talents. But the actor loved indulging in off-stage dramatics, and he seized on this opportunity to pose as the good trouper who generously shoulders the heaviest burden.

'Alphonse d'Este', he said, 'is a sure and brilliant part. Its effects are all concentrated in one act and will carry the actor who plays it. Anybody could make a success of it. Gennaro, on the other hand, is a difficult part. The last scene is especially dangerous with that terrible line: "Ah, so you are my aunt!" Consequently I choose Gennaro.'

The rehearsals went smoothly and quickly. Adèle Hugo recorded that 'M. Frédérick Lemaître, who had the least need of advice, was the most amenable to the author's suggestions. The fact that his was a secondary role did not reduce his interest in the play, and he threw himself into it whole-heartedly. He did everything to help his comrades, saying: "No, that isn't it— look, try saying it this way"—and giving the right intonation. Sometimes, to show them what he meant, he would act their scene for them, making us wish that he could play every character in the drama.'

Meanwhile Harel was advertising the play with all his usual

cunning. The capital was filled with rumours that it was the last word in obscenity, so that the author's enemies sharpened their knives for the kill, while his friends deplored his folly. 'Hugo is about to give us a new play', wrote the sculptor David d'Angers. 'The subject is *Lucrèce Borgia*. He has improved on the original, which is already quite scandalous and abominable enough, by making Lucrezia fall in love with the son she has had by Borgia. There seems every reason to fear that these horrors will revolt the public.' But the public were all agog to see the horrors. Since the Press had prophesied that *Lucrèce Borgia* would suffer the same fate as *Le Roi s'amuse*, there was a scramble for first-night tickets; and the opening performance, on 2 February 1833, was given before a packed, expectant house.

There was a tense moment in the very first scene, when a distinct hiss was heard at one point. Harel, already worried by the enormous cost of the production, asked Hugo what it could mean, and received the proud reply: 'It means that I am the author of the play.' But although there was more hissing at this and subsequent performances, the audience as a whole was fascinated by the drama and refused to be drawn.

Another awkward situation occurred towards the end of the first act, this time on the stage. Gennaro is supposed to throw away his sash in anger on discovering that it is a present from Lucrezia, and as Frédérick was doing this the sash caught on his sword. Someone giggled, and for a moment the fate of the play hung in the balance. Then, with the presence of mind for which he was already famous, Frédérick drew his sword, tore the sash free, and in a combination of real and simulated fury trampled it underfoot. The audience, quick as all nineteenth-century audiences were to appreciate an ingenious subterfuge, applauded him enthusiastically.

Except in this incident, Frédérick attracted little attention during the first two acts of the play. In the third and last act, however, he held the house enthralled. No actor could rival him in the art of using silence to create tension, and while Lucrezia harangued her victims every eye in the theatre was fixed on the motionless figure of Gennaro. His sombre statement: 'You need a sixth, Madame' produced a tremendous sensation, and his playing of the final scene with Mlle George carried the audience by storm. Hugo, in a characteristic plethora of antitheses, declared that 'Frédérick realized the Gennaro the author had dreamt of in a performance of genius. He was elegant and familiar; he was full of grandeur and full of grace, he was fearful and gentle; he was childlike and manly; he charmed and he horrified; he was modest, grim and terrifying.' In a more restrained and meaningful comment on the play[12] Charles Maurice admitted that his old enemy had played Gennaro with 'the most remarkable simplicity, nobility and good taste'. While he joined with his colleagues in praising Frédérick's violent duologue with Mlle George, Maurice chose to pay particular tribute to the actor's performance in the less spectacular scenes. 'We have regiments of Romantic actors', he wrote, 'who are ready to pass for great men because they know how to adapt themselves to the exaggeration of the genre. The mob thinks they are wonderful because they have wonderful parts. But only Frédérick is capable of doing what he does in this play.'

In spite of Maurice's praise, Frédérick went on pretending that Gennaro was a subsidiary role which he had chosen out of sheer altruism. Thus to a friend who told him that he had been superb he wryly answered: 'In my self-abnegation, yes.' But he did not carry self-abnegation to the point of abandoning the search for new effects. On the second night, for instance, when Mlle George shrieked: 'I am your mother!' he reeled back and crumpled to the floor in what appeared to be a dead faint. The jealous George refused to see any merit in this innovation, which had the serious disadvantage in her eyes of drawing attention to her partner at the supreme moment of the play; she therefore got Harel to insist on the omission of what the public called Frédérick's 'Shakespearian fall'. The actor's annoyance at being deprived of his final effect led him to brandish his dagger with unusual energy the next time he had George-Lucrezia at his mercy. He looked so frightening as he leapt upon her, and her conscience was so uneasy, that George lost her nerve. Once again she complained to the manager, and a harmless property dagger was substituted for the all too real weapon Frédérick had been using.

For two whole months *Lucrèce Borgia* was the rage in Paris. It aroused passionate discussion in and out of the Press; its characters were represented in the Carnival masks on Mardi Gras; it was parodied in *Tigresse-Mort-aux-Rats* at the Variétés and *L'Ogresse Gorgia* at the Ambigu; and it broke all box-office records at the Porte-Saint-Martin. What is more, it was a literary as well as a financial success. True, the more perceptive critics complained that Hugo was repeating himself, and that *Marion de Lorme, Le Roi s'amuse* and *Lucrèce Borgia* shared a common theme: moral or physical deformity redeemed by love. But everyone agreed that *Lucrèce Borgia* was the best constructed, most dramatic and most inventive of all his plays. Hugo's triumph was complete.

His friends and disciples lost no opportunity to stress the contrast between his success and Dumas's failure—for the latter author had abandoned the theatre after the *Fils de l'émigré* fiasco and was now turning out historical essays under the title of *Gaule et France*. But Dumas did not mind. He was confident that he could make Paris dance to his tune again whenever he wished; and during the Carnival of 1833 he set out to prove it— literally and figuratively—by throwing a huge fancy-dress ball.[13] The Hugolaters sneered that he was trying to score off their idol, but if the ball was in fact a gesture of defiance it was aimed rather at Louis-Philippe. The King had recently given a fancy-dress ball at the Tuileries from which the artistic and literary celebrities of Paris had been ostentatiously excluded, and Dumas intended his own ball to be a demonstration by the artistic world against the bourgeoisie and their puppet ruler. He therefore sent out invitations to all the actors, painters, writers and musicians that he knew, and those he forgot took care to remind him of their existence. The problem of feeding this multitude was solved by a day's shooting in the State Forest which produced nine deer and three hares; the hares were put into a pâté, three of the deer traded for a gigantic salmon, a fourth bartered for a galantine and the rest roasted whole. The caterer Chevet arranged the buffet and provided the wine: three hundred bottles of bordeaux, three hundred of burgundy and five hundred of champagne. As Dumas's flat in the Square d'Orléans was scarcely big enough to accommodate the food and drink, let alone his guests, a set of four empty rooms on the same floor was taken over for the occasion. The most famous painters in Paris—Eugène Delacroix and Célestin Nanteuil, Louis and Clément Boulanger, Alfred and Tony Johannot, Decamps, Grandville, Jadin and Barye—offered their services to cover the bare walls with suitable canvases, Delacroix completing a vast panel in less than three hours without even bothering to take his coat off or roll up his sleeves. The paint had only just dried by the time the two orchestras struck up and the guests began to arrive.

It was very much a theatrical occasion. Two of the murals showed scenes from *La Tour de Nesle* and *Lucrèce Borgia*. Actors from the Comédie-Française rubbed shoulders with players from the Boulevard theatres. Mlle Mars, Firmin and Joanny had come in the costumes they had worn for *Henri III et sa Cour*; Mlle George was rather incongruously disguised as an Italian peasant-girl; Bocage appeared as Didier, the hero of *Marion de Lorme*; and Frédérick was dressed as Robert Macaire, with spangles scattered all over his rags. But the other arts were well represented too. Delacroix was there as Dante, Rossini as Figaro, Alfred de Musset as Pagliacci, Eugène Sue in a domino, and Petrus Borel, the self-styled Lycanthrope, in an eccentric Jeune-France costume which could easily pass for fancy dress. One aged guest, the Academician Tissot, appeared as an invalid, and the painter Jadin, who was got up as an undertaker's assistant with crepe on his hat, could not resist the temptation to follow him from room to room, hissing: 'I am waiting!' every five minutes until Tissot took to his heels. The gargantuan supper which Dumas had devised was served at three in the morning, and the dancing began again as soon as it was over. It was not until nine o'clock that the ball came to an end, with an orchestra leading the guests into the streets in a wild processional gallop, the head of which reached the Boulevard while the tail was still frisking about in the Square d'Orléans.

Not long after the great Dumas ball, Frédérick put on his Robert Macaire costume again, this time without any spangles, to appear in a revival of *L'Auberge des Adrets* at the Porte-Saint-Martin.[14] For this new production Benjamin Antier and Maurice Alhoy had written a one-act epilogue entitled *Les trois derniers quarts d'heure*, which purported to analyse the feelings experienced by Macaire and Bertrand while waiting to be guillotined; and after the execution came a so-called 'fantastic apotheosis' by a certain Lefebvre, *Le Paradis des voleurs*, in which the two scoundrels were seen occupying places of honour in a thieves' heaven. The epilogue, with its macabre jokes and comic songs, was roundly hissed, but the apotheosis appealed to the audience's sense of humour. It consisted of a huge canvas showing the great robbers of the past and present, from Cartouche, the Dick Turpin of France, to Vidocq, the ex-convict who was then Head of the Sûreté, as well as petty thieves such as lawyers, wine-merchants, cab-drivers and cooks, with notorious haunts of vice like the Hôtel d'Angleterre and the Stock Exchange in the background. Frédérick was probably largely responsible for the composition of this rogues' gallery, which gave the public a foretaste of the social satire he was to practise himself a year later in his play *Robert Macaire*.

Hugo was furious to learn that *Lucrèce Borgia* had been taken off before it had run its full course, to make room for such a threadbare programme. It has been suggested that Harel took the risk of incurring the great man's anger in a desperate attempt to please his leading actor, who was tired of playing Gennaro and hankered after a principal role again.[15] This may be the correct explanation of Harel's odd behaviour, though it seems more probable that Mlle George was feeling the strain of what was then considered a long run, and wanted a rest. In any event, the revival of the *Auberge* did little or nothing to improve relations between Frédérick and Harel. Frédérick, with his generous, spendthrift nature, found it impossible to like or even understand a man as mean and miserly as the manager of the Porte-Saint-Martin. For however unorthodox Harel's way of life might be, he was really a grasping bourgeois at heart, and he would go to extraordinary lengths to avoid paying his creditors or his actors. Once, when he was very hard pressed, he put up a notice which stated: 'Tomorrow the treasury will be open from two forty-five until a quarter to three', and a few slow-witted members of the company waited hopefully for some time before they realized they had been fooled.[16] On another occasion the actor Raucourt, to whom long arrears were owing, tried an appeal to his better nature.[17]

'Monsieur Harel,' he said, 'I haven't had any dinner today.'

'My dear fellow,' replied Harel, 'you will sup all the better.'

'But if I am to sup at all, I must have some money.'

'And haven't you any? But that's your own fault. Go to the treasury—I have given instructions that you should be paid.'

Away went Raucourt to present his account, which amounted to 550 francs. The treasurer gravely counted out 20 francs and offered them to him, saying he was unable to give him a sou more. Raucourt rushed back in a rage to find Harel, but did not come across him till the following day.

'Monsieur Harel,' he spluttered, 'you have been making a fool of me! I went to see the treasurer as you told me to . . .'

'Well, he ought to have paid you.'

'He offered me twenty francs!'

'And you didn't take them?'

'Certainly not!'

'That was foolish of you, my dear fellow, very foolish. I can't offer you so much today.'

Whatever claims might be made on his purse, Harel was never at a loss for an answer. One day a small-time player called Fonbonne came to him and asked for an increase in salary.[18] Harel, who knew his man, replied: 'Monsieur Fonbonne, the

current takings make it impossible for me to raise your salary,
but money is not the sole interest of an artist. Though unable to
satisfy you from a pecuniary point of view, I will at least gratify
your pride. You are at present a walker-on, but henceforth you
shall be an actor; you have hitherto been confined to the second
green-room, but henceforth you shall be admitted to the first.
Go and call Monsieur Frédérick Lemaître comrade; go and
speak on equal terms with Mademoiselle Théodorine. I hope,
Monsieur Fonbonne, you will appreciate what I am doing for
you.' Fonbonne was delighted with his promotion to the first
green-room, but he soon found that not everything was *couleur de
rose* in his new position. Whereas the walkers-on received their
pittance on the first of the month, the actors were not paid till
the fifth or the seventh, so that he was forced to live on credit
for a week.

Only the leading players could hold their own with the little
manager, and Frédérick took a malicious pleasure in extract-
ing money from him as often as possible.[19] Many a night Harel
would have to send someone over to the Banquet d'Anacréon,
the restaurant on the other side of the Boulevard, to tell
Frédérick that the curtain was about to go up. The actor would
fumble in his pockets and an expression of horror would cross
his face.

'Dammit!' he would mutter, 'I haven't got a centime on me.
Look, here's the bill—take it to Harel and say that I'm being
held as hostage.'

Though it went against the grain, Harel had no choice but to
pay up if he wanted the evening performance to take place. Even
when Frédérick dined at home the exchequer suffered, for the
actor would arrive in a cab and ask for a louis to pay the driver.
At last Harel ventured a mild protest.

'My dear fellow,' he said, 'if this is a joke it has gone on long
enough. If you haven't a sou, well dammit, come here on foot!'

Frédérick gave a roar of anger. Then, lifting one leg in the
air, he showed the terrified manager a tattered sole that would
have done credit to Robert Macaire.

'On foot?' he shouted. 'With boots like these?'

Harel did not dare to make any further objections for fear that Frédérick would take umbrage and break his contract. Already Bocage had left the Porte-Saint-Martin to become a *pensionnaire* at the Théâtre-Français, and Dorval was hoping to follow his example. She had not been given an important new part for over a year—George had seen to that—and Vigny maintained that in any event Harel's theatre was an unworthy setting for her genius. He disapproved too of the company she kept. Her dressing-room was always crowded with old friends and lovers such as Frédérick and Dumas, and she often received them wearing her chemise, calling her favourites *mon bon chien* and joking with them in that husky voice of hers which they found so attractive. Vigny, for his part, thought that her laughter was vulgar and out of key with her true nature. 'The gravity of your voice,' he told her,[20] 'your features and your bearing, the natural sadness which is in you—everything marks you out as a tragic actress, and you must think of nothing else.' Meanwhile he plotted with Dumas and Hugo to obtain a place for her in the first theatre in France.

The long-awaited break between Harel and his two great players occurred in the summer of 1833, in connexion with the Marquis de Custine's tragedy *Béatrix Cenci*.[21] Custine, whom Vigny and others called 'the gentleman in petticoats', was generally known to be a homosexual. On this account he had been excluded, some years before, from the salons of the aristocracy, and since then he had devoted his considerable talents and immense wealth to literature. *Béatrix Cenci*, his first play, was based on the story of the Roman girl executed at the end of the sixteenth century for killing her father, Francesco Cenci, who was alleged to have raped her. The Comédie-Française accepted the tragedy; settings were designed at the author's expense by the famous scene-painter Ciceri; and Mlle Mars learnt the heroine's part. But at the last moment the Government refused to allow the play to be presented on the official stage, ostensibly because one of the characters was Pope

Clement VIII, but more probably because the subject of the work and the reputation of the author had alarmed the guardians of public morals. Custine promptly went to see Frédérick, for whom he had a great admiration, and offered him the part of Francesco Cenci if he could find a home for the play. Frédérick read it, liked it and recommended it to Harel, who showed far more interest in the author's financial position than in his dramatic gifts.

'I am willing to accept your play,' he told the Marquis, 'but you know the conditions normally imposed on dramatists who have still to win their spurs. Times are hard for theatre managers, and we are obliged to reject the work of a new author unless he covers the complete cost of the production.'

'That seems perfectly fair', said Custine.

Suppressing a smile of triumph, Harel took pen and paper and proceeded to draw up a bill for sets, costumes, lighting, firemen and other services calculated to frighten anyone except a stage-struck millionaire. But the Marquis de Custine was just that, and he paid up without question. In return he had only one request to make, and that was for Marie Dorval to play the title role. Harel hummed and hawed, took several pinches of snuff, and finally went off to consult Mlle George. He returned all smiles: the management would like nothing better. A less naïve person than the Marquis might have wondered why George had made way so readily for her rival. The sinister explanation was that she had no faith in Custine's play and also felt sure that Dorval, the great exponent of prose drama, would fail miserably in poetic tragedy.

During the rehearsals Harel taxed his ingenuity to discover additional expenses he could charge to the Marquis, who met every new bill uncomplainingly. Finally, on the eve of the first performance, the insatiable manager asked him to buy up all the first-tier boxes and present the tickets to members of the Diplomatic Corps. For a moment it seemed as if Custine was going to refuse, but he was assured that the success of his play was at stake and once again gave in. Frédérick, who had been present at this last conversation, could not resist a cutting comment on Harel's rapacity.

'Surely you're not letting him go?' he said, pointing to the Marquis. 'He has still got his watch!'

By the time the curtain went up on *Béatrix Cenci*, on 21 May, the author had paid out no less than thirty thousand francs. But he felt that it was money well spent as he watched his work come to life on the stage. The settings were luxurious, the actors surpassed themselves, and the audience gave the play an enthusiastic reception. Everyone was surprised, therefore, when it was taken off after only three performances. The trouble was that, contrary to Mlle George's expectations, Marie Dorval had shown a very real aptitude for tragedy and won fulsome tributes from the Press. George was jealous enough of Frédérick: she was even more jealous of Dorval. Nothing less than the complete suppression of *Béatrix Cenci* would soothe her wounded vanity, and Harel obediently sacrificed Custine's play to please her.

Marie Dorval was used to treachery of this sort on the part of her fellow actresses; she simply shrugged her shoulders and went off again on tour. The Marquis de Custine contented himself with taking his play away from the Porte-Saint-Martin and publishing it with an acid note on the manager's conduct. Frédérick's reaction was much more violent. He had it out with Harel and George in an angry scene in which insults and blows were freely exchanged—a scene which Dumas was to reproduce in his drama *Kean*. Soon afterwards he left Paris, fully determined never to appear at the Porte-Saint-Martin again.

Later that summer Harel wrote to him threatening to take retaliatory action if he failed to return. 'My dignity as a man and an artist', says Frédérick,[22] 'compelled me to leave this letter unanswered.' But when a second letter reached him in which Harel asked him to send back some dressing-gowns which he claimed to have lent him, the actor decided that a reply was called for.

'Monsieur,' he wrote, 'I borrow only from my friends, and I do not have the honour of knowing you.'

FRÉDÉRICK AS ROBERT MACAIRE
Lithograph by Langlumé

CHAPTER TEN

ROBERT MACAIRE

AFTER leaving the Porte-Saint-Martin in June 1833, Frédérick set off on a long tour of the provinces, starting with the cities of Sens, Besançon and Grenoble. Every performance he gave was a triumph. At Besançon his playing of Napoleon so impressed the commander of the local garrison that a dinner was held in his honour in the officers' mess; and the next day the Colonel sent a liqueur he had admired round to his hotel,[1] with a note begging him to 'finish off the contents of the enclosed bottle, preferably first thing in the morning'. At Grenoble he presented *La Tour de Nesle* and *Trente ans* to wildly enthusiastic audiences. But when he reached Lyons his pleasure was marred by two items of news he received from home: he had been sentenced in his absence to five days' imprisonment for failing to do his service in the National Guard, and his enemies were spreading a rumour to the effect that he had been arrested on a charge of rape. He immediately sent off the following letter[2] to the Paris Press:

It is with surprise and indignation that I have just heard of the infamous and absurd rumours that are circulating about me. Guilty of rape! Fie! Nothing else besides? What, not even a little dagger-thrust or some other pleasantry of that sort? Oh, it's just too simple for words, and people do right to criticize me for such a trivial offence. But there has been a serious mistake. I don't take to the road for a little thing like that. At Sens I had my two sons killed; at Besançon I committed four murders and the Byzantines had the bad taste to laugh at poor Cerfeuil's death; at Grenoble it was even worse, for the more crimes I committed the happier people were. At

I

Lyons too, where I am staying for the time being, they are giving me every encouragement; a dozen good murders in the second city of France, and my reputation is made! But if all these crimes produce avengers who are out for my blood, they should set about their task better than this. Come now, show a little courage, gentlemen: swords or pistols at dawn can easily settle the matter.

I shall be in Paris on 1 October and not before. I have engagements which I must keep at Lyons, Toulouse and Marseilles; otherwise I should have been at No. 8 Boulevard Saint-Martin today. In my absence you will find there my excellent and virtuous wife, my respectable mother and three charming little children, who already reveal a remarkable taste for committing crimes in imitation of their father—their father who owes nothing to anybody, pays his rent and his taxes, does his guard-duty . . . Ah!—now here's a crime for you—doesn't do his guard-duty regularly. So prison awaits. But let us submit willingly to the decrees of Providence—and the law-courts. . . .

This protest had the required effect. Writing to her husband a few days later,[3] Sophie Lemaître reported that 'the whole theatre thought your letter was witty and delightful and congratulated me on it. Those terrible rumours have stopped, and everybody is now convinced that there was nothing in them— so try and recover the calm you need so badly.' But in spite of the attractive picture of domestic bliss which Frédérick had painted for the public, all was not well with the Lemaîtres. Sophie might provide her husband with a comfortable home and 'charming little children'—a second son, Charles, had been born in January 1830, and another child was expected—but she was temperamentally incapable of supplying the emotional satisfaction that his passionate nature demanded. Balked of the official recognition that most Frenchmen secretly desire, burdened with an acting schedule such as no star player would tolerate today, harried by continual back-stage intrigues and tied to a devoted but spiritless wife, Frédérick showed his frustration in violent fits of temper which became increasingly frequent. It was not for nothing that Sophie urged him to 'try and recover the calm you need so badly'. The rest of her letter is even more significant, for it reveals the basic incompatibility of the volcanic hero of the Romantic theatre and the lymphatic little woman he had married.[4] Sophie went on:

> How happy you made us by the way you referred to us in your letter! How proud I am about it, for I am quite certain that you believe what you wrote. Why is it though that, thinking of me in that way, you often treat me so harshly? But never mind, I would rather put up with your rough words and bad temper than live without you. You know, Frédérick, if only you would treat me a little more kindly, you would find me a very different woman; instead of fearing you and trembling at your approach I should be happy, because I love you, my dear, more than any other woman will ever love you. I know that I am dull and tiresome and terribly trying, but you who are intelligent and good should try and be a little less hard on me. On my side I would do everything in my power to make our home happier in the future. After all, I have a great claim to your consideration in that I am the mother of your children; that is something no other woman can take away from me, and that is what makes me so proud and gives me the courage to speak to you. I hope you will not be angry with me for opening my heart to you like this. . . .

During the months that followed, Frédérick's temper mellowed to a noticeable extent. For one thing, he was delighted to learn, at the end of August, that his wife had given birth to a third son, who was christened Louis-Napoléon.[5] Then, too, his tour continued to be a tremendous success. Paris was already beginning to tire of Romantic drama, but for provincial audiences it was new and exciting. Marie Dorval reported to Vigny[6] that she was 'turning them all into Romantics'; and Frédérick, who often appeared at a theatre within a few days of his old partner, shared in her achievement. 'Now that he rules over the stage,' wrote Adolphe Dumas in the *Revue de Rouen*,[7] 'he travels in royal fashion, like a Roman emperor, visiting his provincial subjects to win the love of the people. He does right: the Empire is not all in Rome, and we must thank him for having thought of us. Our congratulations are a poor return for the admirable performances he is giving us, which, like those by Mme Dorval, will go down in the history of Rouen. But one

gives what one can: the gods accept whatever fruit is in season
—and these are gods indeed.'

It is noteworthy that the most popular productions in which
Frédérick and Dorval appeared were not the historical works
generally supposed to constitute the whole of Romantic drama,
but plays of contemporary life such as *Trente ans* and *Richard
Darlington*. Thus the Marseilles novelist and critic Méry wrote[8]
of Frédérick:

> His tragic genius is even more terrifying than Talma's, in my
> opinion, for the following reason: Talma never dwelt in the sphere
> in which we live our lives; he was the bogy of kings and queens and
> court poisoners; he had a gilded dagger very much in evidence, he
> wore a costume that was not like ours, he spoke a language that was
> never heard in ordinary life; to fear his anger one had to imag-
> ine that one lived in castles and palaces, or turn Greek or Roman.
> Frédérick, on the other hand, dresses as we do, in jacket and waist-
> coat; he speaks our drawing-room language; he takes care to con-
> ceal his dagger. We can meet the bourgeois characters he plays the
> very next day, in our town or country houses, involved by some
> dangerous hazard in our private plans and domestic affairs: the idea
> is enough to make us shake in our shoes. Nobody is afraid of Nero
> when he threatens Britannicus, but any one of us may have a Georges
> de Germany or a Richard Darlington among his friends and rela-
> tions. I have long ago forgotten what sort of nervous spasm crossed
> Talma's face when he took hold of the burial urn in *Hamlet*, but all
> my life I shall remember Frédérick's expression in the last act of
> *Richard Darlington*, when he picks up his wife's hat and plans a
> murder. . . .

Both Méry and Adolphe Dumas deplored the fact that the
two greatest living exponents of modern drama were separated,
and so did Frédérick and Dorval themselves. 'With that
woman,' the actor told a friend,[9] 'I should regain all my old
spirit and energy. . . . She knows the real meaning of art.' As
soon as he got back to Paris, in October 1833, he wrote to tell
her that he was willing to 'go to any lengths with the theatre
managements' to appear at her side. In a delightfully characteristic letter[10] she replied from Rouen:

> Darling Frédérick, do please go to any lengths, and go quickly!

Yes, yes, I heard all about your success, and it made me so happy! Our cause is triumphing! We have stirred up the provinces, but when are we marching on Paris? Ah, that fellow Harel! How right you were to break with him! Let him rot! . . . Adolphe Dumas has written to me, expressing tremendous admiration for you (it was *adoration* for me!). He says you often spoke to him about me. So much the better—that is something I am delighted to know. Is your wife with you now? I should very much like to see her here, with your darling boys. And can I do anything for you? Just give me my instructions. Until I see you again—soon, I hope—have lots of success, lots of money and lots of victims—as many as you can manage! . . . Ah, if Madame Frédérick could hear me!

Unfortunately the only joint appearance that Frédérick managed to arrange was a single benefit performance of *Trente ans* at the Odéon.[11] With no Parisian theatre to play in, he was obliged to turn to the provinces again, and a new itinerary was drawn up. But before setting off on tour, he paid a flying visit to Le Havre to give a few performances in his home town.

His departure from Paris was in the very best Robert Macaire tradition.[12] On the day he was due to leave, everything was ready at six in the morning; his carriage was waiting, the horses had been harnessed, and he was just about to go out when Cabet, the local police commissioner, arrived. He announced that he had brought a warrant for Frédérick's arrest and a cab to take the defaulting National Guardsman to prison. Though he was one of the actor's most devoted admirers, Frédérick's eloquent pleas failed to move him.

'I hate doing this, Monsieur Frédérick,' he said, 'but you must understand that duty has to come first.'

What he did not know, or rather had forgotten, was that the actor's house, like all those between the Ambigu and the Porte-Saint-Martin, had two exits, one on the Boulevard, where his cab was standing, and the other on the Rue de Bondy, where the postilions were waiting for their passenger. Frédérick asked if he might go upstairs to give the necessary instructions to his servants, and Cabet agreed to this, adding with a smile that he himself would remain in the front room, watching the door.

Within a matter of minutes Frédérick had gone up to his bed-room, come down again by the backstairs and climbed into his carriage. By the time Cabet grew tired of waiting and decided to look for his prisoner, he was well on the way to Le Havre.

There he received a letter from his wife telling him that he had been sentenced to another two days' imprisonment.[13] Sophie's other news concerned the Porte-Saint-Martin, where she reported that Mlle George had been passable and Lockroy 'very bad indeed' in *Marie Tudor*. This was Hugo's latest his-torical drama, which he had written simply to provide a vehicle for Mlle George in the title role and Juliette Drouet in the part of Jane Talbot. It was a failure.[14] The public was growing much more critical in its attitude to the Romantic theatre; it was in no mood to accept a réchauffé of an earlier work—in this case Dumas's *Christine*—that was also badly acted, as *Marie Tudor* undoubtedly was. Even George, however dazzling she looked in her diamond crown and red velvet robe, was generally judged to have overplayed her part. As for the other main roles, which would have suited Frédérick and Dorval admirably, Lockroy was utterly inadequate as Gilbert, while poor Juliette, terrorized by her scornful comrades, went to pieces and decided to abandon both her part and her theatrical career. But it was probably the appearance on the stage of the public executioner, a character whom many people thought the Romantics were using to excess, which decided the fate of the play. As soon as he came on, dressed in red and black and carrying his sword across his shoulder, the audience gave 'lively manifestations of disapproval', and the hissing continued until the final curtain.

Angèle, which Harel put on immediately after *Marie Tudor*, was another indifferent work.[15] It had two authors, Dumas and Anicet-Bourgeois, and two heroes, the cynical Alfred and the melancholy Müller, the one a poor copy of Richard Darlington and the other a second-rate Antony. If the public gave it a fairly sympathetic reception, that was probably to compensate for the rough treatment Dumas had recently had in the Press. In November one of Hugo's disciples, Granier de Cassagnac, had published an article in the *Journal des Débats* accusing Dumas of having pillaged other plays, including *Hernani*, to write his own. The accusation was justified, but Hugo himself was no less guilty of plagiarism, and the attack which he had inspired against his old ally rebounded. On the first night of *Marie Tudor* Dumas's friends stirred up feeling against Hugo by passing copies of the offending article round the audience, while Dumas is said to have commented on the applause which greeted *Angèle*: 'It is to Cassagnac that I owe this success.' But *Angèle* was by no means a success of the first order. Lockroy was as poor as ever; Bocage, who had recently returned to the Boulevard after an unhappy year with the Comédie-Française, was judged to be unconvincing; and the plump, mediocre Ida Ferrier, who from being Dumas's mistress was eventually to become his wife, received only ironic praise for her performance as an innocent girl of fifteen. It would need better acting than this and a better play than *Angèle* to erase the memory of *Le Fils de l'émigré* and restore Dumas to public favour.

In the meantime Frédérick had returned to Paris, served his sentence in the so-called Hôtel des Haricots, the special prison for refractory National Guardsmen, and set off again, this time for the South of France.[16] His first long halt was at Bordeaux, where he found 'the theatre good, though with a rococo interior, the actors bad, the public very backward, and the newspapers stagnant and stupid'. After this disappointing start, he was given an enthusiastic reception at Bayonne, where he played for nearly three weeks, and his success grew as he travelled east through Pau, Toulouse, Montpellier and Nîmes. At Marseilles he recorded a 'colossal triumph' in his diary, and letters poured into his dressing-room from young admirers praising the 'poetic beauty' of his costumes and inviting him to go drinking with them and their mistresses.[17] But there were less happy moments. In January 1834 he was nearly killed when his carriage overturned; in February he was injured in an accident and 'cursed all journeys'; his wife, who accompanied him as far as Toulouse, had to go back to Paris, leaving him 'very sad'; and the entry in his diary for 22 February reads simply: 'Continual melancholy'. Moving from one lonely hotel-room to another, he longed to be with his family again. 'I love my children', he wrote in a pathetic, significant note,[18] 'and I live only for them!'

He got back to Paris at the beginning of April, to find the capital in a most inhospitable mood. During his absence Harel had staged a revival of *L'Auberge des Adrets*, with a third-rate actor called Delaistre playing Robert Macaire; and when Serres had protested on Frédérick's behalf, the unscrupulous little manager had blandly accused him of ingratitude, explaining that Delaistre's bad acting would throw his own performance into relief and convince the public that Bertrand was the main part in the play.[19] Harel's object in engaging Delaistre had clearly been to spite Frédérick, but this minor act of vengeance had not been enough to satisfy his wounded vanity. He had also approached all his colleagues and persuaded them to close their theatres to Frédérick, whom he had described in lurid terms as an unreliable, temperamental brute.[20] Luckily for the actor, one member of this managerial union, Mourier of the Folies-Dramatiques, turned blackleg. He went to see Frédérick, told him of Harel's plot to deprive him of his livelihood, and offered to put the tiny Folies-Dramatiques at his disposal. According to the actor's unpublished notes for his memoirs, Mourier thereby laid the foundations of his vast fortune, for he died 'a millionaire twice over'.

It is ironical that the play which did the most to make Mourier a rich man should have been a satire on the lust for money, the mania for speculation, which possessed France at this time. The bourgeoisie had certainly never been more powerful, more prosperous or more acquisitive. In a perceptive comment[21] on what he called the 'repulsive new régime', Heine wrote: 'The thinking men who worked indefatigably throughout the eighteenth century to prepare the French Revolution would blush if they could see personal interest busily building its wretched huts on the site of the ruined palaces, and from these huts a new aristocracy emerging, even more unpleasant than the old—an aristocracy which does not even try to legitimate itself by an idea, by faith in an hereditary virtue, but finds its final justification in acquisitions which one usually owes to a talent for figures if not to the most ignoble qualities.' The German poet went on to stigmatize 'the armed fear which strikes you with an intelligent bayonet when you dare to maintain that the world should be governed only by genius, beauty, love and strength'. The 'intelligent bayonet' of which he spoke was at work again in April 1834. In that month riots broke out in Lyons and Paris which were suppressed with savage cruelty. The bloodiest incident occurred in Paris, at No. 12 Rue Transnonain, where Government troops butchered all the occupants of the house, young and old, without discriminating between rioters and innocent citizens. Appalled by this brutal act of repression, Honoré Daumier drew his most famous lithograph, *The Massacre in the Rue Transnonain*, showing a man dressed in nightshirt and nightcap, covered with bayonet wounds and lying beside his bed across the corpse of a little child. And Frédérick Lemaître, no less horrified, wrote his most famous play, *Robert Macaire*, showing greed and hypocrisy triumphant.

There had already been several attempts to exploit the success of *L'Auberge des Adrets*, both on the stage and in print. The most recent had been an anonymous novel in four volumes, published in 1833, which recounted the adventures of Macaire and Bertrand in a variety of disguises. For a long time Frédérick had been haunted by the idea of turning the figure of Robert Macaire into a great comic type in the tradition of Molière and Beaumarchais, and he was tempted to use this novel as the basis for a dramatic sequel to the *Auberge*. He discovered from the publisher that the author was none other than his friend Maurice Alhoy, who readily agreed to collaborate with Benjamin Antier, Saint-Amand and Frédérick himself in writing a play to be called *Robert Macaire*.[22] The actor sketched out the main lines of the plot and worked out most of the situations in detail; thus the entries in his diary for April 1834 are all suggestions for the play. He was fully justified in claiming, as he did with his collaborators' approval, to be the sole author of the work.

Robert Macaire begins where the *Auberge* ended, with the supposed death of the famous bandit and the arrest of his accomplice Bertrand. But Macaire has only been wounded, while Bertrand succeeds in escaping from his captors. The two rogues come together again and decide to transfer their criminal activities to Paris, where Macaire founds a vast company specializing in insurance against theft. His success attracts the attention of the Baron de Wormspire, who is in fact no baron but a clever confidence-trickster, and his daughter Éloa, who is in fact no relation of his but a common prostitute he has picked up on the streets. Just as Wormspire is taken in by Macaire's apparent wealth and honesty, so Macaire is deceived by the Baron's talk of his huge estates, and he therefore asks for Éloa's hand in marriage. It is only after the wedding ceremony, at which non-existent fortunes have been exchanged, that the two crooks begin to suspect the truth. In the course of a game of écarté which is one of the funniest scenes in nineteenth-century comedy, son-in-law and father-in-law turn up nothing but kings, and each man realizes to his surprise that he is dealing with a practised card-sharper. However, the game is interrupted by the police, who arrest Bertrand, Wormspire and Éloa, and haul them before the local magistrate. But the figure in the cotton nightcap and green spectacles who receives them in his bedroom is really Macaire in disguise. Infuriated by the discovery that Wormspire and Éloa are fellow crooks, he launches into a torrent of abuse, which his father-in-law returns with interest. These mutual recriminations are followed by a parody of the traditional recognition scene, in which Bertrand learns that Éloa is his own daughter, while Wormspire finds that Macaire is the son he abandoned thirty years ago in a spinach-field. Suddenly the indefatigable gendarmes appear once again and chase the criminals on to an open square, where Bertrand and Macaire escape their clutches by literally taking flight—in a balloon.

A bald summary of the plot cannot possibly give an adequate impression of the verve and brilliance of this unique play, which contains every kind of comedy, from social satire to knockabout farce. However improbable the situations may be, the characterization and dialogue reveal the keenest insight into both human nature and the society of the time. Thus the prostitute who glorifies chastity, the thief who extols honour and the swindler who preaches philanthropy are eternal types, but specially representative of what Stendhal called the 'hypocritical nineteenth century'. *Robert Macaire* may not be an edifying play; on the other hand, no one can deny that it is wonderfully entertaining and wonderfully enlightening.

The first performance, on 14 June 1834, was a personal triumph for Frédérick. As soon as he came on to the tiny stage he established an astonishing hold on the audience, and for four hours he kept them laughing uproariously and shouting with delight. There was only one awkward moment in the whole evening. On Frédérick's advice, the actor who had been cast as Wormspire played his part straight, leading the audience to show him a certain sympathy at first. They were rather piqued to discover later that their sympathy had been wasted on a villain, but any annoyance they felt soon passed, and the final curtain fell to the sound of wild applause.

The next day *Robert Macaire* was the talk of the town, and everyone wanted to see Frédérick in his own play. The Folies-Dramatiques was the smallest and least fashionable theatre in Paris; there were no mirrors in the boxes; the benches were covered with worn and greasy plush; and the stench of sweaty humanity was so strong that Arsène Houssaye for one was grateful for the alcoholic fumes spread by a few drunkards in the audience.[23] Yet every night that summer, smart tilburies stopped outside the theatre, liveried servants let down the folding steps, and yellow-gloved dandies escorted their ladies into the smoky, evil-smelling auditorium to sit beside cloth-capped workmen and their girls. As Théodore de Banville remarked,[24] 'when this amazing comedy took the stage, the people shuddered with the consciousness of their strength, just as they had done on seeing the *Mariage de Figaro*, that prologue to *Robert Macaire*, while the carriage classes anxiously flocked to the Boulevard du Temple to see the new play, which they failed to understand, just as they had failed to understand Beaumarchais's masterpiece'.

If the 'carriage classes' really failed to perceive the significance of *Robert Macaire*, that was their own fault, for all the leading critics of the time explained it to their readers. Indeed, when one reads the copious commentaries which were devoted to Frédérick's work in the course of the nineteenth century, one cannot help wondering why present-day literary and political historians should devote so little attention to it. Admittedly *Robert Macaire* does not lend itself easily to the sort of pigeon-holing practised in literary manuals: an Aristophanic comedy arriving plumb in the middle of Romantic drama is a disconcerting phenomenon that tidy academic minds naturally prefer to ignore. The historians have a rather better excuse for not recognizing the play as the *Mariage de Figaro* of the nineteenth century, in that Frédérick was not a famous author like Beaumarchais, and Louis-Philippe did not personally condemn *Robert Macaire* as Louis XVI did when he banned *Figaro*. But even so, it is difficult to see how any conscientious writer on the period can overlook the play in view of the countless tributes which Frédérick's contemporaries paid to its importance.

Thus there was Jules Claretie,[25] who described Macaire as 'that colossal crook who will go down to history as the personification of the appetites of an era'. There was Arsène Houssaye,[26] who asked himself who Macaire might be, and answered: 'He is you, me, everybody—even the King; indeed, I am very much afraid that in him Frédérick has painted the portrait of his age.' And there was Chateaubriand,[27] who declared that 'Robert Macaire's vulgar taunt—"You old humbug!"—is addressed to everybody in France: to the King who grants the Charter and the Minister who violates it; to all those who have betrayed their faith and their principles since the Revolution; to old M. de

Talleyrand and young M. Thiers; to the man who speaks from
the tribune and the man who preaches from the pulpit—for
neither believes what he is saying'. But perhaps the most perceptive appreciation of the play, both as a work of art and as a
social satire, came from Gautier[28] when he wrote:

> Robert Macaire was the great triumph of the revolutionary art
> which followed on the July Revolution. It is the masterpiece of that
> chance literature, born of popular instinct and pitiless Gallic wit,
> which seemed to contain the seeds of the comedy of the future. There
> is something special about this particular comedy, and that is the
> bold and desperate attack it makes on the social order and mankind
> in general. For the character of Robert Macaire, Frédérick Lemaître
> created a truly Shakespearian type of humour—a terrifying gaiety, a
> sinister roar of laughter, a bitter derision, a merciless raillery, a sar-
> casm which leaves the cold-blooded wickedness of Mephistopheles
> far behind—and on top of all that, an astonishing elegance, supple-
> ness and grace which belongs to the aristocracy of vice. What a
> strange and profound satire this is, in which the criticism of society
> is made by a brigand! And what a weird dualism we have here, with
> Orestes and Pylades dressed in convict garb and the perpetual anti-
> thesis of mind and body translated into slang by Robert Macaire and
> Bertrand, the Don Quixote and Sancho Panza of crime!

The caricaturists of the time were immediately attracted by
the figure of Robert Macaire, and none more so than Honoré
Daumier. This was natural enough, for there was a strong temperamental and artistic affinity between Daumier and Frédérick.
As Champfleury observed in his history of modern caricature,[29]
'both men were ardent workers who broke with tradition and
followed only spontaneous inspiration, and both men could in-
fuse grandeur into trival things and by some strange magic en-
noble the rags they picked up out of the gutter'. What is more,
the artist had the greatest admiration for the actor, and Arsène
Houssaye records that when he was in charge of the Comédie-
Française Daumier was forever urging him to take Frédérick
on.[30] The result of this affinity and admiration was Daumier's
finest work, the Cent et un Robert Macaire, a series of cartoons
in which the caricaturist skilfully developed the character

Frédérick had created, showing an intuitive understanding of the original.

Robert Macaire revealed by his example how greed and graft flourished in France under the mask of philanthropy and respectability. But if the common people were disgusted by the hypocrisy and corruption of the moneyed classes there was very little they could do about it, for the Government had made it clear that any insurrection would be put down without mercy. Almost the only means the masses had of showing their contempt for the order of things was through such dances as the *cancan*, which now acquired an added vogue. 'The people', wrote Heine,[31] 'have so lost faith in the high ideals of which our political and literary Tartuffes prate so much that they see in them nothing but empty phrases—*blague* as their saying is. This comfortless outlook is illustrated by Robert Macaire; it is likewise illustrated by the popular dances, which may be regarded as the spirit of Robert Macaire put into mime. Anyone acquainted with the latter will be able to form some idea of these indescribable dances, which are satires not only of sex and society, but of everything that is good and beautiful, of all enthusiasm, patriotism, loyalty, faith, family feeling, heroism and religion.'

The bolder spirits advocated a less subtle, more drastic way of expressing discontent—namely, regicide. Criticism of the bourgeois régime was concentrated on the person of the bourgeois monarch, and he was savagely caricatured as 'the Pear' by cartoonists such as Daumier. At a Republican banquet a young man brandished an open knife in one hand as he proposed a toast to Louis-Philippe, while Cavaignac claimed that he was hard put to it to hold back a hundred would-be assassins in the Société des Droits de l'Homme. In 1835, as the fifth anniversary of the July Revolution drew near, the attacks on the King became more virulent and the incitements to murder more explicit. On 27 July the *Charivari* published a cartoon entitled *The Victims of Despotism*, in which the familiar pear-shaped head of Louis-Philippe was composed of corpses and manacled prisoners; and the same number contained a laconic news-item to the effect that 'the Citizen King and his family returned to Paris yesterday without anybody trying to assassinate them'. It was widely rumoured that on the 28th an attempt would be made to repair the omission.

The Boulevard du Crime thoroughly justified its nickname that day.[32] The King, accompanied by his sons and his staff, had been reviewing his troops all morning, and about midday the cavalcade reached the Boulevard du Temple, where the Eighth Legion was drawn up in front of the Jardin Turc. Suddenly there was a tremendous explosion and a hail of bullets swept the royal party. The people lining the terrace of the Jardin Turc screamed in panic, the horses reared wildly, and for a few minutes there was utter confusion. When the smoke and dust cleared, it was found that seven people, including Marshal Mortier and several spectators, had been killed, and eight wounded. The King himself had been grazed by a bullet but was unhurt; he waved his plumed hat to the crowd, shouted: 'Here I am!' and calmly continued with the review.

Three men were arrested and charged with the crime: Fieschi, a Corsican marksman, and a couple of tradesmen called Pépin and Morey. They had taken a third-floor flat in the house adjoining the Estaminet des Mille Colonnes, and there installed an 'infernal machine' consisting of twenty-five muskets fastened to a frame and primed to go off all at once. Pépin had financed the operation and also helped Fieschi to aim his guns correctly by riding up and down the Boulevard beforehand in a sinister rehearsal of the massacre. As for Morey, his was the brain behind the whole enterprise; he had even taken the sensible precaution of damaging four of the muskets so that they would explode and silence Fieschi. But the Corsican, though badly wounded, lived to reveal the names of his accomplices, and the three conspirators were executed together.

For once a bloody incident had taken place for which the authorities were not responsible, and they set out to exploit it for all it was worth. First they deliberately exaggerated the number of Fieschi's victims, arousing widespread horror and indignation among the general public. Then, on the pretext of protecting the King and the country from further outrages, the Government forced through the repressive measures known as the September Laws, speeding up judicial procedure and imposing strict control over the theatres and the Press. The Charter of 1830 had declared that the censorship was abolished in France and could never be restored. The Law of 9 September 1835 restored it—for 'dramatic works, drawings, engravings and lithographs'.

Robert Macaire was inevitably one of the first dramatic works to incur the censor's disapproval, and it was banned before the year was out. But it was not forgotten. Ten years later, on his way from Fréjus to Antibes, Gustave Flaubert made a special pilgrimage to the original inn of Les Adrets.

'I looked at it', he told his friend Le Poittevin,[33] 'with religious awe, thinking that it was here that the great Robert Macaire had taken wing for the future, here that the greatest symbol of the age, the epitome of our times, had originated. Types like Macaire are not created every day; indeed, I cannot think of a greater one since Don Juan.'

CHAPTER ELEVEN

THE FRENCH KEAN

THE original run of *Robert Macaire* at the Folies-Dramatiqes lasted for seventy-nine performances. It could have gone on indefinitely, but Frédérick decided that it would be more profitable to take the play on tour for a few months. He had refused to allow his collaborators to have it printed, so that he could exploit it to the best advantage, and the provinces were all agog to see it.

Before setting out on this new tour, he satisfied one of his dearest ambitions by buying a country house where he could install his mother, his wife and his four children.[1] Set in nine acres of parkland at Pierrefitte, not far from Paris, it was an imposing two-storied building in brick and stone, with stables and outhouses attached. Frédérick paid 35,000 francs for it, and an architect relative of his called Coussin assured him that it was worth twice as much. But then, Coussin wanted the job of modernizing and redecorating the house, which he said could be done at very little cost. The actor accepted his estimate, commissioned him to make whatever alterations he considered necessary, and took to the road with an easy mind.

He was given an enthusiastic reception at Troyes, Dijon, Auxerre and Dôle; but at Châlons he fell ill and was obliged to return to Paris at the end of December. As soon as he had recovered he left the capital again, this time for London, where Pélissier, the manager of the French company at the Lyceum, had engaged him for a short season.[2] His first offering to the London public, *La Mère et la Fille*, proved unpopular, possibly

K

because it portrayed an Englishman, Lord Talmours, in an unflattering light; as Frédérick noted in his memoirs, 'the English like to be respected'. His second choice, the Ducis adaptation of *Othello*, was just as unfortunate, for no audience familiar with the original could be expected to stomach this watered-down version of Shakespeare's work. As a crowning misfortune, the Lord Chamberlain banned the two plays he was counting on to win over the public, *La Tour de Nesle* and *Richard Darlington*, on the grounds that the former was offensive to the monarchy and the latter caricatured the English election system. For some reason Pélissier was convinced that the only hope of getting the ban lifted lay in an appeal to the Comte Alfred d'Orsay, whom he held in awe as the supreme arbiter of taste and fashion in London, and he urged Frédérick to call on d'Orsay and ask for his help. The great dandy received the great actor with his usual courtesy and kindness, and the two men became firm friends. They were to see more of each other in later years, either in London during Frédérick's subsequent visits to England or in Paris after Louis-Napoleon had come to power, and they were to meet for the last time only a few days before d'Orsay's death in August 1852. At their first meeting the Count had to disabuse Frédérick of the idea that he could melt the Lord Chamberlain's heart.

'I can see', he said, 'that you don't know what the English are like. They are inexorable about anything that concerns their institutions or the monarchy, and those are precisely the things the two prohibited plays attack. I shall see what I can do, for all that. But in the meantime, why don't you give us *Robert Macaire*, whose fame has now spread all over Europe? If you do, you will easily recoup your losses, because I can promise you at least as great a triumph in London as the one you obtained in Paris.'

Frédérick took this advice and followed *Othello* with *L'Auberge des Adrets* and *Robert Macaire*. The results surpassed all his expectations. In a letter to a Paris lawyer who apparently also acted as his publicity agent[3] he wrote in February 1835: 'Please be so good as to put a note in the Press about my success in

London: it is very great, very great indeed —and I am not being
an "old humbug" when I say so!'

While he was still in London, Marie Dorval was triumphing
in Paris, at the Théâtre-Français of all places, in the most famous
role of her career—that of Kitty Bell, the heroine of Vigny's
Chatterton.[4] It was a hard-won victory. When Jouslin de la
Salle, the liberal manager of the Comédie-Française, had engaged Dorval as a *pensionnaire*, there had been a tremendous
outcry from the classical die-hards, the *Constitutionnel*[5] protesting that 'the Théâtre-Français ought not to descend to
grotesque and immoral exhibitions which bring shame on our
times, shock public modesty and deal a deadly blow to society'.
Rather than allow her to make a brilliant début in a revival of
Antony, as stipulated by her contract, the actors of the Rue de
Richelieu had agreed to pay the heavy damages which the courts
awarded Dumas when the production was cancelled. Since then
Mlle Mars had made sure that Dorval was never cast in a part
worthy of her genius. The reading committee even went so
far as to reject *Chatterton* out of hand, despite its obvious merits,
simply because they knew that Vigny had written it for his
mistress and would insist on her having the leading role if they
accepted it. Only the intervention of the Royal Family, who were
well disposed to Vigny, succeeded in imposing first the play
and then the actress on the recalcitrant Comédie.

The odd thing was that *Chatterton* was not a typically Romantic work. There was no violence or colour in it, and the plot was
positively classical in its simplicity. Balzac summarized it as
follows: 1st Act. 'Ought I to kill myself?' 2nd Act. 'I ought to
kill myself.' 3rd Act. 'I kill myself.' On the other hand, the
theme of the poet driven to suicide by an uncomprehending
society had a strong emotional appeal for the melancholy and
idealistic young writers of the time, who recognized themselves
in Chatterton just as their more passionate brethren had recognized themselves in Antony. But it was Dorval's acting which
more than anything else captivated the public and ensured the
success of the play. In the gentle, subdued role of Kitty Bell,

Chatterton's landlady, she touched every heart in the audience. She put all the love she felt for her own daughters into her scenes with Kitty Bell's two children, and all the tender passion of which she was capable into her last conversation with the dying poet. For the final scene, in which Kitty herself dies of grief, she had devised a brilliant piece of stage-play such as she and Frédérick were adept at inventing. She had insisted on the erection of a staircase on the stage, to the derisive amusement of the other actors, who had asked if she was going to give an extract from *Robert Macaire*. When the Quaker followed Chatterton into his room, she dragged herself slowly upstairs and pushed open the door; then, seeing the poet lying dead in the Quaker's arms, she gave a cry, leaned back against the banister rail, and half-slid, half-fell down to the bottom stair, where she collapsed in a pathetic, crumpled heap. The effect on the audience was indescribable. Some people were so overcome that they shouted: 'Enough!' Eugène Labiche choked with emotion. Even Sainte-Beuve felt tears trickling down his fat little cheeks.

But Dorval still had to contend with the hostility of her fellow actors, which was demonstrated again in April 1835, when Hugo gave his *Angelo, tyran de Padoue* to the Comédie-Française and asked for Marie to play one of the two leading feminine roles.[6] It was a poor work, and Désiré Nisard was justified in maintaining that 'an unknown writer making his début with a play like *Angelo* would not see it performed six times'. The critic attributed the success of the play exclusively to the fact that 'Mlle Mars and Mme Dorval stood godmothers to this coarse and puny child of a worn-out imagination'. Certainly what drew the public to *Angelo* was the chance of seeing the queen of traditional comedy and the queen of modern drama engaged in a theatrical duel. Mlle Mars did everything she could to spoil her rival's chances. First she chose for herself the part of the street-girl Tisbe, which had clearly been written for Dorval. Then, at rehearsals, she treated the other woman with what Hugo's wife called 'the aristocratic *hauteur* of an actress of the Théâtre-Français compelled by circumstances to keep low company with a runaway from the Boulevard'. Finally she tried to have some of Dorval's best speeches cut out of the play, and would have had her name printed in small type at the bottom of the bill—as the latest recruit to the Comédie-Française—if Hugo had not protested. Her fury when, in spite of all these man-oeuvres, the critics gave the palm to the younger actress had to be seen to be believed.

It seems that Jouslin de la Salle, encouraged by Dorval's success, would have liked to engage Frédérick as well. But Frédérick knew from Dorval's example what sort of treatment he could expect from the established actors of the Comédie-Française, and he was not the man to suffer as patiently as she did the humiliations they inflicted on unpopular *pensionnaires*. Rather than lick the boots of lesser artists in the first theatre of Paris he preferred to hold sovereign sway over the last, and on his return from England he re-appeared at the Folies-Dramatiques in *Robert Macaire*, playing to packed houses throughout the spring.

In the summer Coussin presented his bill for the work he had done at Pierrefitte. It was far bigger than he had led Frédérick to expect, and the rest of the actor's savings went to paying it. At this point Harel, hearing that he was in financial difficulties, came to see him and proposed a reconciliation. He offered Frédérick a quarter of the takings in return for five performances a week of 'plays taken from the repertory of the Porte-Saint-Martin and the old repertory of the Comédie-Française'. Coming from Harel, this was a surprisingly generous offer, and Frédérick saw no point in rejecting it. He therefore signed a new contract with the Porte-Saint-Martin, to take effect in August.[7]

It was agreed that his first appearance should be in a splendid new production of *Othello*.[8] Fresh scenery was painted, new costumes were designed, a special musical score was written by Piccini, and huge posters were put up inviting the public to welcome their favourite actor back to the Porte-Saint-Martin. But on the opening night, 17 August, while the theatre was filling up, the local police commissioner served a writ on Harel from the Minister of the Interior, calling on him 'to remain within the limits of his licence, which does not permit him to produce any of the works of the Comédie-Française repertory, and accordingly forbidding him to produce the tragedy of *Othello*'. When Frédérick, dressed as the Moor, read out the Minister's decree from the stage, bedlam broke loose, and the curtain had to be raised and lowered half a dozen times before he could make himself heard again. He then announced that the management was prepared to put on another play, *La Berline de l'émigré*, but the audience refused to accept anything but *Othello* and left the theatre. The only protest Frédérick himself made against the action the Comédie-Française had taken was an ironic interpolation in his next production, a revival of *L'Auberge des Adrets*. Asked by the gendarme to state his profession, he answered: 'Ex-tragedian'—and brought the house down.

The *Auberge* was followed in September by its satirical complement, *Robert Macaire*, which gained by being played on a bigger stage with the inimitable Serres taking the part of Bertrand. A month later the Porte-Saint-Martin was closed for repairs, and Harel transferred the play to the empty Odéon, where the aristocratic Faubourg Saint-Germain applauded the great bandit just as enthusiastically as had the popular Boulevard. But it was too much to hope that the partnership between Harel and Frédérick would last for long, and towards the end of the year the two men fell out again as the result of a conversation which deserves to be recorded for the light it throws on their respective characters.[9]

'My dear fellow,' Harel said to Frédérick one day, 'your salary is too big.'

'I beg your pardon?' replied the actor.

'Much too big. It is my intention to cut it by half.'

'I may be very dense, but I don't understand.'

'Look—I shall go on paying you the full sum, while appearing to give you only half.'

'Whatever for?'

'Well, I'm hard pressed for money at the moment, and it would help if you set your comrades an example of self-denial, outwardly at least.'

'But that would be a filthy swindle!' roared the actor. 'And you actually thought that I'd be a party to it? Why, your proposition is an insult to my character!'

Frédérick stormed out in a fury, and the next day tore up his contract with the Porte-Saint-Martin. Harel's unholy alliance of managers promptly came into operation again, so that the actor once more found the Paris theatres closed to him. For a few weeks he did not know where to turn. He could not hope to make much money out of a provincial tour, because the recently established censorship chose this moment to ban his newest and most popular play, which was *Robert Macaire*. If only he had been able to keep *Robert Macaire* out of print he might have avoided this catastrophe, or at least postponed it, but he had been circumvented by an unscrupulous bookseller called Barba. This man had got permission from Saint-Amand, one of Frédérick's collaborators, to publish the play, but the actor had refused to give his authority or to relinquish the manuscript. Undeterred by this rebuff, Barba had hired a stenographer to take the play down in shorthand at one of the Porte-Saint-Martin performances and had published it in *La France Dramatique*, at the same time coolly threatening to prosecute anybody who reproduced the text. In the event it was Barba who was prosecuted, for Frédérick brought an action against him which was heard on the last day of 1835.

The proceedings were enlivened by one amusing incident.[10] Quoting something Frédérick was alleged to have said to him, Barba struck a theatrical attitude and tried to imitate the actor's stentorian voice. At this Frédérick clapped his hands and shouted ironically: 'Bravo, bravo!'

'I am not an actor, monsieur', remarked Barba.

'No, Monsieur Barba,' thundered Frédérick, 'You are a . . .'

He faltered, as though searching for a term of abuse sufficiently virulent to express his opinion of the defendant. The magistrates leaned forward; the lawyers held their breath; Barba turned pale. At last Frédérick's face cleared as he found the word he wanted.

'You are a bookseller', he said—and raised his eyebrows in mock surprise at the laughter that greeted this innocuous statement.

There were more serious moments, as when Frédérick referred to 'an infamous treaty concluded by the theatre managers of Paris which places the actor on a lower social level than the negro', or when—anticipating Flaubert—he declared in ringing tones: 'Robert Macaire, c'est moi!' But although the court gave judgment against Barba and sentenced him to a heavy fine, Frédérick was awarded only the derisory sum of 1,000 francs in damages, instead of the 15,000 francs he had sued for. The future looked as black as ever.

Then, in the middle of January 1836, the Boulevard learnt to its surprise that Frédérick had entered into a two-year contract with the Variétés, a little theatre which Harel had left out of his calculations because it specialized in vaudeville.[11] According to the pundits, this engagement was sure to end in disaster—for the theatre would find it hard to adjust itself to straight drama, while Frédérick would be frustrated by the limitations of a small stage and a company of vaudeville players. But nobody at the Variétés paid any attention to these gloomy prophecies. Indeed, the very day the contract was signed, Emmanuel Théaulon, one of the theatre's accredited authors, set to work writing two plays specially for Frédérick. The first was an historical drama entitled *Le Marquis de Brunoy*, about an eighteenth-century nobleman who spent his fortune on the poor to spite his rich relations. The other was based on the life and legend of Edmund Kean, who had died less than three years before. Describing this work to Frédérick,[12] Théaulon wrote:

It is a five-act play and the title is to be: *Kean, ou Désordre et Génie*. It is a mixture of all the genres. I would willingly give all my successes, past, present and to come, to produce something that satisfied you. . . . My desire to be played by the first actor in Europe is so great, and I am so utterly convinced that the subject of *Kean* will please you, that I promise to deliver the complete play to you by Sunday next—I am going to work at it night and day.

Théaulon kept his word, but unfortunately the result failed to satisfy Frédérick, and another writer, a disciple of Scribe's called Courcy, was called in to doctor the play. When the second version of *Kean* met the same fate as the first, Théaulon and Courcy decided that their best course would be to submit their work to Dumas for judgment. He saw at once the immense possibilities which the subject offered, both for a dramatist of his experience and for an actor of Frédérick's calibre, and he readily agreed to take the play in hand.

Meanwhile, on 14 March, Frédérick made his début at the Variétés in Théaulon's *Marquis de Brunoy*. As a theatrical occasion it was not very exciting, and his only reason for remembering it later was that it was the first time he acted with the woman who was to be his mistress in private life and his partner on the stage for three tempestuous years.[13] Known as Atala Beauchêne, though her real name was Louise Beaudoin, she was a slim, fair-haired beauty of twenty-one, who had been acting ever since childhood. But she was no Dorval. In 1832 a candid and anonymous critic[14] wrote about her:

She is better known in society than in the theatre. And when we say society we mean those gatherings where young men about town get together to squander their parents' money and lead what they call a short life but a merry one. There is not a single one of our good restaurateurs, our jobmasters or our tilbury-drivers who is not well acquainted with the face of Mlle Atala Beauchêne. At the Vaudeville hardly anyone except the manager pays any attention to her, while the public takes no notice of her at all—which is fortunate for her reputation, because if it ever abandoned its present attitude of indifference, she might well discover what it is to be hissed.

The gossip-writers made meaningful references to the fact that, like that other small-time actress Juliette Drouet, she was always expensively dressed; their readers were left to draw the obvious inference. It was rumoured that all the male guests at her supper-parties in the Rue Monsigny had once been her lovers, from wealthy roués like Lord Normanby and the banker Aguado to young dandies like Alfred Tattet and Roger de Beauvoir; and no doubt there was some foundation for the rumour. But these were shallow little men who could never arouse any but shallow emotions, and it is possible that the passion Atala conceived for Frédérick Lemaître was the first real love of her life. He for his part was drawn to her by her beauty, her reputation and her obvious adoration. Even so, he might not have made her his mistress, or at least he might not have flaunted their liaison as openly as he did, if it had not been for his wife. Sophie had never responded adequately to her husband's love; now, at this crucial moment in their relationship, she repulsed his advances. In a letter of capital importance for the understanding of Frédérick's conduct[15] she wrote to him:

You ask me if I would like to spend the night with you? If it were possible, it would make me very happy, but it is out of the question. As a sensible woman, especially at my time of life, I dare not risk the consequences, which are just too frightening. From being the happiest woman in the world I should undoubtedly become the unhappiest within a matter of days, and we should have to separate once more. I did not sleep all last night, I found it so hard to make up my mind, but reason triumphed in the end: as I said before, the consequences are too awful. So since you are kind enough to give me the choice, let us stay as we are; if I am not happy, I shall at least be easy in my mind, and that is a great deal in my position. All that I ask of you is to be as good to me as you have been lately. I shall never utter a word of reproach, whatever you do, for I know that you are too decent to do anything which might hurt your children. . .

Soon after this Frédérick settled a pension on his wife and they parted amicably. In public Sophie continued to give him her loyal support, and in 1852, fearing that his opponents in a legal action might refer to their separation, she wrote him a letter[16] declaring: 'I wish it to be known that for the past fifteen years the state of my health has obliged me to live alone.' In private, however, despite her promise to the contrary, she sometimes reproached him with his behaviour. But it was too late. He had taken her at her word and given himself up completely to his love for Atala. The dark, curly-headed giant and the slim blonde were seen everywhere together, and their liaison became the talk of the town.

The chief topic of conversation on the Boulevard, however, in the spring and summer of 1836, was not Frédérick's affair with Atala Beauchêne but the arrest and trial for murder of his old friend and colleague Jean-Gaspard Deburau.[17] Like Frédérick, the great mime had never been given official recognition, but whereas the actor had won international fame and could command a proportionately high salary, Deburau was known only to the Boulevard public and was still employed at the Funambules for a pittance. In 1832 it had seemed that fortune was going to smile on him at last, for Jules Janin had devoted a book to him and he had been invited to perform in a benefit at the Théâtre du Palais-Royal; but the book had had little effect and the mime's performance had been hissed by the sophisticated Palais-Royal audience. His first wife had died soon after their wedding; the mistress who had taken her place and borne him four children had ended up by deceiving him; and his daughter by his second wife had recently died in infancy. Soured and embittered by sorrow and failure, Deburau went through the motions of murder every night on the Funambules stage: on 18 April 1836 he killed in earnest.

That day, he was out walking with his wife in the country when a young apprentice called Vielin recognized him and started shouting insults at 'Pierrot and his whore'. Goaded beyond endurance, Deburau finally turned on the youth and felled him to the ground with his stick; Vielin died an hour later. The mime was arrested, incarcerated at Sainte-Pélagie, and brought to trial at the Seine Assizes in May. He created a good impression by appearing dressed in black from head to foot and weeping when the charge against him was read out. Witnesses of the killing told how he had been provoked; friends from the Boulevard theatres testified to his gentle disposition; nobody pointed out that he could be quick-tempered and vindictive, or that he had been taught as a boy how to deliver a lethal blow with a stick. The jury found him not guilty.

When he returned to the stage in July, the Boulevard gave him a hero's welcome. Bertrand had the façade of the Funambules specially illuminated for the occasion, and the little theatre was packed to the doors with an enthusiastic audience of writers, actors, artists and working-men. Deburau was moved to tears by his reception: it was as if he were being acquitted all over again. And yet there was something wrong, something missing. The critic of the *Monde Dramatique* put his finger on it when he wrote that 'Deburau might find his costume on the same hook, his ceruse on the same pad, but he would never again encounter the same laughter or the same fervour—because he who normally lashed out with his foot had struck a blow with his hand, and instead of making people cry with laughing, he had made somebody weep with sorrow.' Pierrot had lost none of his skill, but from now on his antics would leave a chill in the heart.

Meanwhile Dumas had completed his version of *Kean* and the play had gone into rehearsal at the Variétés. It was advertised to open on 21 July, then put back a day, and finally postponed indefinitely. Charles Maurice characteristically attributed this delay to Frédérick, whom he accused of threatening to go on his three months' annual leave unless the management paid him heavy compensation.[18] Rebutting this charge in a letter to the Press,[19] the actor claimed that he had sacrificed his leave for nothing in order to play Kean, and that only the indisposition of his two leading ladies was holding up the play. They eventually recovered, but then Dumas was slapped into the Hôtel des Haricots for failing to do his National Guard duty, and *Kean* had to wait for the author's release. At long last, on 31 August 1836, the curtain rose on one of Frédérick's greatest triumphs.

For an account of the play itself, it would be hard to better Thackeray's ironical synopsis.[20] In his *Paris Sketch Book* he writes:

M. Dumas's piece of *Kean* was brought out by the author as a satire upon the French critics, who, to their credit be it spoken, had generally attacked him, and was intended by him, and received by the public, as a faithful portraiture of English manners. As such, it merits special observation and praise. In the first act you find a Countess and an Ambassadress, whose conversation relates purely to the great actor. All the ladies in London are in love with him, especially the two present. As for the Ambassadress, she prefers him to her husband (a matter of course in all French plays), and to a more seducing person still—no less a person than the Prince of Wales! who presently waits on the ladies, and joins in their conversation concerning Kean. 'This man', says His Royal Highness, 'is the very pink of fashion. Brummell is nobody when compared to him; and I myself only an insignificant private gentleman. He has a reputation among ladies, for which I sigh in vain; and spends an income twice as great as mine.' This admirable historic touch at once paints the actor and the Prince; the estimation in which the one was held, and the modest economy for which the other was so notorious.

Then we have Kean at a place called the *Trou de Charbon*, the Coal Hole, where, to the edification of the public, he engages in a fisty combat with a notorious boxer. The scene was received by the audience with loud exclamations of delight, and commented on, by the journals, as a faultless picture of English manners. The Coal Hole being on the banks of the Thames, a nobleman—*Lord Melbourn*! [*sic* for Mewill]—has chosen the tavern as a rendezvous for a gang of pirates, who are to have their ship in waiting, in order to carry off a young lady with whom his Lordship is enamoured. It need not be said that Kean arrives at the nick of time, saves the innocent *Meess Anna*, and exposes the infamy of the Peer. A violent tirade against noblemen ensues, and Lord Melbourn [*sic*] slinks away, disappointed, to meditate revenge. Kean's triumphs continue through all the acts: the Ambassadress falls madly in love with him; the Prince becomes furious at his ill success, and the Ambassador dreadfully jealous. They pursue Kean to his dressing-room at the theatre; where, unluckily, the Ambassadress herself has taken refuge. Dreadful quarrels ensue; the tragedian grows suddenly mad upon the stage, and so cruelly insults the Prince of Wales that His Royal Highness determines to send him to *Botany Bay*. His sentence, however, is commuted to banishment to New York; whither, of course, Miss Anna accompanies him; rewarding him, previously, with her hand and twenty thousand a year!

From this summary it is clear that Dumas's intention in writing or re-writing the play was not so much to satirize the

Press—though both he and his interpreter settled some old scores in Kean's diatribe against venal critics—or to present a realistic picture of English life, as to provide Frédérick with a vehicle designed to show off every aspect of his many-sided genius. If he made Kean get drunk and go mad, play Romeo and Falstaff, make polite conversation and ardent protestations of love, fight with a pugilist and shout abuse at the Prince of Wales, it was because Frédérick was equally at home as drunkard, madman, brawler, lover, wit, tragic actor or broken-hearted clown. 'Never', said Gautier,[21] 'has a better role been written for Frédérick Lemaître.'

He filled the part to perfection. Dumas wrote to him[22] as soon as he got home that night: 'A long time ago I told you that in my eyes you were the only dramatic artist of our age; all that I can do now is repeat what I said to you then.' And Gautier declared: 'At this moment Frédérick is undoubtedly the greatest actor in the world; no one has ever had a wider range. He is a veritable Proteus, a truly Shakespearian player, as great and simple and multiform as Nature herself.'

A good many critics remarked that Frédérick bore an uncanny likeness to the real Edmund Kean, despite the difference in build between the two men. Thus in a letter to the editor of a Stuttgart periodical[23] Heinrich Heine wrote:

> The whole production is wonderfully true to life. It took me right back in spirit to old England, and I really thought I was watching the late Edmund Kean again, whom I saw so often over there. The illusion was doubtless largely due to the actor who played the leading role, although Frédérick Lemaître is a tall, imposing figure and Kean was short and stocky. But there was something in the latter's personality and acting which is also to be found in Frédérick Lemaître. He is a sublime buffoon whose sinister clowning turns Thalia pale with fear and Melpomene radiant with happiness.

The resemblance between the two actors extended beyond their art to their private lives: they were both notorious for their heavy debts and their heavy drinking. Like Kean, Frédérick had taken to drink on account of the frustrations and disappointments he had suffered, and the habit had hardened into a vice. Stories about his addiction to the bottle were legion. It was said that he used to break every window on the staircase when he returned to his flat after a night's drinking; that he sometimes became so intoxicated he would forget the part he was acting and declaim passages from another play; that he had a miniature wine-cellar installed in his carriage and could be seen driving round Paris holding a bottle to his lips as if it were a cigar.[24] Many of these tales were invented by his enemies or by journalists who were short of copy; some of them were undoubtedly true.

Unlike Clément,[25] the notorious alcoholic whose contract with the Funambules stipulated that on Mondays he should be allowed 'to abandon himself freely to his irresistible passion for the vine', Frédérick drank copiously and regularly every day: his wine bills, which are in the present author's possession, show that even in old age, when he was living alone, he consumed twenty-five bottles of bordeaux a week. He used to take a couple of bottles into his dressing-room at the theatre before every performance and tip the contents into a huge salad-bowl; between acts he would gulp down great draughts of wine and by the end of the evening the salad-bowl was always empty.[26] He obtained the same sort of stimulus from wine as Edmund Kean had done, and sometimes it enabled him to achieve extraordinary effects.

This was shown particularly at one of the first performances of *Kean*.[27] Frédérick kept the audience waiting three-quarters of an hour, and when at last he arrived at the theatre he was so drunk he could scarcely stand. Dumas and the stage-manager both tried to stop him from going on, but he pushed them aside and shouted for the curtain to be raised. Then, with a tremendous effort of will-power, he gained control of his limbs and made a magnificent entrance, subjugating the angry audience and winning a round of applause. When he came to the passage in which Kean deplores his intemperance, the relevance of what he was saying to his own situation was suddenly borne in on him; and abandoning Dumas's text, he launched into an improvisation of such pathos and sincerity that the audience rose from their seats and cheered him for several minutes.

'Kean himself', said Gautier,[28] 'could not have played his own part any better.'

There could be no higher praise than that.

CHAPTER TWELVE

RUY BLAS

'KEAN' played to packed houses until late in November. But it was an actor's rather than an author's success, and by itself it could not halt the decline of Romantic drama. That decline was due partly to a change in public taste, which had begun to react strongly against the violence and passion of the Romantic plays, and partly to the defection or degeneration of the leading Romantic dramatists. Thus Vigny had apparently gone into retirement, Hugo had produced nothing since the scandalous *Angelo*, while Dumas and his collaborators were turning out spectacular pot-boilers such as *Don Juan de Marana* and *Caligula*.[1] The former was put on at the Porte-Saint-Martin in April 1836, with angels and ghosts flying through the air and the Virgin presiding over the heavenly host; it cost 80,000 francs and was a dismal failure. As for *Caligula*, the Comédie-Française gave it a lavish production at the end of 1837, though they refused to let Dumas have the four horses he wanted for the Prologue; he consoled himself by putting souvenir medallions on sale in the foyer, which shocked the *sociétaires* to the core. But expensive scenery and souvenir medallions could not save the play from ridicule, and it was taken off after a few weeks.

The *Caligula* fiasco convinced the Comédie-Française that Romantic drama was dead, and the *sociétaires* congratulated themselves on having recently driven Marie Dorval out of the theatre. It remained to be seen whether classical comedy and tragedy could be resurrected. As an experiment, *Tartuffe* was put on early in 1838, with Mlle Mars as Elmire, and to every-

L

body's surprise and delight it drew full houses. But tragedy was a different matter, for there was nobody at the Théâtre-Français capable of infusing life into the plays of Racine and Corneille. Then, on 12 June 1838, a seventeen-year-old Jewish girl called Rachel Félix, whom Samson had trained and introduced to the Rue de Richelieu, made her début as Camille in *Horace*, and hope was rekindled.[2] In August Jules Janin, now dramatic critic of the *Journal des Débats*, saw Rachel on his return from Italy, and acclaimed her acting in an enthusiastic article which established her reputation. Crowds flocked to the Théâtre-Français to judge for themselves, and were conquered by her frail beauty, her blazing eyes, her clear firm voice. In November she received the royal accolade. Louis-Philippe went to see her in *Cinna*, and told her afterwards: 'My duties rarely allow me to go to the theatre, but I shall see you again. You have brought back the great days of French tragedy.'

Banished from the Rue de Richelieu, the Romantic dramatists found that they were no longer welcome on the Boulevard, where musicians and animals now reigned supreme. In 1836 the proprietor of the Jardin Turc had modernized his garden, dismissed his old conductor, increased his orchestra to sixty, and put a young man called Jullien in charge of it.[3] Jullien's concerts had immediately become all the rage, putting even Musard in the shade. For one thing, the newcomer was extremely good-looking, with his crimped hair, well-cut clothes, diamond tie-pin and yellow gloves; he was also a brilliant conductor and a born showman. He specialized in sensational visual and acoustic effects, using flashing lights, bells and musketry for the quadrille he had adapted from Meyerbeer's *Huguenots*, the sound of barking dogs for a quadrille entitled *St. Hubert* (the patron saint of hunting), and a so-called 'nocturnorama' of coloured transparents for his *Belshazzar's Feast*. Poor Musard's pistol shots and broken chairs were left far behind.

The Boulevard theatres were hard put to it to counter the attraction of Jullien's concerts in the Jardin Turc. Some of them relied heavily on the masked balls which they held at night after the show and which were becoming increasingly popular. 'Scarcely anyone goes to the theatre now', remarked Gautier,[4] 'except to dance; people are obviously eager to get the evening performance over, and the stage-hands lay the dance-floor across the pit in such a hurry that it seems as if a slow-moving play-goer is bound to be trapped under it.' Harel, however, preferred to turn his theatre into a circus rather than a dance-hall. Almost any play was good enough for him, provided it gave him a pre-text to show some animal on the stage. 'Performing dogs,' wrote one critic,[5] 'white elephants, musical hares, everything on four feet has appeared at the Porte-Saint-Martin. Future generations will refer to this theatre as Harel's Ark.' After *Don Juan de Marana*, Harel closed his door against the Romantic playwrights, declaring that the 'literary drama' had ruined him and that henceforth he was 'shamefacedly but resolutely' going to make money out of less exalted but more profitable genres.[6]

The only hope that remained to the Romantics was to found a theatre of their own where they would be able to stage their plays without having to trouble about the whims of managers or *sociétaires*. Hugo and Dumas decided to sink their differences and work together to achieve this object. Their friend the young Duc d'Orléans, to whom they appealed for help, spoke to the Minister Guizot on their behalf, and he eventually agreed to grant a licence for a theatre specializing in drama to one of Hugo's protégés, Anténor Joly, the editor of the theatrical magazine *Vert-Vert*. Unfortunately Joly had no money of his own, and the only backer he could find was a certain Fernand de Villeneuve, a retired undertaker with a passion for comic opera.[7] The omens were not auspicious; nor were the conditions Villeneuve laid down. He insisted that he should be co-manager of the new theatre with Joly, and that the licence should auth-orize comic opera as well as drama. Hugo had serious mis-givings about allowing music anything more than a subordinate role, but in the end he gave way.

There remained the problem of finding a theatre and a com-pany. Hugo and Dumas hoped at first to be able to build a new playhouse on the Boulevard Saint-Denis, no doubt to be able to oppose a Porte-Saint-Denis to Harel's Porte-Saint-Martin, but for financial reasons they had to be content with the Théâtre Ventadour, which until recently had housed the Opéra-Comique, and which they renamed the Théâtre de la Renaissance. They were similarly disappointed in their hopes of engaging the three greatest Romantic players, Marie Dorval, Bocage and Frédérick Lemaître. Dorval was bound by contract to the Gymnase, the little vaudeville theatre she had entered on leaving the Comédie-Française, and she would not be able to escape to the Renaissance for another year; Bocage was in the same position; only Frédérick was available. After *Kean* he had appeared in a few less successful productions before leaving the Variétés in the autumn of 1837. 'My great regret', the manager had told him,[8] 'is to be unable to provide you with a vast stage on which your powerful talents could develop freely.' When Joly offered him the chance of interpreting the Romantic dramatists on the vast stage of the Renaissance, he accepted it eagerly.[9]

At the same time Frédérick persuaded Joly to engage Atala Beauchêne, who had been touring the provinces with him, to play leads at the Renaissance. This was not as outrageous as it might appear, for with the help of careful coaching by her lover Atala's acting had improved beyond recognition. 'Till now', a critic had written at the time of *Kean*,[10] 'she simply did not know that she was a very good actress; but she must know it now that she has played Anna Damby with such sensibility and distinction.' She was certainly a better actress than the other leading ladies at the Renaissance: Ida Ferrier, whom Dumas had forced on Joly, and Juliette Drouet, who was hankering after the stage again. While Hugo was busy writing the play which was to inaugurate the new theatre, the three mistresses jockeyed for position, with Adèle Hugo watching anxiously from the wings. Joly began to wish he had never left his editorial chair.

The play was *Ruy Blas*, the finest of all Hugo's dramas.[11] It is the splendidly improbable story of a seventeenth-century valet with a noble soul and a brilliant mind who falls in love

with the Queen of Spain, Maria de Neuburg, and obtains
supreme power over the country thanks to her protection and his
genius. He is helped at the outset by his villainous master, Don
Salluste, a former Minister whom the Queen has dismissed
and who is out for revenge. Finally Don Salluste reveals the
truth to the horrified Maria and is killed by Ruy Blas, who then
takes poison himself, winning the Queen's forgiveness before
he dies. In the best Hugolian tradition, all the genres are represented: tragedy by Ruy Blas, drama by Don Salluste, and
comedy by a swashbuckling vagabond nobleman called Don
César de Bazan, who bears a suspicious resemblance to Robert
Macaire. As for the central theme of the play, Hugo's preface
offers us a choice of three interpretations: 'The philosophical
subject of Ruy Blas is the common people aspiring to higher
spheres; the human subject is a man in love with a woman; the
dramatic subject is a lackey in love with a queen.'

On the draft contract relating to *Ruy Blas*, Hugo had scrib-
bled: 'Mlle George and M. Frédérick Lemaître are to play the
leading parts.' The contract itself bore Frédérick's name alone.
This was understandable, for Maria de Neuburg is a very
different role from Marie Tudor or Lucrèce Borgia. It seems in
fact to have been designed for Juliette Drouet, who in mid-
August[12] wrote to Hugo: 'Ever since you hinted to me that I
might have the chance of acting in your entrancing play, I have
been like a poor sleepwalker who has been given lots of champagne to drink.' But this arrangement was not at all to Adèle
Hugo's liking, and when her husband went off for a week's
holiday with Juliette, she appealed to Joly to give the part to
some other actress,[13] alleging that she was 'concerned only for
the success of the play'. Joly knew of course that her real motive
was jealousy, but he also knew what a poor actress Juliette was,
and he resolved to talk Hugo out of starring his mistress in this
important opening production. Secretly rather relieved, the poet
gave way after putting up only a token show of resistance, and
since he refused to consider employing Ida, who as Dumas's
mistress might be tempted to sabotage the play, it was decided

to offer the part of the Queen to Atala Beauchêne. Juliette was
heart-broken. 'So Maria de Neuburg will never live through me
and for me', she wrote to Hugo.[14] 'I am more deeply grieved than
you can possibly imagine. The loss of this one last hope has
struck me to the ground.' But out of loyalty to her lover she was
to attend the first night of the play in which she had hoped to
star, and even split her gloves applauding the woman who had
supplanted her.

Frédérick was cast as Ruy Blas. The draft contract shows that
Hugo had written this part specially for him, but even if he had
not, Frédérick would have been the obvious choice: there was
no one else in the Renaissance company, or indeed in Paris,
capable of doing justice to a role which combines tenderness,
ambition, fury and despair, or of sustaining the magnificent
tirade in the third act—a speech over a hundred lines long—in
which Ruy Blas describes the degradation of Spain and stig-
matizes the venality of the King's Ministers. But he had not been
told anything about his part by the time the cast met at Hugo's
Place Royale house, on 30 August, to hear the poet read his
play.[15] In her book about Hugo his wife writes:

M. Frédérick looked radiant with joy during the reading of the
first three acts, worried during the fourth and positively gloomy
during the fifth. He left without a word.

As it was impossible to rehearse at the theatre, M. Anténor Joly
had borrowed the Conservatoire, and it was there that the author
handed out the parts the next day. M. Frédérick Lemaître took his
with an air of resignation, but he had no sooner glanced at it than
he gave a cry of pleasure and surprise.

'So it's Ruy Blas I'm playing!' he exclaimed.

He had thought it was Don César. As always happens with great
successes, his tremendous creation of Robert Macaire was forever
being cast in his teeth; people kept telling him that he would never
be able to play anything else, that he was incapable of taking a
serious role. Seeing how Don César was developing in the fourth
act, he had told himself that M. Victor Hugo held the same opinion
and meant him to have the comic part. It was a good part, of course,
but it was none the less that of a vagabond, whereas Ruy Blas would
rid him of Robert Macaire's rags and tatters. He rushed up to M.

Victor Hugo and thanked him effusively for delivering him at last from irony and derision and reconciling him with passion and poetry.

At rehearsals Frédérick was the dominant figure, advising the other actors on their parts, which he knew as well as his own, and even proposing changes in the text to the author.[16] Several scenes of *Ruy Blas* were in fact rewritten in accordance with Frédérick's suggestions; the part of Don Guritan was given greater importance and further comic touches added to that of Don César. Only once did author and actor clash. Frédérick had been criticizing Atala for a piece of by-play which Hugo had suggested, and when the poet accused him of misinterpreting the passage in question he stormed out of the theatre in a fury. But the next day he was all contrition.

'Monsieur Victor Hugo,' he said, 'I read *Ruy Blas* attentively last night and I discovered that you were right: I was mistaken in the advice I gave Madame. What is more, I failed to show you the respect which an actor owes an author, and which a man of talent owes a man of genius. I therefore offer you a humble apology.'

'Monsieur Frédérick,' replied Hugo, not to be outdone in courtesy, 'only a man of real merit can acknowledge a mistake with such simplicity and dignity. Your apology does you so much honour that I am almost glad that mistake was made.'

Adèle Hugo records that Frédérick treated all his fellow actors kindly and considerately, with one exception—and that was his mistress Atala. He was so determined to extract a great performance from a woman who was no more than a very competent actress that he drove her mercilessly, criticizing her every gesture and inflexion. Once he lost all patience with her and shook her up and down in front of the whole company.

'You blockhead!' he shouted. 'Nobody would ever suspect that you were speaking the most beautiful language on earth! But watch out: the author is there, listening to you and judging your stupidity!'

His cruel behaviour to Atala was in fact a sure sign of his

affection. There is a story—which may be apocryphal but is none the less significant—that her mother found him one day giving his mistress a thrashing, and begged him to beat her instead. He stopped for a moment, much to Atala's relief, and looked at the older woman in amazement.

'Beat *you*?' he repeated. 'But why should I, Madame? I don't love you, do I?'

But at long last Atala's purgatory came to an end, and on 8 November 1838 *Ruy Blas* was presented to the public. This first night was one of the greatest occasions in the history of Romantic drama. True, Hugo's arrogant egotism had alienated most of his old followers, and he could no longer count on the veterans of the Battle of *Hernani*, but the combination of his name and Frédérick's had drawn a full and distinguished house. The newly decorated theatre, all white-and-gold with sky-blue boxes and red carpets, looked magnificent; and Gautier noted approvingly that the attendants were unusually young and pretty.[17] There was only one flaw: the heating system was not functioning and the place was like an ice-box. The women draped themselves in their coats and furs; the men, with the solitary exception of the hardy Duc d'Orléans, kept their overcoats on. But the audience soon forgot their discomfort in the excitement of the play.

The first three acts were well received, especially the hero's great speech to the Ministers, which brought salvoes of applause. The fourth act, on the other hand, was disappointing: the actor who had been cast as Don César, Ferré Saint-Firmin, lacked the necessary gusto to make this comic but unessential character either credible or acceptable. But Frédérick brought the play to a triumphant close with his playing of the last act.[18] Adèle Hugo records that 'the way in which he tore off the coat covering his livery, bolted the door, struck the table with the sword, spoke to Don Salluste, begged the Queen's forgiveness and drank the poison was grandiose, true to life, splendid and profound, and the poet had the rare satisfaction of seeing the character he had imagined live before his eyes'.

The Press on the whole treated the play harshly.[19] Gustave
Planche, for instance, described it as 'a challenge to good sense
and good taste, a childish accumulation of impossible episodes';
Chaudes-Aigues asked when the author was going to be committed to the lunatic asylum at Charenton; and while Jules
Sandeau admitted that the audience had enjoyed *Ruy Blas*, he
hastened to add that they had made a resolution 'to go the next
day and drink at the purer springs of Racine and Corneille'. But
even the most hostile critics had nothing but praise for Frédérick's performance. Granier de Cassagnac declared that he was
'undoubtedly far and away the greatest artist of our age'; Roger
de Beauvoir put him above Kemble and Macready and stated
that 'with this role Frédérick has risen to unheard-of heights';
and in the *Presse* Théophile Gautier wrote:

> Robert Macaire is no more! From that heap of rags, like a God
> leaving the tomb, Frédérick has reappeared, the real Frédérick we
> know so well, the melancholy and passionate Frédérick, full of
> strength and grandeur, who can summon up tears to move you and
> thunder to terrify you, who in voice and look and gesture is the
> greatest comedian and the greatest tragedian of modern times.
> This is a wonderful piece of good fortune for dramatic art.

Hugo himself was well aware what a tremendous debt he
owed his great interpreter, and in his postface to the published
text of *Ruy Blas*, after playing tribute to the other players, he
wrote:

> As for M. Frédérick Lemaître, how can I praise him better than
> the public, whose enthusiastic acclamations greet him as soon as
> he comes on the stage and follow him after the final curtain? Dreamy
> and thoughtful in the first act, melancholy in the second, grandiose,
> passionate and sublime in the third, he rises in the fifth act to one
> of those prodigious tragic effects from whose lofty eminence the
> radiant actor dominates all the memories of his art. For old men,
> he is Lekain and Garrick in one; for us, his coevals, he is Kean's
> action combined with Talma's emotion. Then too, amid the lightning
> flashes of his acting, M. Frédérick sheds tears, those real tears which
> make others weep, those tears of which Horace speaks: *Si vis me
> flere, dolendum est primum ipsi tibi.* In *Ruy Blas* M. Frédérick realizes

for us the ideal of the great actor. There can be no doubt that his whole career, past as well as future, will be illuminated by this brilliant creation. For M. Frédérick, the performance of 8 November 1838 was not a theatrical occasion but a transfiguration.

Frédérick certainly considered Ruy Blas one of the finest parts he ever created, and he could not countenance the idea of anyone else playing it. Thus in 1849, when the Porte-Saint-Martin, which had revived the play, was threatened with bankruptcy, he wrote[20] to Hugo: 'If I should sign a contract with another theatre, can you and will you guarantee that Ruy Blas would pass to the theatre to which I belonged?' He need not have worried: the other leading actors of his time were terrified of measuring themselves against him in the part, and as late as 1869 Mélingue confessed[21] that he would never dare to play Ruy Blas 'because apart from the magnitude of the role there was the memory of Frédérick to contend with'.

No one in the theatrical world could forget the story which Alexandre Mauzin, the original Don Salluste, used to tell, to show how completely Frédérick identified himself with Hugo's hero.[22] Every night, at the point in the third act of Ruy Blas at which Don Salluste orders the lackey-minister to shut a window, the Renaissance audience burst into thunderous applause; but Mauzin, sitting in an arm-chair with his back to Frédérick, could not see what the great actor was doing to get this response from his public. Finally, unable to contain his curiosity any longer, he looked round one night as soon as the cheering started. Frédérick was standing behind him, his face ghastly pale, and genuine tears of humiliation rolling down his cheeks.

There was hissing as well as applause at nearly every performance of Ruy Blas, and Joly soon discovered that it was being organized by his co-manager Villeneuve.[23] In the interests of his beloved musical comedy, the retired undertaker was doing everything in his power to bury Romantic drama. Whenever Ruy Blas was presented, the heating broke down, the orchestra played out of tune and people with complimentary tickets hissed. On the other hand, whenever the musical comedy Lady Melvil

was put on, the theatre was comfortably warm, the orchestra
behaved itself and a powerful claque rallied the audience. The
drama company fought back manfully, and once, when Frédérick
caught sight of the leader of the *Lady Melvil* claque blowing a
whistle in the third act of *Ruy Blas,* he went down to the footlights and turned the full blast of his invective on the frightened
little man. But the war between music and drama continued unabated. Joly did not dare to protest, since Villeneuve held the
purse-strings. Small wonder that in December he confided to
Frédérick[24] that he was 'exhausted by managerial problems and
at the same time alarmed by the course the theatre is taking!'

Ruy Blas was eventually taken off after fifty performances and
replaced in April 1839 by a new Dumas play.[25] Dumas had
offered Joly a choice between two works: *Mademoiselle de Belle-
Isle,* a delightful comedy in prose which recalls Marivaux and
Beaumarchais, and *L'Alchimiste,* a turgid drama in clumsy
Alexandrines which clearly owes a great deal to Hugo's *Angelo.*
Joly, remembering the well-meaning advice Gautier had given
him at the beginning of the Renaissance venture—'Don't have
any prose: just verse, more verse and still more verse!'—had
taken *L'Alchimiste.* It was a disastrous choice.

Frédérick did his best with the play. His own acting copy is
covered with close-written notes in which he criticizes forced
rhymes such as *tétrarque* and *Pétrarque,* points out weaknesses in
characterization and suggests cuts in the more verbose passages.
But he could not turn a mediocre drama into a masterpiece, and
it was given a cool reception by the first-night audience. The
critics praised Frédérick's miming in certain episodes but recognized that the title-role was the poorest Dumas had ever written
and gave little or no scope to the actor's talents. They were
far less indulgent to Ida, who played the heroine, and made
cruel jokes about her figure: her part was not too big for her,
they said, but she was too big for her part.[26] *L'Alchimiste* had
only seventeen performances.

The failure of Dumas's play spelt the beginning of the end for
the Renaissance. With the public flocking to see Rachel in

classical tragedy at the Français, and Romantic drama obviously moribund and discredited, Joly's theatre could not hope to survive for very long. Though it dragged out an ignominious existence for another two years, its fate was really settled when Frédérick left in June 1839.

For some time past, Atala's mother, who had never approved of her liaison with Frédérick, had been urging her to take a new lover of ampler means and gentler manners.[27] In May the girl decided to follow this advice. She came to an arrangement with a man whom her biographers describe as 'a Liberal count', promising to join him after the last performance of *L'Alchimiste*, which was due to take place on the 20th. That night she played the part of Maddalena, the lovely courtesan who seduces the alchemist, more passionately than ever before, and then slipped out of the theatre at the end of the fourth act, leaving a brutal letter for Frédérick with the concierge.

Like the true Romantic hero he was, both on and off the stage, Frédérick gave himself up to a frenzy of grief. He told Joly that he could not bear to remain at the Renaissance, where everything reminded him of his unfaithful mistress. His contract expired at the end of May, and he asked to be released from a promise he had given to stay on into the summer. At the manager's request he put off his departure for a few weeks, but on 18 June[28] he wrote to Joly:

> My dear Anténor, it is quite impossible for me to remain any longer in the cruel position in which I find myself. Please think seriously about it, and let us make an end of the matter. If you had had me play *Ruy Blas* two or three times I think I might have posesssed my soul in patience a little longer, though even then I don't know how I should have managed. But with my arms folded, my purse empty and my heart broken!!—as I said before, we must make an end of it.

A few days later[29] he addressed an even more impassioned appeal to the manager: 'Since you have the power to allay my despair, do so, I beg you. Take pity on a lunatic, a madman, whom love has made forgetful of everything else.' And this time Joly relented.

Throughout the summer and autumn Frédérick toured the provinces with *Ruy Blas*. On his return to Paris in December he signed a contract with Harel to play leads at the Porte-Saint-Martin from the beginning of February 1840 to the end of March 1841.[30] At the same time Harel engaged Sophie Lemaître, who had not appeared on the stage for some years, to play 'leading roles and young mothers in comedy, drama and tragedy'.

The theatrical world was astonished by this reconciliation between two men whose enmity had become a by-word in Paris. But it was self-interest that brought Harel and Frédérick together again. The manager had a profitable affair in view, and the actor a great new role. Balzac had promised a play to the Porte-Saint-Martin.

CHAPTER THIRTEEN

BALZAC

AT the triumphant first night of Dumas's *Mademoiselle de Belle-Isle*, Balzac came face to face with the author on the staircase of the Théâtre-Français.[1]

'When I'm worn out,' he said sourly, 'I shall start writing for the theatre.'

'Then you'd better start straight away', retorted Dumas.

In fact Balzac had been writing plays, or rather attempting to write plays, for nearly twenty years—but without success. For one thing, he had no experience of theatrical technique and found his tumultous imagination cramped by the narrow limits of the stage. For another, he regarded novel-writing as the chief purpose of his life and considered play-writing merely as a means of making money quickly and easily. The idea that any special skill or effort might be called for never occurred to him. With a few ideas for a plot, and a cheap literary hack to turn them into dialogue, he felt sure he could produce a dozen or so plays a year, any one of which might make his fortune.

His latest attempt to put this theory into practice had ended in disaster. Anténor Joly had promised him 6,000 francs on the delivery and acceptance of a play to be called *L'École des Ménages*, and Balzac had promptly started looking for a collaborator. He had found one in a feeble-minded young man called Charles Lassailly, whom he had lured out to his country house, Les Jardies, on the understanding that he should have free board and lodging in return for roughing out the script. The wretched Lassailly had very soon discovered that collaborating with Balzac meant going to bed at six in the evening, getting up at midnight, slaving away till seven on black coffee, snatching a few hours' sleep, working another stint in the afternoon, and then starting all over again. After a few days and nights of this routine he had felt that he was losing his reason—he eventually died insane— and had sneaked away, leaving Balzac to finish *L'École des Ménages* himself. And then, to the novelist's surprise and disgust, Joly had rejected the play.

In Balzac's opinion his great mistake had been to waste precious time writing a play without making certain that it would be accepted, and he resolved not to make the same mistake again. When he heard that Harel was in dire financial straits and looking for a sensational play that would save his theatre from ruin, he went to the Porte-Saint-Martin and proposed a dramatic version of Vautrin's adventures, on condition that Harel agreed to take the work on trust. The little manager was so desperate for money that he would have agreed to almost anything. Besides, he thought that Balzac's first play was bound to draw huge audiences, especially if it was about the most popular of all his characters. He accordingly accepted the novelist's terms, even promising to engage Frédérick, whom Balzac considered to be the greatest of living actors, to play the title role. By the time they parted, the two men had convinced each other that all their troubles were over.

Balzac's, however, were only just beginning, for he still had to write the play. He moved into his tailor's house in the Rue de Richelieu, to be close to the Boulevard, and summoned no less than four prospective collaborators to a hurried conference.[2] Gautier, who was one of them, has left us this entertaining account of what happened when he arrived:

'Ah, so here you are at last, Théo!' cried Balzac. 'You tardigrade, you slow-coach, you lazy-bones, you! Hurry up now and sit down. You ought to have been here an hour ago. I've got to read a five-act play to Harel tomorrow.'
'So you want my advice on it?' I asked, settling into an arm-chair in preparation for a lengthy reading.

Balzac guessed my thoughts from the position I had taken up, and answered simply: 'The play isn't written yet.'

'The deuce it isn't!' I said. 'Well, in that case you'll have to put the reading off for six weeks.'

'No, we are going to turn out a dramorama straight away, so that we can collect the cash. I've got a lot of bills falling due pretty soon.'

'But you'll never be able to produce a play by tomorrow! Why, there isn't even time to have it copied out.'

'Let me explain how it's going to be done. You will write one act, Ourliac another, Laurent-Jan the third, Belloy the fourth, I'll take care of the fifth, and at midday tomorrow I shall read the whole play as arranged. An act doesn't contain more than four or five hundred lines, and anyone can turn out five hundred lines of dialogue in a day and a night.'

I was rather taken aback, but I replied: 'Tell me what it's about, let me have some idea how the plot develops, sketch out the characters for me, and I'll set to work.'

'Oh!' he cried, with magnificent disdain and a superb air of weariness. 'If I've got to tell you the story, we shall never be finished.'

It had not occurred to me that I was being indiscreet in asking for this information, but Balzac thought it was just idle curiosity on my part.

With tremendous difficulty I managed to extract some brief particulars from him, and I used these to draft a scene of which only a few words remained in the final version. This, as may well be imagined, was not read to Harel the next day after all. I cannot say exactly what the other collaborators did, but the only one who really worked hard on the play was Laurent-Jan, to whom it is dedicated.

Laurent-Jan later claimed in fact to have done nearly all the work himself,[3] and wryly complained that 'Balzac began by referring to *Vautrin* as "your play", then as "our play", and finally as "my play"'. But even if Laurent-Jan was responsible for the greater part of the first draft, it is probable that Balzac rewrote most of it in the course of rehearsals. For the novelist was beginning to realize the difficulties involved in writing for the stage. Every day Frédérick or Harel suggested some change in the text, and every day he got a little thinner from worry and overwork. 'Two and a half months of rehearsals', writes his

BALZAC, FRÉDÉRICK AND GAUTIER AT PIERREFITTE
Water-colour by Gautier

CLARISSE MIROY IN
La Grâce de Dieu

friend Léon Gozlan,[4] 'had made him quite unrecognizable, and
his fatigue had become so notorious that many people, knowing
the time he used to go home from the theatre, used to wait for
him to pass by. His huge blue coat, his nut-brown Cossack
trousers, his white waistcoat, and above all his enormous shoes
with their leather tongues hanging out—all these clothes of his,
heavy, mud-stained and far too big for him, spoke of the confusion, the disorder, the fearful upheaval which the theatre had
produced in his life.'

The same impression was given by Balzac when he wrote[5]
to Mme Hanska:

> *Vautrin* is an exhausting business; I have a rehearsal every day.
> In a single evening I shall be playing for a fortune in money and
> fame. Frédérick Lemaître guarantees that it will be a success. Harel,
> the manager, is sure of it. As for myself, I began to despair ten
> days ago; I thought the play was stupid and I was right. I have
> completely rewritten it and now I think it might do. But it will
> always be a poor play. I yielded to the temptation to transfer a
> character from the novel to the stage, and that was a mistake.

Vautrin is indeed a poor play, with a tedious, improbable plot.
As for the principal character, he differs somewhat from the
Vautrin of *Le Père Goriot*, for Balzac modelled him not only on
Vidocq, the convict turned policeman, but also on Robert
Macaire, whom he, like Flaubert, regarded as the greatest
dramatic creation of the age.[6] Curiously enough, the hero of
Frédérick's play likewise owes something to Vidocq, since he
too is an ex-convict who at one point proposes to become Chief
of Police. But then both Balzac and Frédérick knew the great
detective well. Among the actor's unpublished papers[7] there is a
tantalizing note which reads: 'Vidocq! His confidences! He con-
sults me. He wants to go on the stage!' It is tempting to think
that perhaps Balzac or Frédérick invited the theatrically-minded
Head of the Sûreté to rehearsals at the Porte-Saint-Martin,
where he could in fact see himself on the stage—in the person of
Vautrin.

There were other officials present at the rehearsals of Balzac's

M

play who were not as welcome as Vidocq. The censor had rejected *Vautrin* three times, and when Rémusat, the sympathetic
Minister of the Interior, finally gave permission for the play to
be performed, he stipulated that if the analogy between *Vautrin*
and *Robert Macaire* led to disturbances in the theatre, the ban
would immediately be re-imposed.[8] Three commissioners
appointed by the censor attended the dress rehearsal and left
without making any criticisms. But on this occasion an incident
had occurred which was to have disastrous consequences for
everyone concerned.

The plot of *Vautrin* required Frédérick to assume a variety of
elaborate disguises, and in the fourth act he had to appear as a
Mexican envoy called General Crustamente. When he came on
to the stage wearing a gorgeous uniform designed by Louis
Boulanger and a cone-shaped wig, the three commissioners saw
nothing remarkable in his appearance. But Moëssard, the stage-
manager of the Porte-Saint-Martin, did.[9]

'Don't you think', he whispered to Harel, 'that Frédérick
looks like Louis-Philippe?'

'Quiet!' hissed Harel, struck by a sudden inspiration. 'That
will be the making of the play!'

Unknown to Frédérick, he summoned the theatre hairdresser
to his office and instructed him to alter Crustamente's wig so as
to bring out the resemblance to Louis-Philippe's famous pear-
shaped coiffure. On no account, he said, was the man to let
Frédérick see what he was doing: it was going to be a wonderful
surprise.

The first performance of *Vautrin* had been fixed for 14 March
1840. For days beforehand, Paris talked of nothing else. 'Not
since the great first nights of Victor Hugo's dramas', says
Gozlan,[10] 'had the public's curiosity been so aroused. It was an
event.' Almost the only person who had not heard of it was
Lamartine,[11] who invited Balzac to spend the evening of the 14th
with him at his house, and received the good-humoured reply:
'Monsieur, the politician in you has absorbed the writer to such
an extent that I can well understand your not knowing what is

happening in a little Boulevard theatre. I therefore have the
honour to inform you that tomorrow I am putting on a five-
act drama at the Porte-Saint-Martin. If, as I hope, it falls flat
early in the evening, I shall hasten to ask for your friendly
condolences.'

Despite the fact that there was a farewell performance at the
Opéra and a Scribe *première* at the Gymnase, the Porte-Saint-
Martin was packed to suffocation on the 14th. The first three
acts of Balzac's play were received coldly but quietly, but as soon
as Frédérick came on in the fourth there was a storm of catcalls
and hisses. For a moment the actor could not understand what
had roused the audience; then he heard murmurs of: 'The King!
Louis-Philippe!' and saw people pointing at his wig. He remembered noticing something odd about it when he was putting it on,
and suddenly realized what it was.[12] But it was too late to do
anything about it. The Duc d'Orléans had got up and walked out
of his box, and the audience, according to Gozlan,[13] had 'lost all
dignity, all calm, all respect; every box was a mouth of a great
volcano of which the pit was the crater: a volcano of laughter
and mockery, blasphemy and abuse, and also threats—for there
were a few loyal friends here and there who remained faithful to
the author in the midst of all this frantic anger, this unbridled
rage'.

The play was savagely mauled by the Press. Jules Janin, for
instance, described it[14] as 'a work of desolation, barbarism and
ineptitude, completely lacking in wit, style, urbanity, invention
and common sense'. But every critic without exception hailed
Frédérick's performance as a masterpiece. Gautier declared[15] that
he was 'prodigious, astounding, beyond all praise: in his mouth
commonplace words acquire new meaning and importance, and
from an apparently insignificant phrase he strikes a strange, lurid
spark which lights up the whole play'. And Édouard Thierry,
after an ironical summary of the plot,[16] wrote:

> Frédérick was admirable throughout: a supple actor, full of re-
> sourcefulness and subtlety, revealing for the first time a gift for
> transformation and transfiguration which he had reserved for this

new phase of his theatrical career. Trivial and sublime in one and the same gesture, melancholy and brutal, radiant with folly or imbued with unction, Frédérick made this perhaps his most comprehensive creation to date. And I use the word 'creation' advisedly, for when he acts another man's work he gives unsparingly of himself.

The briefest reference to the play was probably that made by the official Government paper, the *Moniteur universel*. It stated simply: 'The Minister of the Interior has banned further performances of the play presented yesterday at the Théâtre de la Porte-Saint-Martin under the title of *Vautrin*.'

The Government pretended that the reason for the ban was the alleged immorality of Balzac's play, but everyone knew that it was really Frédérick's wig. Apparently the Duc d'Orléans had gone home to the Tuileries, woken Louis-Philippe up and said to him: 'Father, they are playing you at the theatre. Are you going to stand for it?' Louis-Philippe was not. He acted swiftly. And Frédérick's friends received a black-edged card[17] bearing the following inscription:

FRÉDÉRICK LEMAÎTRE
regrets to inform you of the loss which the most productive of our novelists has just suffered in the person of Monsieur Vautrin, *alias* Trompe-la-Mort, ex-convict, who has died suddenly at the Théâtre de la Porte-Saint-Martin, where he has been buried in the prompter's box.

This probably struck Balzac as altogether too flippant in the circumstances, and for a while it seems that he held the actor responsible for the banning of the play. 'Frédérick was sublime', he told Mme Hanska.[18] 'But the business of the resemblance to Louis-Philippe may have been a deliberate attempt to bring about Harel's fall, which he wanted in order to take his place as manager of the Porte-Saint-Martin.' This suspicion was characteristic of Balzac, but it was completely unfounded. In fact Frédérick did everything he could to save the play, and as soon as the ban was announced he went to the Ministry of the Interior to try and have it lifted.[19]

The Ministry officials greeted him with roars of laughter.

'You were wonderful!' they cried; and Cavé, the Director of Fine Arts, slapped him on the back and said admiringly: 'In years to come they will say that Louis-Philippe lived in the reign of Robert Macaire!' But he explained that the Ministry was powerless to countermand a decision taken by the King. The inevitable result was that a few days later Harel went bankrupt and the Porte-Saint-Martin closed its doors.

Balzac was appalled by the news, not only on his own account but also because of the actors and stage-hands who had been thrown out of work. In the hope of saving them and himself, he promptly started writing two new plays, this time choosing Frédérick as his collaborator.[20] The first was a 'popular drama' called *Richard Cœur-d'Éponge* which Balzac had been talking about since 1830. The second was a more ambitious work, a five-act comedy entitled *Mercadet* which, so he told Frédérick, was to be 'a new *Robert Macaire*, a compound of *Vautrin* and *Tartuffe* and anything else you like, provided it personifies what is going on around us'. Frédérick was to take the leading part in both plays.

The actor was luckier than the unfortunate Lassailly had been: his share in the partnership was limited to revising Balzac's work. He has left us this brief record[21] of his collaboration with the novelist:

Balzac was the best of authors to deal with: if you pointed out a dangerous scene, he would rewrite it; if you told him that an act did not follow on properly from the preceding one, he would start it all over again without the least objection.

One day he wrote to me: 'Dear Master, tonight at ten o'clock I shall come and read you our new dénouement; I think it is as close to Molière as anything could be!'

He came and read his dénouement: it was impossible. And when I had explained why I thought so, he calmly put his manuscript in his pocket and said: 'All right. I'll do it again when I get home.'

Besides being good-natured he was fully aware of his genius; he spoke about it simply and majestically, without any overweening pride.

'*Eugénie Grandet* is a wonderful book', I said to him in the course of one of our long conversations. 'It is as good as Molière.'

'It is probably better', he replied. 'Molière wrote *L'Avare*, and I have written *L'Avarice.*'

Actor and author saw a great deal of each other during the spring and summer of 1840. One day Balzac went out to Frédérick's house at Pierrefitte, accompanied by Gautier and Porcher, the theatrical agent and impresario. It was probably on this occasion[22] that Gautier heard Balzac read a few scenes from *Mercadet*, 'finding a different voice for each character, speaking, declaiming, miming, and bringing a whole world to life with a feverish turbulence that carried one away.' The versatile poet painted a water-colour of Balzac, Frédérick and himself in the garden at Pierrefitte, and it was presented to Porcher 'as a souvenir of this memorable day'.

At other times Frédérick would visit Balzac at Les Jardies.[23] He saw the famous charcoal inscriptions on the bare walls: 'Here an Aubusson tapestry . . . Here a Venetian mirror . . . Here a painting by Raphael . . . ' He inspected the famous boundary wall which had fallen on to the adjoining property so many times that Balzac had finally bought a strip of land just beyond it—'so that the poor thing can at least die in its own bed'. He heard about the famous schemes for making a fortune from pineapples, for installing a lake at Les Jardies, for breaking the bank at Baden Casino. And now and then, when he managed to get a word in, he brought up the subject of Balzac's work for the theatre.

Richard Cœur-d'Éponge was completed in May 1840 but rejected by Frédérick as unlikely to have any success.[24] The actor kept the manuscript for some time and then, at Balzac's request, handed it over to the publisher Paulin as security for a loan the novelist wished to negotiate.[25] Balzac tried to regain possession of the play in 1848, but it is not known whether he succeeded. Certainly the manuscript has never been seen since.

As for *Mercadet*, it seems that Frédérick offered it to the Comédie-Française on Balzac's behalf, for the present author possesses a letter which Cavé wrote to the actor in June 1840,[26] saying that 'it might well be possible for the play to be put into rehearsal at the Théâtre-Français without delay'. Whether Frédérick himself hoped to gain entrance to the Comédie-Française at the same time as *Mercadet* is not clear; in any event, he reckoned without Balzac. The novelist put off finishing his play again and again, until at last Frédérick wrote to him[27] in exasperation:

> Let us bring the affair to a speedy conclusion. Believe me, you will be pleased with it, and above all do not forget (I say this as a friend) that I, who am completely devoted to you, have been idle now for *four months*, simply and solely because I liked you and listened to you. *Be reasonable*—and that does not mean be careless. *Be reasonable*—by which I mean consult your interests and mine, the interests of your glory and my little reputation.
>
> I have just met Hugo, to whom I have *told everything*, and who truly and sincerely hopes that everything will turn out well.

It was all in vain. *Mercadet* had to wait another eleven years before it reached the stage. In August 1851 it was presented at the Gymnase in a three-act version prepared by Adolphe Dennery, and scored a tremendous success. But Geoffroy, not Frédérick, played the title role. And Balzac was dead.

CHAPTER FOURTEEN

TO ENGLAND

BAD luck seemed to dog the theatres with which Frédérick was connected at the beginning of the eighteen-forties. In March 1840 the Porte-Saint-Martin closed after the first and last performance of *Vautrin*. In November 1840 the Ambigu went bankrupt after Frédérick had staged a number of successful revivals there and before a contract he had signed with the management could come into effect.[1] And in May 1841 the Renaissance, which had opened triumphantly with his creation of *Ruy Blas*, closed ignominiously with his creation of *Zacharie, ou l'Avare de Florence*.[2]

This was a flimsy melodrama by a certain Rosier for which Joly had engaged Frédérick in the hope that the actor might save his theatre from bankruptcy. But Frédérick was not the right man for the part, as Gautier explained[3] when he wrote:

> Frédérick disappointed us: apart from a few flashes of genius such as he always reveals, he completely failed to put over the character of the miser. Of course, his physique and his talents are ill suited to the part. Frédérick, the man of life and expansiveness *par excellence*, is the last person one should choose to play a miser. He has always been prodigal of his talent, his genius, his glory and his beauty; he is the actor of the sudden gesture and the unexpected spark; he can portray ambition, gambling fever and all the fiery passions which find expression in frenzied raptures and dithyrambic rages; he can carry sarcasm and irony to their furthest limits; but he will always fail in parts of petty wickedness, in cold, sinister roles.

According to the critic, Frédérick gave a far better performance in a speech he made to the first-night audience than in the

play itself. It so happened that Joly had recently taken him to
court for throwing up the part of Zacharie, and he had been
ordered to fulfil his obligations to the Renaissance by returning
to the theatre. The public, angered by the resultant delay, decided to show their displeasure by hissing him as soon as he came
on. But he knew how to deal with them.

'Gentlemen,' he said, placing his hand on his heart, 'touched
by your kindly welcome, I should like to state that I have
never departed from the path of honour and virtue any more than
I have from the respect which every actor owes his public.'

The audience were satisfied with this declaration and
applauded wildly. Only a few suspicious souls noticed the ambi-
guity of the formula Frédérick had chosen.

From the Renaissance he returned to the Porte-Saint-Martin,
which had just reopened under the management of the Cogniard
brothers, Théodore and Hippolyte.[4] The conditions of his contract were extremely generous, but even so his salary was not
big enough to allow him to live as extravagantly as he did and
at the same time settle the huge debts he had accumulated in
recent years. He therefore decided to sell Pierrefitte, where,
according to a contemporary account, 'banquets, firework displays and entertainments of all kinds had been held for six years,
to the delight of the local inhabitants, but to the prejudice of the
actor-proprietor'. The sale realized 42,000 francs, which
promptly disappeared into the pockets of Frédérick's creditors.[5]

For his first production under the Cogniard management
Frédérick picked *Ruy Blas*, which opened in August 1841;
and it was while Hugo's play was in rehearsal that he met the
great love of his life, a woman who was to be his mistress for
thirteen years, entirely supplanting Sophie Lemaître in his
affections and those of his mother and children.

The Gaîté had just put on a melodrama called *La Grâce de
Dieu*, which was having a remarkable success. Frédérick went
to see it and was captivated by the beauty of the actress playing
the leading part. He could easily have made her acquaintance by
going back-stage to speak to her, but he decided to attract her

attention in a less conventional way. Every evening he took a
seat in the front row of the stalls, and from time to time during
the performance he dropped his stick on the floor. This annoyed
the rest of the audience intensely, but it had the required effect
of arousing the actress's curiosity. One night Frédérick was
seen to arrive at the Gaîté without his stick: it was no longer
needed.

The name of his new mistress was Clarisse Miroy.[6] Born in
1820, she had gone on the stage at the age of fifteen, and had
played at various Paris theatres from the Gymnase-Enfantin to
the Ambigu. But it was *La Grâce de Dieu* which first brought her
to the notice of public and critics. Gautier, in his article on the
play,[7] wrote: 'Mlle Clarisse, who plays the part of Marie, is a
pretty young person, all pink and fair, which is a rare distinction
in this age of dusky complexions and raven locks. She has con-
considerable sensibility and intelligence, and deserves to blossom out in a better theatre than the Gaîté.' Frédérick, for more
personal reasons, shared his opinion.

For the time being, however, Clarisse was bound by contract
to the Gaîté, and it was Marie Dorval whom the Cogniard
brothers engaged a year later at Frédérick's suggestion.[8] The
two great artists had been separated for nine years, but they had
lost none of their affection and admiration for each other. 'To
play with you again', Dorval wrote to her old partner, 'would be
my delight.' Play together they did: first in a revival of the perennial favourite which they had created, *Trente ans*, and then in
La Mère et la Fille, *La Tour de Nesle* and *Ruy Blas*. The Boulevard gave them a rapturous reception.

Both of them hankered after the opportunity to play in the
classics of the old repertory as well as of the new, but they were
constantly thwarted in this ambition by the Comédie-Française.
In October 1842 Dorval performed *Phèdre* at the Odéon, and
though she acted with less than her usual fire she was sufficiently
successful to incite the jealous Rachel to attempt the part a few
months later.[9] Frédérick had to wait rather longer. From 1841
to 1843 he announced at various times that he was going to

appear in *Don Juan*, *Le Misanthrope*, *Les Fourberies de Scapin* and *Tartuffe*, and every announcement drew a veto from the Comédie-Française which the Press understandably attributed to a fear of comparison. Then one day, either because Frédérick had been particularly insistent or because the *sociétaires* dreaded him less in tragedy than in comedy, he was granted permission to play in *Andromaque*. A benefit performance of Racine's tragedy was given in November 1843 at the Gaîté, in aid of Clarisse Miroy.[10] Frédérick played the part of Orestes, Dorval took the title role, and Clarisse herself was Hermione. The critics reported that they had 'some remarkable inspirations'. But it was an isolated success.

In England that same year, Bulwer's Licensing Act deprived the Patent Houses, Covent Garden and Drury Lane, of their monopoly, which meant that any actor could perform the classics in any theatre. In France, the monopoly of the official theatres was fully maintained, while at the same time the supply of Romantic dramas to the Boulevard theatres dried up at the source. Vigny had long since broken with Marie Dorval and stopped writing for the stage. Dumas had turned his attention to the historical novel, an even more lucrative genre than the drama, and any plays he wrote in the future would be just adaptations of his stories. As for Hugo, the catastrophic failure in March 1843 of his epic drama *Les Burgraves*, which he had written for Frédérick and Dorval, but which was poorly acted at the Théâtre-Français by Beauvallet and Mme Mélingue, marked the end of his theatrical career.[11] The result was that Frédérick had to be content with appearing in revivals of the great Romantic dramas and in new works of little or no literary merit. In 1844, for example, the three productions with which he managed to fill the Porte-Saint-Martin thoughout the year were shoddy plays which owed their success almost entirely to his superlative acting.

The first was *Les Mystères de Paris*, which was adapted from Eugène Sue's famous novel by Sue himself and the author of *Trente ans*, and staged on 13 February 1844.[12] It was probably a poor play to begin with, for the task of condensing twenty volumes into five acts was enough to daunt even that skilled practitioner Prosper Goubaux; but it was made even worse by the censor, who cut certain scenes, altered characters and tampered with the dialogue. However, the fame of the original novel, which had been serialized over two years and recently published in book form, was so great that Sue and Goubaux felt sure that there would be a packed house on the first night at least. They were right. In the morning there was a huge queue stretching from the theatre to the Rue de Bondy; at two in the afternoon traffic on the Boulevard was interrupted; at six in the evening people were paying 200 francs for an orchestra stall.

The play itself was almost inevitably a disappointment to the audience, and some scenes were roundly hissed. But Frédérick saved the show and started it on a long run by means of a tremendous performance as Jacques Ferrand which was all the more remarkable in that he was ill when he gave it. Balzac, who saw him earlier in the day, wrote to Mme Hanska[13] on the 14th:

> *Les Mystères* finished this morning at half-past one. Frédérick was afraid of having a stroke. I found him in bed yesterday at noon; he had just been in a mustard-bath up to his knees; the day before he had lost his sight twice. *Les Mystères* is the worst play in the world, but Frédérick's performance is bound to give the novel a new lease of life. His acting was really sublime: one cannot describe such effects, they have to be seen to be believed.

Goubaux's friend Ernest Legouvé has told how, when rehearsing the scene in which Ferrand declares his passionate love for the helpless Fleur-de-Marie, Frédérick paced up and down like a caged animal, and finally asked Sue if he could not have a heap of straw in one corner of the stage, so that the audience would be afraid he was going to throw the heroine on to it. 'He did not get his heap of straw,' writes Legouvé, 'but he was none the less terrifying in his ferocious sensuality.'

Audience and critics were particularly struck by the skill with which Frédérick rang the changes between Ferrand the lusty bandit, Ferrand the doddering solicitor and Ferrand the fanatical miser. As Gautier watched him gloating over his hoard of gold, he was forced to revise the opinion he had expressed after *Zacharie*: that the actor was incapable of representing avarice.[14] 'His strong arms,' wrote the critic, 'arms which have suddenly grown as wiry as those of Milo of Crotona, are plunged into this golden bath with demoniacal delight, with the spasmodic ecstasy of a tiger eating a living prey.'

But the most impressive moment in the whole play was generally agreed to be in the last scene, where Ferrand's eyes are put out by his accomplices. 'You must see Frédérick at the end,' wrote Janin,[15] 'with his hands groping about wildly, his head bent, his voice broken with sobs, furious, defeated, crushed, crying: "Mercy! Pity!" and casting a hideous glance here and there from his bleeding eyes. It is frightful, but also very beautiful. The actor who has attained this artistic pinnacle is truly drama incarnate.' And Gautier declared: 'In the blinding scene he reaches the uttermost limits of terror; he is as beautiful and awe-inspiring as the Œdipus of antiquity. To understand and play a part like this, one needs more than just talent, one must have genius.'

Les Mystères de Paris was followed in July 1844 by *Don César de Bazan*, a drama specially written for Frédérick by Dumanoir and Dennery to allow him to play Hugo's vagabond nobleman without abandoning the part of Ruy Blas to another actor. The role of the gay, generous, swashbuckling adventurer was admirably suited to Frédérick's gifts, but the play had no merits except as a vehicle. Gautier made this point well[16] when he wrote:

> Frédérick is such an accomplished actor that the value of the plays in which he accepts a part is almost immaterial. Provided he has a rag to throw across his shoulder, a cloak to wear over his sword, a chair to move about and a pretext to go from left to right or from right to left, that is all he needs. For the vague figure lightly sketched out by the theatrical purveyor he will substitute a living silhouette worthy of Salvator Rosa or Callot. A smile does duty for the non-existent jest, a flash of the eyes for the missing passion.

And how he kneads and twists the doughy dialogue to turn it into what he wants! Listening to him you really imagine you are hearing stylistic phrases, coherent sentences, something resembling a language; and when he sings, even though he has very little voice and what he has is cracked, he convinces you that the couplets strung together by MM. Dennery and Dumanoir are poetry!

For the past three years Frédérick had been taking Clarisse Miroy with him on his provincial tours and coaching her as he had once coached Atala Beauchêne, in preparation for the day when the Gaîté would release her and he could recommend her to the Cogniard brothers. That day had now come, and Clarisse made her début at the Porte-Saint-Martin in *Don César*, playing the part of the heroine Maritana. She created a favourable impression on the public, though one ungracious critic[17] declared that she was 'not equal to acting opposite Frédérick, and half-sang, half-whimpered her role in an unbearably childish way'.

After *Don César*, which ran for three months, the Cogniards put on *La Dame de Saint-Tropez*, a five-act drama based on the notorious Lafarge murder of 1840 and upholding the innocence of Marie Lafarge, who was now serving the sentence of life imprisonment imposed on her for the crime. It was one of Adolphe Dennery's poorest plays, and even the fascination which the case had for the public would not have saved it without Frédérick's remarkable performance as the murder victim. In the final scene the dying husband looks in a mirror and surprises his best friend pouring poison into his medicine; and here Frédérick's miming and the terrible cry he gave sent a shudder of terror through the audience.[18] The critics claimed that it was this episode above all which made the play a success. Whatever the reason, *La Dame de Saint-Tropez* held the stage for sixty nights.

By now Frédérick was the subject of scores of anecdotes, and every year produced a fresh crop of stories, most of them illustrating his love of the bottle and his wicked sense of humour. It was said, for instance, that one night when he had wined ınd dined too well, he launched into the famous tirade from *Ruy Blas* in the middle of a performance of *Don César de Bazan*.[19] The prompter made frantic efforts to tell him of his mistake and ;ive him his proper cue, but all in vain. Then suddenly Frédé-ʾick noticed the red face bobbing up and down in the box at his ʾeet, and stopped dead in amazement.

'By heaven,' he said indignantly to the audience, 'I do believe :his fellow's drunk!'

On another occasion, at a theatre in the provinces, he had ;carcely taken his first sip of stage 'champagne' than he spat it ɔut and roared for the manager.[20]

'Approach', he said in solemn tones when that worthy ıppeared. 'What is the meaning of this stupid prank, Mon-;ieur? Do you think me capable of acting as your accomplice and ʰelping you to deceive the public?'

'What, me?' squeaked the manager.

'Yes, you, Monsieur!' And turning towards the audience, he explained: 'You doubtless imagine, gentlemen, that I am drink-ing champagne. But this is not champagne—this is soda-water!'

'Monsieur Frédérick,' said the manager, 'I'll go and get you some champagne straight away. I shan't be a minute. It's all a dreadful mistake, I swear it is.'

And away he went, leaving Frédérick to discourse to the de-lighted audience on the horrors of soda-water and the iniquities of theatre managers.

But perhaps the most intriguing story told about Frédérick at this period of his life is one which concerns the English actor Macready and his partner Helen Faucit.[21] Frédérick's bio-grapher Georges Duval recounts it as follows:

> Every night for some time Frédérick noticed a fair-haired young woman, as assiduous as Anna Damby in *Kean*, sitting in the left-hand stage-box at the Porte-Saint-Martin. At first he took her to be an ordinary admirer of his talent, but then he began to wonder if her perseverance might not be due to some more tender feeling. He had the young woman followed by one of his friends, and dis-covered that she lived in the Rue de la Paix. The next day he went to see her.

'Madame or Mademoiselle,' he said, 'I am Frédérick Lemaître. I believe it is out of love that you come to the theatre every day. If I am wrong, tell me at once, so that I may abandon the hope which inspires me. If I am right, do not torment me, but let me respond to the best of my ability to a sentiment of which I shall endeavour to prove myself worthy.'

One can easily imagine the lady's stupefaction. However, being English, she gave no hint of any untoward emotion, but calmly replied: 'I do not know if it is love that I feel, Monsieur. All I can say is that it began by being admiration. I am an actress known as Miss Helen, I have played opposite Macready for the last five years, and I am waiting for him now. To be quite frank with you, he is my lover. I thought that it was impossible for anyone to surpass him, but now I see that I was mistaken.'

As she said this a blush rose to her cheeks which did not escape Frédérick's notice. Miss Helen was twenty at this time, and without exactly being beautiful she possessed great charm, that somewhat mannered English charm of Keepsakes and Books of Beauty. You know what I mean: a vague smile, moist eyes, lank hair, sloping shoulders, and a costume composed of a happy medley of gauze, ribbons and feathers.

Frédérick soon fell a victim to this charm of hers, and legend has it that he and Miss Helen concluded a love-pact which stipulated that everything should be forgotten from the day Macready set foot in France. That day was not long in coming, and a month later the Salle Ventadour billed *Othello* with the English actor in the title role and Miss Helen as Desdemona.

Frédérick had given his word, and in order to avoid being tempted to break it, he left for London to conquer there the laurels which Macready, his rival in two respects, had come to win from him in France.

He was about to set out on the return journey when he learnt that Macready was back. Immediately he signed a new engagement with his manager and had Ducis's *Othello* billed for the next day.

Macready was in one of the stage-boxes with Miss Helen, like the Prince of Wales with the Countess of Kaefeld. Frédérick, however, was able to control his passions better than Kean, and was applauded to the echo before Macready and his sometime mistress.

What happened then? No one knows. But the next day Miss Helen threw herself into the Thames.

Like all good stories, this one contains a modicum of truth. Macready and Helen Faucit *did* open a season at the Ventadour in December 1844,[22] and Frédérick *did* play in London soon afterwards. But it is extremely doubtful whether Helen Faucit was ever Macready's mistress, let alone Frédérick's; the French actor knew better by now than to offer Ducis's *Othello* to the English public; and if 'Miss Helen' threw herself into the wintry Thames for love of Frédérick, she obviously suffered no ill-effects from the experience, since she lived to the age of seventy-eight and died the highly respected wife of Sir Theodore Martin, Lord Rector of St Andrew's.

On the other hand, both Macready and Helen Faucit were probably drawn to see Frédérick act in London, for the four-week season which he did at the St. James's in February and March 1845 was a triumph from beginning to end.[23] It was very nearly cancelled: the actor's carriage overturned in a ditch on the way to Boulogne, and Frédérick was badly hurt. But as a cold-blooded journalist put it,[24] 'medical aid came to his relief, and now he will be quite in character for the performance of *Don César de Bazan*, his scarred visage giving him just the appearance of having recently arrived from a fray with alguazils, or a duel with some vainglorious Don of the Escurial'.

In fact, he opened on 17 February with the 'French toxicological drama' *La Dame de Saint-Tropez*, which was playing simultaneously at no less than three other London theatres, in English versions variously entitled *The Deed of Horror*, *The Bride of Woe* and *The Poisoners and the Victim*. It obtained 'a complete and decided success', though the English critics,[25] like their French colleagues, attributed this success solely to 'the extraordinary acting of M. Lemaître, who in the fourth and fifth acts gave one of the most frightfully vivid pictures of gradual death resulting from poison that was ever witnessed — so terrible, yet so faithful in every detail, and so completely enthralling the attention of the audience, that the revolting nature of the drama was entirely lost sight of'.

After this 'arsenicated piece' he appeared in *Don César de Bazan*, a play which the English public found both edifying and amusing. The critic of the *Illustrated London News*[26] stated

N

approvingly that Frédérick 'never lost sight of the gentleman: even in his most dissipated phases the high spirit of honour continually broke through'. He would have been pleased to know that Queen Victoria, who went to see *Don César* on the 24th, was of precisely the same opinion.[27] In her diary she wrote:

> At eight we went to the French Play, where we were delighted with Frédérick Lemaître's beautiful acting in *Don César de Bazan*, a most interesting play in five acts. Lemaître is no longer young, I should say past fifty; he depicted quite admirably the *aventurier* character of Don César—full of noble and generous feelings. The others all acted their parts very well, and the costumes were very fine and correct. We got home at half-past eleven, having greatly enjoyed our evening.

The next week the Queen paid another visit to the St. James's,[28] and afterwards recorded in her diary: 'We saw a very interesting, but dreadful piece called *Trente ans ou la Vie d'un joueur*. It is divided into three Tableaux, between each of which at least fifteen years elapse. The piece is very moral, but terrible. Lemaître acted admirably, and so did Mlle Clarisse.' Perhaps the piece was too terrible, for according to the Press 'exclamations of horror burst from every part of the house, and the play has not since been repeated, albeit the applause at the fall of the curtain was loud and continuous'.

Frédérick wanted to put on *Ruy Blas* next, but the play was banned as likely to shock the Queen.[29] He therefore fell back for his last production on *L'Auberge des Adrets*, which proved to have lost none of its appeal for the English public. 'His representation of the renowned Robert Macaire', stated one periodical,[30] 'was perfect, and kept the audience in a roar of laughter whenever he was on the stage.' And Queen Victoria described the play in her diary[31] as 'a most amusing piece in which Lemaître was quite admirable, acting beautifully and inimitably, as a swindler, thief and even murderer'.

His London season had in fact been a complete success, and the English Press gave him unstinted praise. 'No actor', wrote one critic,[32] 'possesses a talent so varied, original and perceptive; there is no other so full of sentiment, power, and terrible energy.' Yet he was a prophet without honour in his own country, for the Comédie-Française still refused to admit him to the Rue de Richelieu. This dog-in-the-manger attitude gave rise to an increasing number of protests from the Press and the public, and the present author possesses a typical letter from one of Frédérick's admirers[33] asking: 'Will good M. Buloz always be blind, and will he never understand that the greatest actor of the times is indispensable to the first stage of France? Poor Théâtre-Français!'

At long last, in October 1845, threatened with Rachel's departure and Firmin's retirement, the *sociétaires* swallowed their repugnance and made a tentative offer to the actor whom the critics had been recommending to them for years past. The news of this offer aroused widespread approval, and Alexandre Dumas was so delighted that he promised Frédérick to write the play in which he should make his début at the Théâtre-Français.[34] But Frédérick soon discovered that the established actors of the Comédie-Française had no intention of relinquishing any of the leading roles in the repertory to their prospective colleague. Geffroy clung doggedly to Tartuffe, Provost to Harpagon, Samson and Régnier to Scapin and Figaro. In these circumstances, with no hope of playing the parts in which he was most likely to shine, and every prospect of becoming involved in humiliating quarrels, Frédérick hesitated; and before he could come to a decision the *sociétaires* withdrew their offer.

Soon after this fiasco the sculptor Bonnassieux did a bust of Frédérick which is now in the present author's possession. It is a revealing study. The head is as erect as ever, the hair as luxuriant, the jaw as firm and rock-like. But the corners of the mouth are turned down, and the lips are set in a thin, bitter line.

CHAPTER FIFTEEN

ROMANTIC DECLINE

AFTER his triumphant season in London, and a no less successful stay in Brussels,[1] Frédérick spent the summer and autumn of 1845 touring the French provinces.

Playgoers in the towns where he was billed to appear looked forward to his visit with delight, but theatre managers waited for him in fear and trembling. Weeks before he was expected, he would send on detailed lists of his requirements, explaining to one manager[2] that 'I don't like making a mess of things, partly because I'm a man of method and partly because of the love I have for my art'. And he had scarcely got out of his carriage before he was organizing rehearsals, browbeating the stage-hands, altering the props, criticizing the scenery and changing the lighting. Sometimes he met opposition from the theatre personnel, but he always overcame it. For instance, two or three days after his arrival in Lyons he asked the orchestra at the Théâtre des Célestins to run through the incidental tunes for one of his plays.[3]

'But we never rehearse things like that', said the conductor. 'Why, yesterday we played the whole of the *Barber of Seville* without rehearsing it beforehand.'

'So I noticed', said Frédérick drily.

The conductor took the hint.

Back in Paris in November, the first thing the actor saw was a playbill advertising a new piece by Dennery, *Marie-Jeanne, ou la Femme du peuple*, which was due to open at the Porte-Saint-Martin on the 11th, with Dorval in the title role. Like the plays

in which Frédérick had recently been appearing, it was a commonplace melodrama, the tearful story of a working-class
mother who loses her child and eventually finds it again; but
Dorval, like Frédérick, had the gift of turning dross into gold.
'For this play', wrote George Sand,[4] 'she found cries which
seared the soul, accents of grief and passion which will never
again be heard in the theatre, because they could come only
from that one heart and that one body, because they would be
monstrous and grotesque coming from anyone else, and because
her temperament alone could make them terrifying and sublime.'
And Jules Janin declared[5] that 'never before had her genius been
so poignant or so human'.

During one of the intervals Frédérick went back-stage to
Dorval's dressing-room, where Gautier and Dumas were congratulating her on her performance.[6] 'The two great artists',
writes Gautier, 'could find no words to express their emotion;
they embraced and started weeping.'

'No other woman', Dumas told Marie Dorval, 'has ever
been acclaimed by the public as you have tonight.'

'That', she replied huskily, 'is because the others give them
only their talent, and I give them my life.'

The men said nothing: they were too deeply moved. For it
was painfully clear to them that Dorval, worn out by the passions and sorrows of a tumultuous existence on and off the stage,
had little life left to give. In April 1846, in fact, she fell ill and
had to abandon the part of Marie-Jeanne, which was taken over
by Clarisse Miroy in July. An English critic[7] observed that 'to
say she played the character as well as her predecessor would be
incorrect, nothing finer than Mme Dorval's performance of the
bereaved mother having been seen for many a day, but her
Marie-Jeanne was not the less a clever piece of acting'. On the
other hand, a French periodical[8] stated that 'her youthful talent
has eclipsed the memory of Mme Dorval, and that in one of the
latter's finest roles'. Poor Dorval's heart must have bled if she
came across this notice.

Frédérick appeared in two new plays in 1846. One was an

austere verse-drama entitled *Michel Brémond*, by the Academician Viennet, which attracted a distinguished and appreciative
audience on the first night but failed to please the Boulevard
public.[9] The other was an Anicet-Bourgeois melodrama, *Le
Docteur noir*, in which Frédérick did wonders with the part of a
brave mulatto who dies to save the woman he loves.[10] Balzac
described the play as 'the height of stupidity, mediocrity in its
saturnalia', but it had a great success.

In January 1847 Frédérick took Clarisse to London for
another six-week season at the St. James's. He presented *La
Dame de Saint-Tropez* again, at the express command of Queen
Victoria,[11] and his performance was judged to be 'so terribly
real that one would not readily see it repeated; only, however,
from the desire not to have the truthfulness of its representation
weakened by a second delineation'. The Queen also went to see
Le Docteur noir, which she described in her diary[12] as 'a very
interesting but sad piece in seven acts, in which Lemaître and
Mlle Clarisse acted beautifully'. The other new play which
Frédérick put on — *Les Mystères de Paris* — had less success. The
Queen was probably voicing the general opinion when she called
it[13] 'a rather disagreeable piece and badly adapted'; she added
that 'Lemaître acted well, but the character of Jacques Ferrand,
which he represented, was quite horrid — too revolting'. It was
left to that perennial favourite, *L'Auberge des Adrets*, to re-
awaken the public's enthusiasm. 'As the termination of M.
Lemaître's engagement draws nigh,' said the *Illustrated London
News*,[14] 'we would recommend our playloving readers not to
lose the chance of seeing the most extraordinary actor in the
world. Even if they cannot follow his language very readily, they
can shake their sides at his grand extravagant waltz, and in fact
at all his pantomime and drollery of action.' Once again Frédérick left England in a blaze of glory.

On his return to Paris he began rehearsing a play by the
socialist author Félix Pyat, *Le Chiffonnier de Paris*, about a
drunken but virtuous rag-picker called Jean who outwits the
rich murderer Garousse, *alias* Baron Hoffmann, and saves the

daughter of Garousse's first victim from arrest and execution for his latest crime. Frédérick studied the part of Jean with all his usual care. He even sought out the philosopher-rag-picker Liard, a legendary figure of the Paris streets who was renowned for his absolute honesty and his wide classical learning, and consulted him on the correct way of using the tools of his trade — the lantern, the rag-bag and the hook.[15] By May the *Chiffonnier* was ready to be put on, and the opening performance was fixed for the 11th.

There was a packed house at the Porte-Saint-Martin on the first night. Some of the audience had been attracted by rumours that Pyat's drama was a revolutionary work; most of them had come simply to see Frédérick in his new part. For an idea of the drawing-power which he exerted at this period of his career one cannot do better than read Gautier's notice of *Le Chiffonnier de Paris*,[16] in which the critic writes:

> The creation of a new role by Frédérick Lemaître is an event which stirs even those who are the least susceptible to dramatic emotions. That evening, society folk and artists, critics and poets, genuine and imitation duchesses, the regular first-night public in fact, fill the theatre long before the orchestra have taken their places. What is more—and this is a miracle no one else can achieve! —the ladies are dressed in time. Even if their rebellious bandeaux reveal a few stray curls from hastily loosened plaits, even if their hats are slightly askew, their necklaces awry, their posies loosely fastened to their corsages and their shawls badly draped, off they go to the theatre, impatiently pushing fingers loaded with rings into gloves which are too tight for them. 'What if we were to miss Frédérick's entrance!'—that is what worries them all, and no one would get over it if it happened. The coquettes are even driven to the point of forgetting their beauty care; in any event they know that once the great actor is on the stage every eye will be fixed upon him, and that the intervals will be devoted to calling for him, applauding him and cheering him.
>
> If Frédérick arouses such lively curiosity in the fashionable and artistic worlds, he exerts just as great an influence on the rough, uncultured section of the public. As early as three in the afternoon the angels in caps and overalls who adorn the 'gods' with a ring of far from seraphic faces are fighting and jostling at the door of the

theatre; for Frédérick has the remarkable power of speaking to the highest intelligence as well as to the crudest instinct. Victor Hugo and the grocer's boy, Jules Janin and the duty fireman, George Sand and the attendant who peers through one of the windows in the boxes, are all equally impressed and applaud him with equal enthusiasm; Rachel, her face a pallid mask, leans out of her stage-box, panting with emotion; the actors at the other theatres hurry over after rushing through their parts, scarcely pausing to wipe off their make-up, or else regretfully tear themselves away when the time comes for them to go on-stage themselves; even if it is only for a single act, a single situation, a single line, everyone wants to enjoy the emotion and education of a first performance by Frédérick Lemaître.

The first performance of the *Chiffonnier* was one of Frédérick's greatest triumphs. He was called back at the end of every act and given a tremendous ovation at the final curtain. 'It was a frenzy, a furore', reported Gautier. 'The astonished claque sat back and let the rest of the audience do their work for them, marvelling at the force of the clapping, the loudness of the cheering, the unity of the whole house, which had not even rehearsed its acclamations the night before.' But the enthusiasm of the first-night audience was not aroused solely by Frédérick's playing, superlative though that was: it owed a great deal to the appeal of Félix Pyat's brand of sentimental socialism.[17] His story of virtuous poverty defeating vicious wealth matched the spirit of 1847 to perfection. Rag-picker Jean became the hero of Paris.

Night after night, month after month, Pyat's drama drew huge audiences to the Porte-Saint-Martin. During the summer, fans were put on sale bearing a portrait of the author and four scenes from his play. A parody, *Le Chiffon-nié de par ici*, was staged at the Théâtre Beaumarchais. The Cogniard brothers presented Frédérick with a valuable clock as a token of their gratitude. And the *Chiffonnier* was still running in 1848 when the February Revolution broke out.

It was not unexpected. For years France had become increasingly bored with the Government's foreign policy and increasingly discontented with its conduct of home affairs. In 1846 and 1847 the failure of the corn harvests had led to a shortage of food among the lower classes, a serious industrial depression and widespread unemployment. At the same time the country had been shocked by two great scandals: the revelation of the corrupt practices of a former Minister called Teste, a real-life Robert Macaire, and the murder of the Duchesse de Choiseul-Praslin by her husband, a real-life Garousse. But Louis-Philippe and his Minister Guizot, like Charles X and Polignac before them, regarded the situation with astonishing complacency. No social legislation was introduced to alleviate the distress caused by the economic crisis; no attempt was made to widen the franchise, which was confined to the very wealthy. 'Get rich', said Guizot, and left it at that.

Yet even so the Revolution might never have occurred but for an accident. Thiers and other Opposition leaders had organized a succession of banquets to campaign for parliamentary reform, and the last and biggest of these, which was due to be held in Paris on 22 February, was banned by the Government. However, crowds gathered at the meeting-place in spite of the ban, the National Guard mutinied, and the King, losing his nerve, dismissed Guizot and called on Thiers to form a new government. At this point it seemed that everything was over and that the Opposition had won the bloodless constitutional victory it wanted; but in the evening of the 23rd an ugly incident developed outside the Ministry of Foreign Affairs and the troops fired on the mob. From then on there was no holding the Parisians. Barricades were set up, armed crowds bore down on the Tuileries, and Louis-Philippe fled ignominiously in a cab. His last official act had been to abdicate in favour of his ten-year-old grandson, the Comte de Paris, but this time the Republicans were in no mood to give way to the Orléans family. On 24 February the Second French Republic was proclaimed at the Hôtel de Ville.

A new era seemed to have opened, and Paris abandoned itself to an orgy of delirious celebration. Trees of liberty were planted, popular banquets arranged, idealistic speeches made, high-sounding toasts proposed and drunk. Nowhere was there greater enthusiasm than at the Porte-Saint-Martin, the first theatre to open its doors again after the Revolution. There, in the afternoon of 26 February, a free performance of the *Chiffonnier* was given to the people of Paris.[18] After Moëssard had led the house in the singing of the *Marseillaise* and the re- volutionary *Chant du départ*, Frédérick acted out Pyat's stirring drama. When he opened his rag-bag at the end and pulled out first the crown and then a police notice stating: 'The Banquets are banned', the audience went wild with delight. Recalling the scene in later years, Frédérick described it as 'a truly sublime spectacle', and Félix Pyat, banished from France for his political activities, declared that 'a life of exile is a small price to pay for a day like that'.

The censorship having been abolished with the monarchy, the Cogniard brothers decided to follow the *Chiffonnier* with a revival of the two Macaire dramas. For several months Frédé- rick presented *L'Auberge des Adrets* and *Robert Macaire* on alternate nights, improvising new jokes or allusions to suit every turn of events and every audience.[19] Once, when the public failed to call for him at the end of a performance of *Robert Macaire*, he had the curtain raised and strode up to the foot- lights.

'Gentlemen,' he said, 'is Monsieur Auguste in the house?'
No reply.
'Or Monsieur Antoine?'
Still no reply.
'Well, gentlemen,' he continued, 'I'm the victim of some sharp practice on the part of the leader of the claque and his deputy. I gave them forty francs this morning to call for me, and neither of them is here. As you can see for yourselves, gentlemen, I've been swindled!'

He was not always as light-hearted as this, however. On 16 April the workers of Paris staged a vast demonstration in favour of postponing the elections to a Constituent Assembly, for the Socialists had suddenly realized that giving the vote to a largely

rural population would probably produce a predominantly conservative Chamber. Frédérick, who was entirely in sympathy
with the demonstrators, was so deeply moved that he only
agreed to play that night under protest, and interrupted his performance to declare that 'it was shameful to act the fool at a time
when Paris was in arms'. The audience, who had paid their
money to be amused and not harangued, hissed him off the
stage.

His fears proved to be well founded. The elections, held on
23 April, were a victory for the moderate Republicans and a disaster for the Socialists. In June the new Government, sure of its
strength, decided to put an end to the Socialist experiment of
the National Workshops for the unemployed, and offered the
young workers a choice between conscription and starvation.
The workers promptly rose in arms, and the barricades went up
again in the eastern districts of Paris. General Cavaignac was
ordered to suppress the insurrection at all costs, troops were
rushed into the capital by train, and for three days the Army and
the bourgeois National Guard fought the workers in the
bloodiest civil warfare France had ever known. Hundreds of
rioters were killed, over fifteen thousand imprisoned and four
thousand deported. And a breach was created between the bourgeoisie and the working class which has never been healed.

This was scarcely a time for jesting, yet the June Days
were scarcely over before the Porte-Saint-Martin put on a
Romantic verse-comedy by Auguste Vacquerie entitled *Tragaldabas*.[20] Vacquerie was an ardent disciple of Hugo's, and Balzac
was not being unjust when he described his play[21] as 'an exe-
crable work of the funny-Hugo type'. It was a catastrophic
failure. Even with Frédérick giving of his best as the drunken
vagabond of a hero, the public was not prepared to accept this
pretentious example of late-Romantic humour, especially in the
wake of civil war. But the first night had its comic moments,
some of them unintentional. Balzac, who was there with Hugo,
George Sand, Dumas and Gautier, wrote afterwards to Mme
Hanska:

I have never in my life seen anything funnier than the way Frédérick Lemaître came forward at the end of this ultra-stormy performance and announced: 'Ladies and gentleman (much bowing and scraping), the play we have just had the honour to perform for you is by Citizen Auguste Vacquerie'—unless it was Hugo forgetting the Battle of *Hernani* and reproving the author's friends for shouting at the hissers and calling them silly asses. . . .

Vacquerie himself had not really expected his play to be a success. All he wanted, he told Frédérick beforehand, was a lively performance. His wish was certainly granted. In his memoirs[22] he writes:

> The curtain would have been rung down a score of times if it had not been for my young defenders. They in the audience and Frédérick on the stage put up a heroic resistance. I was in the wings, listening and watching, proud to have revived something of the great battles of old, full of admiration for Frédérick. In the first acts he was amazing; towards the end he was sublime. Never before, not even in *Robert Macaire*, had he shown such astonishing verve, such glorious buffoonery. He was the lightning in this storm. The failure, thank heavens, was only the author's. How I was hissed by Monsieur What's-his-name and Monsieur So-and-so! But how Frédérick was applauded by Hugo and Balzac!
>
> In the last act the noise never stopped. To make an end of it, put out by the hissing and exhausted by his strenuous performance, Frédérick went up to the footlights in his ass's skin and indicated that he had something to say. Silence descended on the theatre. He then made three bows whose gravity was somewhat attenuated by the ass's head which nodded every time with his own, and pronounced these memorable words: 'Citizens and gentlemen, now more than ever is the time to cry: *Vive la République!*'
>
> At this the tumult stopped short! The Porte-Saint-Martin was no longer a theatre, but a club. We were really and truly in a Republic!

Few Parisians would have agreed with this last opinion, least of all Frédérick, who was in despair at the way events were shaping. The jails and forts were still full of political prisoners, mass deportations were continuing, the right of public meeting was severely limited, clubs were placed under supervision and the old restrictions on the Press were reintroduced. 'This', said *Le Peuple constituant* in its last issue, 'is not the Republic, but the saturnalia of reaction around its bloodstained tomb.' And when, in December, five million electors voted for the only name that was known to them all and made Prince Louis-Napoleon Bonaparte their President, it became abundantly clear that France was a Republic in name only.

Meanwhile, in the smaller world of the theatre, all Frédérick's attempts to put his Republican ideas into practice had likewise ended in failure.[23] He had thrown himself enthusiastically into the activities of a Republican club for actors, which was opened in the Passage Jouffroy; but the club was closed down by the authorities. He had given his support to a project for a Dramatic Congress which was to watch over the common interests of authors, actors and managers; but quarrels arose between the three groups and the scheme had to be abandoned. He had been the moving spirit in the formation of a co-operative society to run the Porte-Saint-Martin, with Théodore Cogniard acting as financial adviser; but the society went bankrupt. At last, in April 1849, dispirited and disillusioned, he set off on a tour of the provinces. He was at Lyons when news reached him from Paris which put the finishing touch to his unhappiness. Marie Dorval was dead.

She was not the first of the great theatrical figures of the Boulevard to disappear. Three years before, on 17 June 1846, Jean-Gaspard Deburau, the beloved Pierrot of the Funambules, had died at the age of forty-nine.[24] He had been suffering from asthma for some time, and during his last performance he became so exhausted that he asked the conductor of the Funambules orchestra to omit several of his dances, particularly a wild *chahut* which was very popular with the public. The audience objected loudly, but they relented when they saw tears staining his flour-covered cheeks, and cried: 'No, no! No *chahut!*' According to Champfleury, he left the theatre at midnight still holding the bouquet of flowers he had carried throughout *Les Noces de Pierrot*—'a bouquet for his wedding with Death'.

At Deburau's funeral, all the theatre people of the Boulevard followed Pierrot on his last journey from his home in the Faubourg du Temple to the church of Sainte-Élisabeth and thence to Père-Lachaise. The coffin was carried, not by the usual under-taker's assistants but by the stage-hands of the Funambules, who wanted to pay their dead comrade this last tribute. The streets were lined and the windows filled with people who mur-mured: 'Deburau!' as he passed. It was a solemn, moving occa-sion, marred only by one hideous incident. The manager of the Funambules, Bertrand's nephew Billion, who had refused to close the theatre on the night Deburau died and had forced Paul Legrand to play Pierrot despite his protests, gave the grave-diggers a two-franc tip and then asked the mime's widow to re-fund the money.

Harel would have approved—but by this time Harel was insane, and he died a month after Deburau.[25] In his last years he had taken to literature, producing a eulogy of Voltaire which pleased the Académie Française and convinced his enemies that his brain was softening. As long as his reason held out he accompanied Mlle George on her provincial tours, relying on his old publicity methods to draw the public. 'Mlle George will be wearing jewels worth 60,000 francs', announced the play-bills; 'and Mlle George wears nothing artificial!' But even if George's jewels were genuine, they were certainly not worth 60,000 francs; and without Harel to manage her affairs she was lost. The State, it is true, accorded her a pension of 2,000 francs a year, but the pension was never paid.

'A crust of bread', she called it[26] when she saw Hugo in the autumn of 1847; 'and then I don't get my teeth into it! They wanted to have me at the Théâtre Historique, but I said no. What should I do among all those silhouettes—a fat woman like me? And then, where are the authors? Where are the plays? Where are the parts? As for the provinces, I tried them last year, but it's just impossible without Harel. I simply don't know what to do with the actors. How can I be expected to deal with those crooks?'

Two years later, after trying in vain to have an audience of the Prince-President, she went to see Rachel, to ask the young actress to play *Rodogune* with her for her benefit. Rachel, triumphant and vindictive, refused to see her and asked her to write.

'Well, I shan't!' George told Hugo.[27] 'I haven't sunk as low as that! I'm a queen of the theatre like her, I've been a beautiful whore like her, and one day she'll be a poor old woman like me. She forgets that she was a beggar-girl once, and she can't imagine ever being a beggar again. But in another thirty years she won't have a sou to her name, and she'll go slopping through the mud in down-at-heel shoes. Oh, no, I shan't write to her. I haven't anything to eat. I owe my concierge ten francs. I've been obliged to sell some diamond buttons the Emperor gave me. I play at the Théâtre Saint-Marcel, I play at Les Batignolles, I play in the suburbs, and I haven't enough money to pay for a cab. But I shan't write to Rachel—I shall just throw myself in the river!'

Events were to prove her wrong. Rachel died in luxury less than ten years later, while George herself dragged out her life in poverty and misery for another eighteen years. Towards the end she became a grotesque caricature of the majestic figure she had been in the hey-day of Romantic drama. Jules Claretie recalls in his memoirs being taken as a boy to see her perform in the theatre at Limoges.[28] The play was *Marie Tudor*. At one point George went down on her knees and then found that she could not get up again. All his life Claretie carried in his mind the pitiful memory of the old actress stranded on the stage, her eyes rolling wildly and tears running down her cheeks, while the audience rocked with laughter.

Dorval's decline was swifter and even more pathetic than George's. After the triumph of *Marie-Jeanne* she descended to smaller parts and smaller theatres. In 1847 George, now her sister in misfortune, said of her: 'Poor Dorval, she really does deserve to be pitied. She's playing all over the place to earn her living—at Toulouse and Carpentras, in derelict barns! Like me she's reduced to displaying her bald head and dragging her old bones about on ramshackle boards lit by a few tallow candles, with buskers who've either been in jail or ought to be sent there.'²⁹

Her only consolation was her little grandson Georges, and when he died in May 1848 her mind was affected. She spent whole days in the Montparnasse Cemetery, sitting on a folding-stool beside his grave, talking to the dead child until the hour the gates were closed. When she went on tour again she visited the cemetery in every town she played, and put flowers on the children's tombs.³⁰

A short while before she died she appealed to the Comédie-Française to make her a *pensionnaire*.³¹ For the meagre stipend of 6,000 francs a year the woman who had been Kitty Bell and Adèle d'Hervey promised to play anything the Comédie wished, even walking-on parts; she added that she did not expect to be a burden on the exchequer for very long. The *sociétaires* rejected her appeal. Seveste, who brought her their answer, said that the lighting system at the Théâtre-Français was going to be altered, and offered Dorval the small sum of money he hoped to save every month on oil. It was meant kindly, but she could not bring herself to accept.

In the spring of 1849 she travelled to Caen to fulfil an engagement there with her son-in-law, the actor René Luguet.³² But as soon as she arrived she had to take to her bed with an ulcerated liver. After nursing her devotedly for several weeks, Luguet brought her back to Paris, where she died in her little Rue de Varenne flat·on 20 May. Samson, the *doyen* of the Comédie-Française, attended the funeral, but left without paying the customary graveside tribute to the dead actress. Rachel did not trouble to come.

Of all the men who had known and loved Marie Dorval, two were particularly grief-stricken. One was Alexandre Dumas, who with typical generosity pledged his decorations to cover the funeral expenses, wrote a pamphlet to pay for a permanent grave and a memorial, and opened a subscription so that the actress's jewels could be bought back from the pawnbroker and given to her surviving grandchildren. The other was Frédérick

FRÉDÉRICK IN 1846
Bust by Bonnassieu

FRENCH PLAYS,
ST. JAMES'S THEATRE, KING STREET, ST. JAMES'S.
Lessee, Mr. JOHN MITCHELL, 33, Old Bond Street.

SEVENTH APPEARANCE OF THE EMINENT ACTOR,
MONSᴿ
FREDERICK LEMAITRE,
AND
Madᶫᶫᵉ CLARISSE,
WHO WILL APPEAR FOR THE SECOND TIME, THIS EVENING,
IN VICTOR HUGO'S PLAY OF
RUY BLAS.

This Evening, Monday, March 22, 1852,
THE ENTERTAINMENTS WILL COMMENCE
AT HALF-PAST SEVEN O'CLOCK,
WITH,
(FOR THE SECOND TIME IN THIS COUNTRY),
VICTOR HUGO'S CELEBRATED DRAME OF
RUY BLAS
EN CINQ ACTES, ET EN VERS.

DISTRIBUTION:

Ruy Blas	M. F. LEMAITRE.
DON SALLUSTE DE BAZAN	M. DELORIS.
DON CESAR DE BAZAN	M. ARMAND VILLOT.
DON GURITAN	M. ST. MARIN.
LE COMTE DE CAMPOREAL	M. LEON.
LE MARQUIS DE SANTA-CRUZ	M. TOURILLON.
LE MARQUIS DEL BASTO	M. FAUVRE.
COVADENGA	M. LANGEVAL.
LE COMTE D'ALBE	M. ARMAND (FILS).
LE MARQUIS DE PRIEGO	M. LUCIEN.
GUDIEL - M. VICTOR.	UN LAQUAIS - M. THIRON.
UN HUISSIER - M. THEOPHILE.	UN ALCADE - M. CLARENCE.
DONA MARIA DE NEUBOURG (reine d'espagne)	Madᶫᶫᵉ CLARISSE.
LA DUCHESSE D'ALBUQUERQUE	Madᵉ THIBAULT.
CASILDA	Madᶫᶫᵉ ST. GEORGES.
UNE DUEGNE	Madᵉ MANCINI.
UN PAGE	Madᶫᶫᵉ CAUVIN.

WEDNESDAY NEXT, MARCH 24,
THE POPULAR AND FAVORITE PLAY OF
L'AUBERGE DES ADRETS.

Doors will be opened at Seven o'Clock, and the Performance commence at Half-past Seven.

Prices of Admission:
BOXES, 6ˢ. PIT, 3ˢ. AMPHITHEATRE, 2ˢ.

PRIVATE BOXES, STALLS, AND TICKETS MAY BE OBTAINED AT
Mr. MITCHELL'S ROYAL LIBRARY, 33, Old Bond Street;
AND AT
The Box Office of the Theatre, which is open Daily, from 11 till 5 o'clock.

Printed by W. J. GOLBOURN, 6, Princes Street, Leicester Square.

Royal Library: Windsor Castle
QUEEN VICTORIA'S PROGRAMME
FOR *Ruy Blas*

Lemaître. When he heard the news of Dorval's death he was silent for a moment, remembering the happiness they had known together and the triumphs they had enjoyed.[33] Then he spoke.

'Now she has gone,' he said, 'I feel like a widower.'

CHAPTER SIXTEEN

DEATH OF THE BOULEVARD

THE eighteen-fifties saw Frédérick's career go into a decline. It was not that he lost any of his skill or was surpassed by another player: he remained undisputably the first actor of France. But the times had changed, and the theatre with them. The heroism and idealism, the panache and gusto of the Romantic era had been finally extinguished in the bloody repression of the June Days; mediocrity and frivolity took their place. High drama and uproarious comedy were supplanted by thesis-play and operetta, the giants of Romanticism by dwarfs such as Dumas *fils* and Augier, Meilhac and Halévy. And Frédérick, still excluded from the Comédie-Française, inevitably found that suitable roles were harder to find, and audiences smaller.

One last great part in the Romantic tradition came his way at the end of 1849, when Lamartine offered him the title role in his *Toussaint Louverture*, a dramatic poem—it could scarcely be called a play—about the negro slave who became commander-in-chief in Haiti during the French Revolution.[1] Lamartine had originally written this work in 1834 as a piece of propaganda in favour of the emancipation of the slaves in French colonies. As propaganda it was now superfluous, since the poet-politician had had the satisfaction of proclaiming the abolition of slavery before his recent fall from power; but he was so deep in debt that he accepted an offer for it from the publisher Lévy, and a proposal by the new manager of the Porte-Saint-Martin, Charles Fournier, to put it on at his theatre. It was still far from stage-worthy, however—Lamartine once admitted that he was 'clearly not born for the poetry of character and situation they call drama'—so Frédérick was called in to help rewrite it. In December 1849 he travelled to Lamartine's home, the Château de Monceaux, accompanied by his son Charles and Michel Lévy.

He soon found that collaborating with Lamartine was a very different matter from working with Balzac. Charles Alexandre, one of Lamartine's friends who was staying at Monceaux at the time, has told how 'the poet would retire to a room adjoining the main gallery to embroider the canvas prepared by the actor. There he would meditate, and a few minutes later he would return holding several large sheets of paper covered with his lyrical writing, on which magnificent verses had been thrown like gold coins from a gambler's hand.' As soon as this semi-mystical process of revision had been completed, Frédérick went back to Paris with the precious manuscript, and rehearsals began at the Porte-Saint-Martin.

Toussaint Louverture was presented there on 6 April 1850, and given an enthusiastic reception. All the critics agreed, however, that it was lyrical rather than dramatic in form, and that no one but Frédérick could have succeeded in putting it across the footlights. 'Never', wrote Auguste Vacquerie, 'has the supreme actor given better proof of his genius than in this impossible part, for with speeches and monologues to declaim which would have seemed interminable in anyone else's mouth he endowed Lamartine's uniform poetry with astonishing variety.' And the author himself, in his preface to *Toussaint Louverture*, paid this generous tribute to his interpreter:

A great actor concealed beneath the splendour of his genius the imperfections of this work. Frédérick Lemaître was the Talma of the blacks, a Talma of the tropics, as great an artist (though of a fiercer, more passionate, more explosive character) as the Talma of Tacitus, whom we have seen in our own home posing, walking, thinking and talking like the living statue of classical history. The public might well say of Frédérick Lemaître what the French said of Toussaint: 'This man is a nation.'

Shortly before leaving for Monceaux in December 1849,

Frédérick had received a visit from Arsène Houssaye, who had just been given charge of the Comédie-Française and came to offer him a place in the Rue de Richelieu company.[2] 'Frédérick embraced me', he wrote later, 'at the thought of playing *Tartuffe* at the Théâtre-Français, but to his great regret he was not free. He could not cancel his Boulevard contract at a moment's notice, so he put me off for three months.' But Houssaye was reckoning without the *sociétaires*, who naturally imposed their veto as soon as they learnt of his proposal. The result was that when the Porte-Saint-Martin went bankrupt again in June, it was not to the Théâtre-Français that Frédérick went but to the Gaîté.

There, after reviving several of the old works in his repertory, he created a new role in November 1850, playing the broken-hearted clown in *Paillasse*, a sentimental drama by Dennery and Fournier.[3] The critics brought out all their superlatives for the occasion. 'With a single leap', wrote Janin in the *Débats*, 'Frédérick has returned to the peak of his art. What a man!' In the *Siècle*, Matharel de Fiennes declared that 'the play is Frédérick—Frédérick in the most brilliant, most sublime representation of paternal love ever seen on the stage'. And in the *Constitutionnel*, describing the most moving moment in the play, when Paillasse comes out of his wife's room after discovering that she has left him, Auguste Lireux wrote:

> It is quite impossible to say to what sublime heights Frédérick Lemaître rose in this scene. The art of acting can go no further. This is nature itself in its most terrifying reality. No straining, no cries, no gestures. But the stupefaction of the face, the drooping of the arms, the sudden flow of tears, the broken attitude of the body, the sound of the voice, the mask of suffering and despair—no one but this actor, the greatest of his time, could achieve such an effect.

Paillasse had exactly a hundred performances, after which Frédérick left Paris to fulfil a series of engagements in Brussels and the provinces.[4] On his return he quarrelled with the management of the Gaîté and moved to the Théâtre National, where he was due to open in *Richard Darlington* on 4 December 1851.

But on the 2nd, the anniversary of Austerlitz, Louis-Napoleon dissolved the Assembly and called on the French people to approve his assumption of personal power in a referendum. Frédérick, alarmed by the arrests of prominent Republicans which had taken place, decided to follow the example set by Hugo and Dumas, and took refuge in Belgium.

He spent a month in Brussels, enjoying one of the most suc-cessful seasons of his career.[5] After a fortnight the playbills announced his 'last performance', a few days later his 'farewell performance', then his 'definitely final appearance', followed by an 'extra performance at the public's request'. But at last the time came for Frédérick's 'irrevocable farewell', and he left for London to do a season with Clarisse at the St. James's.

His audiences here were as enthusiastic as ever, except over one play, *Ruy Blas*, which the Lord Chamberlain had finally given him permission to perform. Hugo's story of the lackey who loves a queen shocked the English public's sense of social propriety; it horrified Queen Victoria.[6] On her return to Buckingham Palace from the St. James's she wrote indignantly in her diary:

> We went to the French Play and were not edified by the four long acts of the five-act play of *Ruy Blas*, by Victor Hugo. It is false in sentiment and throughout devoid of all right and noble feeling; it is really of the worst tendency, placing the unfortunate Queen of Spain in the most humiliating position imaginable. Ruy Blas, the hero, was very badly acted by Lemaître, who besides being very old, without a tooth in his head, which rendered him scarcely intelligible, and with a cracked voice, is devoid of all dignity. It was a disagreeable performance. Mlle Clarisse acted the part of the Queen well.

After this, Frédérick could do nothing right in Her Majesty's eyes. When he put on *Paillasse*, the London Press[7] declared that 'the delicacy, the nature, the facility with which every change of mood, sentiment and situation is produced by this incomparable performer are indescribable', and that actor and man had blended in 'an union perfect in its elements and irresistible in its results'. But the Queen complained[8] that the play 'lasted fully four hours, was overstrained, and very painful, and rendered less interesting by Lemaître's slow and disagreeable acting'.

There is a famous anecdote which all Frédérick's French biographers tell with relish, about an encounter which is supposed to have taken place at this time between the actor and the Queen.[9] According to this tale, Queen Victoria was so impressed by his performance in *Le Chiffonnier de Paris* that she summoned him to her box and offered him her congratulations, adding: 'But what dreadfully poor people you have in Paris!'

'Your Majesty,' said Frédérick, 'those are our Irish.'

It is a good story, but it appears to have no foundation in fact. As far as is known, Frédérick never performed the *Chiffonnier* before Queen Victoria, either at the St. James's or at Buckingham Palace or Windsor. And even if he did, and the event has gone unrecorded, it is unlikely that the Queen had a kind word to say to him after *Ruy Blas*.

In April 1852 he decided that it was safe for him to return to Paris, where he entered into an engagement with the Variétés. He was no luckier here, however, than he had been in the eighteen-thirties, for the only new parts he was given were in a mediocre comedy and a trashy vaudeville. After hearing him sing in this last work, Jules Janin[10] wrote sympathetically: 'He belongs to that race of actors who rightly hold that there is nothing too low for a great artist.' This was a well deserved compliment, but it was small consolation to Frédérick.

Just as he was beginning to despair of finding a good new role, most of his old favourites were taken from him; for the Second Empire had scarcely been proclaimed in December 1852 before the Imperial censorship banned all public performances of *Richard Darlington*, *L'Auberge des Adrets*, *Robert Macaire*, *Ruy Blas* and *Le Chiffonnier de Paris*. But then two dramatists whose plays he had often acted, Dumanoir and Dennery, came to his rescue and wrote a drama specially designed to display his remarkable mimic gifts. Ever since his days at the Funambules with Deburau, Frédérick had longed for an opportunity to show what he could do with mime alone, and now this chance was given to him with *Le Vieux Caporal*, a play about an old soldier who is dumb for three out of five acts.

As soon as he was released from his engagement with the Variétés, he signed a short-term contract with the Porte-Saint-Martin, where *Le Vieux Caporal* was presented in May 1853.[11] It was a tremendous personal triumph for the actor-mime, particularly the scene in which the hero tells in dumb show the story of his captivity in Siberia. One critic, Jules de Prémaray of the *Patrie*, went so far as to declare: 'Without a voice or a pen, Frédérick Lemaître sang and wrote— for this silence of his will live in the annals of the theatre—a poem as great as the *Iliad* or the *Odyssey*. Nor am I overpraising him: Frédérick dumb can only be compared to Homer blind.' And Gautier, who long before had expressed the hope that Frédérick might one day perform a complete pantomime,[12] wrote in the *Presse*:

> You must see Frédérick in the marvellous scene where he reveals his identity. He adopts a series of poses so beautiful, so noble, so antique that each attitude ought to be perpetuated by a statue: one imagines Michelangelo sculpting in marble the symbolical figures of Heroism, Suffering, Resignation and Captivity. Certainly his fettered slaves are no more beautiful than Frédérick with his wrists pressed together, his head bowed, his eyes downcast, his back bent, his steps shortened, on his way to Siberia. And when, coming out of the mines, he sees the light again, how he shudders like an old eagle spreading its stiff wings once more, shaking its wet feathers and blinking its dazzled eyes! For the moment when Simon recovers the power of speech, Frédérick has found a magnificent effect. Waves of frantic joy pass over him from head to foot, and he cries: 'I can speak!' in a truly superhuman voice. Eleven years of misery are burnt and shrivelled up in that cry like blotting-paper in a fire. Never has happiness shone forth with such brilliant radiance. . . .

Despite the rapturous reception which public and critics gave the play, *Le Vieux Caporal* had fewer than fifty performances, and Frédérick was obliged to spend the autumn and winter 'resting.' He did not return to the stage until April 1854, when he appeared at the Gaîté in an adaptation of an Eugène Sue novel, *La Bonne Aventure*, the last play in which he and Clarisse Miroy were billed together.[13]

For the past thirteen years Clarisse had been a devoted mistress and companion to him, watching over his comfort, nursing his ageing mother, looking after his youngest children, managing his household affairs. She was no longer beautiful, for she suffered from a heart ailment which had made her pathetically fat; indeed, as far back as 1847 an English critic,[14] recalling that she was once known as *la rose du Boulevard*, had ungallantly remarked that 'she now resembles a full blown rather than a budding rose'. But Frédérick still felt a deep affection for her, treating her with that mixture of tenderness and violence which he reserved for the women he loved. One of the very few letters he wrote to her which remain extant bears a striking resemblance to the letters he sent his wife soon after they were married, yet it dates from the last period of his liaison with Clarisse.[15] In it he wrote:

> I have just this minute received your two letters. They have caused me so much happiness and made my heart beat so violently that I don't know what I am writing. It is now five o'clock: instead of having dinner I am going to go for a walk in the country and read your letters again—and tonight I shall take up my pen and try to make you understand how much you mean to me.

Recently, however, Clarisse had fallen in love with a handsome but untalented young actor called Jenneval, who was commonly known as 'the poor man's Frédérick Lemaître'. On the first night of *La Bonne Aventure*, Frédérick intercepted a love-letter from Jenneval which left no doubt in his mind that his mistress was deceiving him.[16] He went home immediately after the performance, threw all Clarisse's belongings on to the landing outside their flat, and locked her out. She wept and pleaded with him, bombarded him with pitiful letters and begged his children to intercede on her behalf, but all in vain: he refused to take her back. A year later, disillusioned with Jenneval and furious to see her best parts given to Marie Laurent, she stole into Frédérick's dressing-room one night and emptied a bottle of laudanum into his bordeaux. Only the fact that someone saw her coming out of the room and warned

Frédérick saved him from death by poison in the best traditions of Romantic drama.

He never spoke of this attempt to kill him until after Clarisse had died, fourteen years later. Indeed, he did his best to appear unconcerned and even amused by her betrayal of him with Jenneval. When he was told that Jenneval had slapped her face in public, he roared with laughter and said: 'No, not really! He's taken my parts, he's taken my mistress, and now he's taken my way of dealing with Clarisse Miroy! That small-town Frédérick Lemaître obviously can't do anything original!' But in reality he was deeply hurt.

Later that same year his daughter Caroline was married to a cashier called Élie Thiébaut at the church of Saint-Joseph in the Faubourg du Temple.[17] Legend has it that Frédérick originally offered to provide her with a dowry and also pay for her trousseau, but then decided that he could not afford to spend so much money. When the two families met to sign the marriage contract, he abruptly withdrew half his offer.

'Frédérick Lemaître's daughter', he said, 'has no need of a dowry: her maiden name will serve instead. Let us therefore leave out the dowry.'

Thiébaut, who had a ready wit, rose to the occasion.

'Frédérick Lemaître's daughter', he retorted, 'has no need of clothing: she can drape herself in her father's glory. Let us therefore leave out the trousseau.'

In the end the matter was amicably arranged. Caroline did not receive a dowry, but her father provided her with a trousseau, gave her a present of a diamond ring, and paid for a splendid wedding breakfast at Véry's.

A few months later, in January 1855, Frédérick opened a six-month season at the Ambigu, presenting revivals of *Paillasse*, *Trente ans*, *La Dame de Saint-Tropez*, *Kean* and *Don César*, in a successful attempt to save the manager, his friend Charles Desnoyers, from bankruptcy.[18] This was the year of Napoleon III's first Great Exhibition, and Paris was crowded with visitors. Among them were Charles Dickens and Wilkie Collins, and one night the two novelists went together to the Ambigu to see Frédérick playing in *Trente ans*. It was a revelation to them. Years afterwards, Collins could still remember every detail of the evening,[19] and told Frank Archer how 'at the end of one of the acts we were so utterly overcome that we both sat for a time perfectly silent'. As for Dickens, he set down an account of the performance which deserves to be quoted at length in that it is undoubtedly the most vivid description we have of Frédérick's acting.[20] He wrote:

Incomparably the finest acting I ever saw, I saw last night at the Ambigu. They have revived that old piece, once immensely popular in London under the name of *Thirty Years of a Gambler's Life*. Old Lemaître plays his famous character, and never did I see anything, in art, so exaltedly horrible and awful. In the earlier acts he was so well made up, and so light and active, that he really looked sufficiently young. But in the last two, when he had grown old and miserable, he did the finest things, I really believe, that are within the power of acting. Two or three times a great cry of horror went all round the house. When he met, in the inn yard, the traveller whom he murders, and first saw his money, the manner in which the crime came into his head—and eyes—was as truthful as it was terrific. This traveller, being a good fellow, gives him wine. You should see the dim remembrance of his better days that comes over him as he takes the glass, and in a strange dazed way makes as if he were going to touch the other man's or to do some airy thing with it; and then stops and flings the contents down his hot throat, as if he were pouring it into a lime-kiln. But this was nothing to what follows after he has done the murder, and comes home, with a basket of provisions, a ragged pocket full of money, and a badly-washed bloody right hand which his little girl finds out. After the child asked him if he had hurt his hand, his going aside, turning himself round, and looking over all his clothes for spots, was so inexpressibly dreadful that it really scared one. He called for wine, and the sickness that came over him when he saw the colour was one of the things that brought out the curious cry I have spoken of from the audience. Then he fell into a sort of bloody mist, and went on to the end groping about, with no mind for anything, except making his fortune by staking this money, and a faint dull kind of love for the child. It is quite impossible to satisfy one's self by saying enough of this magnificent performance. He said two things in a way that alone

would put him far apart from other actors. One to his wife, when he
has exultingly shown her the money, and she has asked him how
he got it—'I found it'—and the other to his old companion and
tempter, when he was charged by him with having killed that
traveller, and suddenly went headlong mad and took him by the
throat and howled out: 'It wasn't I who murdered him—it was
Misery!' And such a dress, such a face, and, above all, such an
extraordinarily guilty wicked thing as he made of a knotted branch
of a tree which was his walking-stick, from the moment when the
idea of the murder came into his head! I could write pages about
him. It is an impression quite ineffaceable. He got half-boastful of
that walking-staff to himself, and half afraid of it; and didn't know
whether to be grimly pleased that it had the jagged end, or to hate
it and be horrified at it. He sat at a little table in the inn yard, drinking with the traveller; and this horrible stick got between them
like the Devil, while he counted on his fingers the uses he could
put the money to.

If they had but known it, Dickens and Collins could have seen
another of the great figures of the Romantic theatre while they
were in Paris, though not on the stage. Mlle George, desperate
to find employment, had applied to the Exhibition authorities
for the job of superintending the umbrella counter at the
Champ de Mars.[21] As it happened, that position was already
filled, but they had another one to offer her. She accepted it.
And the queen of tragedy who had been an emperor's mistress
was put in charge of the public lavatories.

Frédérick had not yet fallen as low as that, but he was growing unhappier year by year. He was also completely out of
sympathy with the spirit of the times. Expansion and enjoyment
were the watchwords of Paris in the middle-fifties. Trade and
industry were booming; department stores and public buildings
were going up everywhere; houses and apartment blocks were
being erected at such a rate that the wits said Paris was becoming uninhabitable. Worth introduced the perfected crino-
line, and soon the boulevards were full of elegant women in
huge calix skirts. Foreign diplomats flocked to the French capital
for the Congress of Paris. There were firework displays and
free entertainments to celebrate the birth of a son to Napoleon

III and the Empress Eugénie. At the newly opened Bouffes-Parisiens packed houses applauded the first Offenbach-Halévy production, a *chinoiserie musicale* called *Ba-ta-clan*. But except when he had to be at the theatre, Frédérick stayed morosely at home.

The sadness of his life at this time is well conveyed by a letter he sent in February 1856 to his son Charles, who was fulfilling an engagement at Lisbon.[22] In it he reported:

> I am not writing these days, but thinking . . . thinking too much indeed, and there is nothing more tiring, nothing more enervating, nothing which makes you less capable of action. It is a disease, a disease often born, in solitude, of regrets and disappointments. Here, there is not much news. Caroline is ill. Napoléon does nothing but play the fool. As for me, I spend my time rehearsing, cooking and darning. . . .

The play he was rehearsing was the first of the great Romantic dramas, *Henri III et sa Cour*, which was revived at the Gaîté with Frédérick as the Duc de Guise, Mme Naptal as the Duchess and Laferrière as Saint-Mégrin.[23] There was an unfortunate incident at the end of one performance. Frédérick was in the habit of changing into a black velvet dressing-gown immediately after the last scene, and one night this delayed the curtain-call so long that Mme Naptal said to Laferrière: 'Must we always wait for the old man?' The 'old man' arrived at that moment, heard what she said, and stormed off to his dressing-room. When Mme Naptal went to see him and apologize, he relented, saying: 'What won't we forgive a woman—especially a woman as pretty as you?' But the thrust had gone home.

Henri III was followed by two nondescript plays: a revival of Bouchardy's old melodrama *Le Sonneur de Saint-Paul* at the Gaîté, and a new work by Victor Séjour, *André Gérard*, at the Odéon.[24] Then, in the summer of 1857, Frédérick fell ill with anaemia and had to go into a hydropathic establishment at Bellevue, where he stayed throughout the autumn and winter.[25]

He returned to the stage in March 1858, with a successful revival of *Don César de Bazan*, before moving to the Ambigu to
create the title role in Paul Meurice's play *Le Maître d'école*
a year later.[26]

His performance as the humble village schoolmaster in this
last work, particularly in a scene where he read and explained
La Fontaine's fable *La Cigale et la Fourmi* to a child, surprised
and captivated a public accustomed to seeing him in more
violent roles. The great Michelet was so deeply moved by his
acting that he wrote to the author: 'I am grateful to you for
having given that immortal man such a wonderful opportunity
to reveal a second youth. He could not have played the part
any earlier, at least not with that adorable tenderness which
touched every heart in the audience, mine most of all.' And
Paul de Saint-Victor wrote in the *Presse*:

> Frédérick shows himself in a completely new light in *Le Maître
> d'école*. His voice has become softer, his gestures ampler, his acting
> veiled with melancholy. This is the pale, pure autumn of a great
> talent growing calmer after the storms of summer. There is a cer-
> tain chiaroscuro in his look and in his speech. One is irresistibly
> reminded of those extraordinary evenings whose twilights are
> phenomenal.

Frédérick's next production, *Le Marchand de coco*, which he
presented at the Ambigu at the end of the year, was far less
successful, largely on account of the play's faulty characterization and clumsy dialogue.[27] There was an angry scene at the
actor's flat after the first performance, Charles having been
unwise enough to invite a friend home to supper.[28] Frédérick
glowered ominously throughout the meal, finally hurling a wing
of chicken into the air so that it landed on the unwanted guest,
ordering the man out of the house, and laying a solemn curse
on Charles and Napoléon when they ventured to protest. But
his temper cooled during the night. At dawn the next day, dressed
in a black suit and a white cravat, he woke his sons and drove
them to Saint-Germain-l'Auxerrois, where he made them kneel
down before the high altar.

'Lord,' an astonished sacristan heard him say, 'yesterday, in a moment of folly, I cursed these children of mine. Lord, I take back my curse. . . . Now get up, you two!'

And he marched them out of the church again.

He knew, of course, that in spite of dubious successes like *Le Marchand de coco*, he still retained the admiration of a small, utterly devoted public, for he kept receiving letters of fulsome and even blasphemous praise. One admirer[29] went so far as to ask him point-blank: 'Oh Monsieur Frédérick, to stir souls so deeply, could it be that you are God Himself?' But he was beginning to fail in both health and courage, and about this time a series of events occurred which thoroughly disheartened him.

First Laferrière, a colleague whom he had helped and advised in the early stages of his career, usurped the title role of *Richard Darlington*, which had recently been authorized by the censor, and played it at the Porte-Saint-Martin in spite of all Frédérick's protests to actor, authors and management.[30] Then his beloved mother died, at a time when he himself was ill in bed, so that he could not accompany her on her last journey.[31] And finally the Boulevard du Temple, which had seen so many of his triumphs, was obliterated by that most ruthless of all town-planners, Baron Haussmann.

In July 1862 posters went up advertising sales of theatrical equipment and furniture ranging from costumes and properties to benches and statues. On the 15th the seven doomed theatres on the left-hand side of the Boulevard gave their last performances to packed houses. Some, like the Gaîté, pretended that nothing out of the ordinary was happening, and put on plays from their normal repertory. But the Folies-Dramatiques had a topical production called *Les Adieux du Boulevard du Temple*; and the Funambules staged a farewell pantomime, *Les Mémoires de Pierrot*, with Deburau *fils* playing Pierrot dressed in black.

On 7 December that same year, the Emperor and the Empress formally inaugurated the new Boulevard du Prince Eugène by driving in state over what had once been the Petit-Lazari, the Délassements-Comiques, the Funambules, the Gaîté, the Folies-Dramatiques, the Cirque-Olympique and the Théâtre-Lyrique. The crowds cheered. And Frédérick watched with bitterness in his heart.

CHAPTER SEVENTEEN

THE OLD LION

In August 1862 Frederick gave the worst performance of his career at the Théâtre du Palais-Royal.[1] The play was *Les Saltimbanques*, the part that of the clown Bilboquet, which the great comedian Odry had created.

Ten years earlier, Frédérick had refused to play Bilboquet at the Variétés, asserting that he would 'never touch an irreproachable creation'. If he changed his mind in 1862, it was partly because he could not afford to reject the offer the Palais-Royal made him, and partly because he wanted to play a trick on the Imperial censorship by turning Bilboquet into another Robert Macaire. But his fellow actors had no desire to see the play banned and they threatened to walk out unless he gave up the idea. Prevented from interpreting the role as he had originally intended, he lost all interest in it. The result was a disaster.

'The audience came close to hissing me in *Les Saltimbanques*,' he told Henry Lecomte one day, 'and they were right. Once it had been pointed out to me that I could not play the part as a Macaire, I had been forced to look for another interpretation, which had to be different from Odry's because I possessed neither his ordinary build nor his grotesque appearance. I made a poor choice, and I was very bad, well-nigh ridiculous.'

Balm was administered to his wounded pride early the next year,[2] when the Government took the unprecedented step of granting him an annual pension of 2,000 francs, 'as a token of sympathy and esteem in appreciation of your long and brilliant career'. In his official letter informing Frédérick of the award,

FRÉDÉRICK CARICATURED BY GILL

FRÉDÉRICK IN OLD AGE

the Minister of State expressed the hope that that career was
not yet over. The actor had in fact decided to retire after the
failure of *Les Saltimbanques*, but the pull of the stage proved too
strong for him in the end.

'The theatre', he wrote in the notes for his memoirs,[3] 'is like
a mistress you have sworn never to see or think of again; you
have no sooner heard the rustle of her dress outside or her timid
knock than you rush to open the door to her. Its joys, its emotions,
even its sorrows make it forever dear to you. After the success
of *Le Comte de Saulles* I found that all my fine resolutions about
retiring had been banished by a little applause. Art had re-
asserted its rights.'

Le Comte de Saulles, a play by Édouard Plouvier, was presented at the Ambigu in April 1864.[4] Frédérick scored a tremendous personal triumph in the title role, earning much more
than the 'little applause' he mentioned in his notes. To obtain
an idea of the impression he made on his audience, one cannot do
better than consult François Coppée,[5] who first saw him act
about this time and wrote some years later:

He was now just a physical wreck. The striking mask, once so
handsome and so often discomposed by the mimicry of every passion, would collapse when he was tired into a sour grimace of fatigue
and disgust. The famous Louis-Philippe toupet now crowned a forehead slashed by deep wrinkles. The eyes had not lost their bright-
ness, but they were bloodshot and watery, and half-covered by heavy
lids. Under the chin, which still stuck out proudly, there hung an
old man's dewlap; and from the mouth, which was turned down at
the corners and encumbered with false teeth, the voice emerged
only with difficulty, sounding faint and distant.

But as soon as the play got under way and came to some violent
situation, Frédérick underwent a transfiguration. He made a
sudden effort, an effort of genius, and gave himself up entirely to
the pathetic situation expressed by the author in nondescript phrases;
he lived and felt his part with all his thoughts, his nerves, his heart.
Aged and exhausted by a life of disorder and excess, he regained
the strength and agility of youth. He sprang about, filling the
stage with his ample, supple gestures and his giant strides. They
were real tears that he shed, and the flame of passion burned in his

P

eyes. His face flushed with genuine anger, went pale with real terror, softened with sincere pity. His voice, so faint to begin with, burst forth in cries, groans and sobs. This was truth itself, since it was life, but truth as it should be revealed to the people, that is to say magnified by art, poetic, poignant and grandiose!

Ten years before, at one of the annual Molière banquets which were attended by the leading actors and writers of the day,[6] Frédérick had proposed a toast to 'that immense genius' and expressed 'the ardent wish that in the future no one should be denied the glorious right to interpret him'. Now at long last the Government abolished the monopoly of the two official theatres, and Frédérick's friends promptly urged him to seize the opportunity to play the great traditional parts. 'You are only sixty-three', one correspondent wrote,[7] 'and now that the theatres are free we beg you to let us admire new aspects of your prodigious genius.' But it was too late. The popular theatres no longer had any desire to stage the classics; and though the Odéon management engaged him to play Harpagon and Tartuffe, it made the engagement conditional on the failure of George Sand's *Marquis de Villemer*.[8] Unfortunately for Frédérick, the *Marquis* did remarkably well, and he reluctantly gave up hope of ever appearing in a Molière comedy.

In its new-found enthusiasm for the theatre the Government also decided at this time to bestow the Légion d'honneur on an actor.[9] This honour had never before been paid to a member of the theatrical profession, and everyone expected the decoration to go to Frédérick, as the greatest living player. In the event, it was Samson, the *doyen* of the Théâtre-Français, who was rewarded with the red ribbon. The pundits explained that it was an understandable choice. Frédérick, after all, had not led such a blameless, respectable life as Samson; more serious still, though admittedly this was not his fault, he had never 'played the old repertory'. But there were protests in the Press. And Frédérick himself made no secret of his disappointment.

'It is my cross', he said, 'that Monsieur Samson is going to wear.'

He became increasingly depressed, quicker-tempered, more eccentric in his ways. Frédéric Febvre, who played opposite him several times, has left us a vivid impression of the old actor in his memoirs,[10] where he writes:

In the evening, while he was getting ready to go on, he would often send for me and ask me to play a few pieces of religious music on a little harmonium which he kept in his dressing-room. It thus happened that I witnessed countless highly comic scenes—with the hairdresser, for example, on nights when Frédérick was nervous.

When the man had put curl-papers all over the right-hand half of his head, Frédérick would suddenly jump up and shout in a voice of thunder: 'That's enough! Now get out!'

'But Monsieur Frédérick . . . what about the other side?'

'That's enough, I said. Away you go!' And before the poor fellow could move, Frédérick would take him by the shoulders and throw him out.

Then he would turn to me and say: 'That *De profundis* was really beautiful. Play it again.' And while I was finishing the Hymn of the Dead, I could see him in the looking-glass prinking up the hair in curl-papers and smoothing down the rest, to produce the oddest coiffure imaginable. . . .

For three years Frédérick 'rested', appearing only in a revival of *Trente ans* at the Ambigu and a number of benefit performances. The effect on his finances can be seen from his account-book.[11] In 1854 he had savings of over 130,000 francs, including 50,000 in rouleaux of gold coins hidden in the cellar. By 1862 he was down to 42,000 francs, and the rouleaux of gold had gone. In 1867 he made a brief, final entry—'000: Total 0!!!' —and slammed the book shut, smudging the ink on the opposite page.

Ironically enough, the year that he faced poverty and ruin was the year that French prosperity and pride reached its zenith. It was the year of the second Universal Exhibition, when the whole world appeared to be flocking to Haussmann's splendid *ville lumière*, and Paris worked itself into a last wild paroxysm of gaiety before the debacle—a debacle foreshadowed by the ominous Prussian exhibit, the biggest cannon from the Rhine fortifications.

In the theatre, it saw the disappearance of Mlle George, who died on 11 January, sixty-four years to the day since her first meeting with Napoleon.[12] It saw the brilliant début and humiliating eclipse of Cora Pearl, Prince Napoleon's Plymouth-born mistress, who appeared at the Bouffes as Cupid in a revival of *Orphée aux enfers*, sang a few numbers with a pronounced English accent and was eventually hissed off the stage.[13] Above all, it saw the amazing triumph of Hortense Schneider in Offenbach's latest operetta, *La Grande Duchesse de Gérolstein*.[14]

There were times when it seemed as if *La Grande Duchesse* and not the Exhibition was the chief attraction in Paris. Everyone was humming the tunes from the show; everyone had seen it or wanted to see it. Bismarck and Moltke changed out of uniform into evening dress straight after Napoleon III's great parade in the Bois, and hurried off to the Variétés to hear Schneider singing: '*Ah! que j'aime les militaires!*' The Kings of Prussia, Portugal, Bavaria and Sweden went too. The Prince of Wales applied directly to Schneider for a box at the theatre on the very day he arrived in Exhibition Paris. The Tsar of Russia was even more impatient: he sent a telegram to his Ambassador from Cologne, ordering him to obtain a box for him immediately. Small wonder that Hortense Schneider felt entitled to drive her carriage into the Exhibition, a privilege reserved for royalty, calling out as she did so: 'Make way! I am the Grande Duchesse de Gérolstein!'

No foreign potentates went to the Folies-Dramatiques in June to see Frédérick in his new play, *Le Père Gachette*, but the critics and his old admirers were there in strength to welcome him back to the theatre.[15] As he made his entrance, walking slowly down a staircase erected on the stage, the whole house rose to him, cheering and clapping wildly. 'It was not just a man we were applauding,' wrote Paul Foucher,[16] 'but the memory of the melodrama regenerated, the Boulevard ennobled, a new art revealed and consecrated; it was sixty years of fervour and genius coming down those plaster steps.'

The play itself, by Paulin Deslandes, was a poor thing, but

Frédérick's acting made the improbable plot seem almost plausible. There was one moment in particular when he roused the audience to frantic enthusiasm without even facing them. In the final scene the locksmith Gachette finds his pipe in a private park, remembers that he has been there before, and suddenly realizes that the heroine of the piece is imprisoned in the summer-house in the background. At this point Frédérick said nothing but simply peeled off his jacket. 'We could only see his back,' wrote Francisque Sarcey, 'but the gesture with which he removed his jacket was so powerful; it said so clearly: "Ah! I have it! It won't be long now!" and it revealed such formidable determination, such implacable energy, that there was a single cry from the stalls to the gallery.'

It was the simplicity of Frédérick's effects which most impressed the master-critic Barbey d'Aurevilly, who wrote in the *Nain Jaune*:

> In his most brilliantly written and cleverly devised roles Frédérick has never acted better than in the wretched *Père Gachette*, where he showed himself in a completely new light. By dint of concentration, reflection and artistry, the Frédérick of *Le Père Gachette* has become even more surprising than the Frédérick we used to know. The latter was what I should call 'a lyricist of the stage', who sometimes bordered on grandiloquence—and that indeed was the only criticism one could dare to make of this formidable man, when one was not absolutely hypnotized by the fascinating force of his acting. But the Frédérick of *Le Père Gachette* is the Frédérick of simplicity, a simplicity which he has at last discovered and snatched from the Sphinx of Art, whose final secret it is. All the qualities which went to make the Frédérick of old are still here, but employed with a discretion, a restraint, an assurance and a depth of feeling which one cannot praise too highly, and which are the signs of a sovereign artist.

To some extent, of course, this new restraint was enforced by old age. 'As your physical powers diminish,' an anonymous admirer told the actor,[17] 'you replace them with a wonderful sureness of touch, a remarkable sense of light and shade, and miming that is at once subtle and energetic.' Frédérick himself was certainly extremely conscious of his advancing years. When the magazine *La Lune* asked for authority to publish a cartoon of him by André Gill, he gave the editor the necessary permission,[18] but added wryly: '*Lune*, caricature the young—time will take care of the old.' And when he came across a notice calling him 'the old lion'—a phrase which the Press now applied to him whenever he appeared on the stage—he remarked: 'Old lion? No, I'm just an old duffer. You see, the cruel thing about acting is that when you can you don't know how, and when you know how you can't any more!'[19]

But this was false modesty on his part, as he proved in February 1868, when he won one of the greatest triumphs of his career in a melodrama at the Ambigu called *Le Crime de Faverne*.[20] His part, that of the notary Maître Séraphin, was only an episodic role, which could have been omitted without seriously damaging the plot; but he played it with such brilliance that it became the leading role in the play. Gentle and kindly to begin with, Séraphin suddenly goes mad towards the end, when he discovers that his dead wife had been unfaithful to him. The critics were used to madness scenes, particularly in Frédérick's plays, but his performance in this one amazed them. Louis Ulbach went so far as to say that 'this man, giggling and singing his shame, dancing his despair, frolicking on the tomb of his dead life, drags us into the sublime depths whose entry is guarded by the great dramatic geniuses, and introduces Shakespeare into a play by MM. Théodore Barrière and Beauvallet'.

As in *Le Père Gachette*, there was one point in *Le Crime de Faverne* when Frédérick carried away his audience with a simple, effective touch. Georges Cain, who was taken to see the play as a boy,[21] remembered it years later:

> Haggard and roaring with rage, he angrily hurled into the fire all the countless souvenirs which he had treasured so fondly. 'Into the fire with her wedding bouquet! . . . Into the fire with her little silk cloak! . . . Into the fire with her locks of hair! . . . Into the fire with her ribbons!' And then suddenly he stopped. 'This picture of her

was painted after her death.' It was not the dead woman who had deceived him. And this brief moment of emotion was enough to allow the great actor to leave an unforgettable memory with every member of the audience.

It was his last great triumph. There were over seventy performances given to cheering audiences. The Empress Eugénie came to see the play during the first week it was on, and Frédérick told his son Charles[22] that she 'wet three handkerchiefs'. And the *Figaro* called upon the public to 'bow down before Frédérick, salute him, acclaim him and recognize in him the unconquered master of the drama, the Mirabeau of the Romantic theatre, defying the old, electrifying the young, and throwing himself like a tempest into the flat calm of our paltry plays and dreary plots'.

In September the Ambigu put on a revival of *Trente ans*.[23] There still exists a pathetic note in shaky handwriting, signed 'Georges de Germany', in which Frédérick wrote that he placed himself 'at the disposal of my new Amélie tomorrow at three o'clock'. It was now nearly twenty years since his first Amélie had died.

Early in the run he had a letter from Caroline Thiébaut reporting that her mother, who had recently gone into Dr. Blanche's asylum, was dangerously ill.[24] Thiébaut had had her examined by his own doctor, who 'found her in such a serious condition, not mentally but physically, that we must expect the worst at any moment'. Sophie lingered on for nearly two months and died on 16 November. She was buried on the 18th in the Montmartre Cemetery, where Frédérick spoke a few words of farewell at the graveside.[25]

'Here', he said, 'lies the body of my beloved mother. Here too are to rest the remains of one who was a devoted daughter, a faithful wife and a tender mother. Her soul has returned to the Creator; may she intercede with Him on our behalf!'

It sounds a little theatrical to modern ears, but Frédérick's grief was probably quite sincere.

A few months later, the author-actor Fechter wrote to him

from England inviting him to come to London to discuss a proposed adaptation of Wilkie Collins' book *The Woman in White*.[26] The play was destined for the Ambigu, where Frédérick and Marie Laurent were to take the leading roles. But although Marie Laurent was enthusiastic, Frédérick was not, and the idea was dropped.

In April 1869 the Ambigu decided to put on a revival of *Vautrin*, which had not been performed in Paris for nineteen years.[27] The first night was a disaster, the audience sitting in stony silence from beginning to end. In one of the intervals, Frédérick complained angrily to a friend: 'It's sheer prejudice! The critics have condemned Balzac as a dramatist so often that they simply refuse to see anything interesting in his play.' But the public shared the critics' poor opinion of *Vautrin*, and Frédérick himself no longer had the voice or the energy required to make a success of the exhausting title role. Within a fortnight the play was taken off.

After this failure Frédérick 'rested' for several months. In September the Ambigu obtained permission to revive *L'Auberge des Adrets*, but just as the play was about to go into rehearsal a sensational murder took place at Pantin, and Frédérick decided that this was no time to put on a burlesque of killing and banditry.[28] When at last he returned to the stage, in February 1870, it was not at the Ambigu but at the little Théâtre des Menus-Plaisirs, where he created the role of General Forestier in a new play by Théodore Barrière, *Malheur aux vaincus*.[29] The play was not a success, but Frédérick's performance as the old general was widely acclaimed. In the *Parlement* Barbey d'Aurevilly wrote:

Frédérick here is paternal love—that old theatrical sentiment which has been twisted, squeezed and worn until there is scarcely any of it left, and which Frédérick himself has represented a hundred times—but paternal love refreshed and restored this hundred-and-first time by a talent which can transfigure the most commonplace feelings. Frédérick was original where other actors are merely touching, and that is what I call the mark of genius. He played not only the father, but also the good man and the old soldier, and he succeeded in giving a new lease of life to these hackneyed types. From the beginning to the end of his role he was on a level with himself, with his past, with his glorious reputation.

By a hideous stroke of irony, Frédérick had scarcely finished playing this part of the loving father before he lost his favourite son.[30] Charles was acting in a revival of *Lucrèce Borgia* at the Porte-Saint-Martin when he was struck down in March by smallpox. On the 15th, when the fever reached its peak, he threw himself out of the window of his flat in the Boulevard de Strasbourg and was killed instantly.

Frédérick was overwhelmed with grief. Oblivious of the danger he was running, he himself prepared the body for burial; and on the 17th, though weak with emotion and fatigue, he led the funeral procession all the way from the church of Saint-Laurent to the Montmartre Cemetery, where Charles was laid to rest beside his mother.

That evening Frédérick had an unexpected visitor.[31] It was Clarisse Miroy, come to offer him her sympathy. The two sometime partners and lovers embraced and wept. For an hour or so they sat together, talking sadly of old times; then Clarisse said goodbye and went down the stairs and out of Frédérick's life.

She died in September that year in a nursing-home in the Avenue du Roule. During her last months she used to entertain her fellow patients by reciting the famous parts she had played with the great Frédérick Lemaître. They found her very amusing.

CHAPTER EIGHTEEN

LAST YEARS

IN July 1870 France declared war on Prussia, and with the mobs shouting: 'A Berlin!' thousands of troops left Paris for the frontier, allegedly 'ready down to the last gaiter button', but in fact disastrously under-equipped and hopelessly ill-trained. Less than two months later, on 2 September, the Emperor surrendered at Sedan with over eighty thousand men. On the 4th, a new Republic was proclaimed in Paris.

Frédérick, in common with most of his fellow citizens, was appalled by the news of what he characteristically called a 'truly Imperial skitter', but overjoyed at the foundation of the Third Republic.[1] Though the Prussians were reported to be advancing on Paris, and no one could have blamed him for taking refuge in the country, he decided that it was his duty to remain in the capital and help as best he could in its defence.

On the 5th, Victor Hugo returned from exile, bringing with him the ferocious book of poems in which he had scourged the 'little Napoleon' and prophesied his downfall: *Les Châtiments*. The Society of Authors, like every other society in Paris, wanted to buy a cannon for the new 'Government of National Defence', and hit upon the idea of raising the money by holding a reading of Hugo's satires. The leading actors and actresses in the capital were invited to take part, and were given the opportunity to choose whichever poems they preferred. Frédérick's choice was significant. He picked that quiet, bitter, deadly poem which tells of a little boy killed during Louis-Napoleon's *coup d'état: Souvenir de la nuit du 4 décembre*.

The great Romantic poet and the great Romantic actor were

reunited at one of the rehearsals.[2] Hugo listened to Frédérick
reading his poem, shook him warmly by the hand, and told him:
'You have lost nothing since I last saw you.'

It was in fact Frédérick who obtained the greatest success
of all at the public reading, which took place at the Porte-Saint-
Martin on 5 November. As soon as he appeared, quietly dressed
in a frock-coat and grey trousers, the audience rose to a man
and cheered him. He looked round the theatre, put on his
spectacles, adjusted the reading lamp and began the famous tale:

L'enfant avait reçu deux balles dans la tête. . . .

But he had scarcely read the first few lines before he abandoned his script and began acting the tragedy of the child's
death and its grandmother's grief, with such poignant effect
that there was an explosion of enthusiasm from the whole house
when he finished.

He repeated this unforgettable performance at a second reading a week later, and then at various charity shows at the Opéra
and the Porte-Saint-Martin. On each of these occasions he received a tremendous ovation from the audience, a letter of fulsome praise from the organizers, and of course no remuneration.
Indeed, the only money he earned during the four-month siege
of Paris was from a few performances of *Trente ans* at the Ambigu. It was scarcely enough to allow him to buy food on the
black market, and except for occasional gifts of fruit or poultry
from admirers such as Paul Meurice, he had to subsist on the
tiny official ration. There is extant a pathetic letter he wrote
to the mayor of his arrondissement, asking if it was true that the
rationing regulations allowed an extra portion of meat to sep-
tuagenarians.[3] Life on a starvation diet in a beleaguered city
during one of the cruellest winters of the century must have been
sheer misery for the old actor.

He was sustained by the patriotic fervour which had inspired
the people of Paris ever since they had set up the Republic in
September. But at the end of January Paris capitulated and an
armistice was signed.

There was worse to follow. In March, alarmed by the election of a largely Royalist Assembly by rural France, disgusted by the terms of a peace treaty which abandoned Alsace and Lorraine to Germany, and provoked by the head of the new Government, the detested Thiers, Paris rose in revolt and founded the ill-fated Commune. In May, the Government troops from Versailles invaded the capital and fought their way through the burning city, killing without mercy. As usual, the last barricades were in theatre-land; and at the height of the fighting Frédérick saw the Porte-Saint-Martin, the scene of some of his greatest triumphs, go up in flames. He saw, too, the fearful vengeance which Thiers's army took on Paris during the 'Bloody Week': the thousands of summary executions, the mortuaries piled high with bodies. He was sickened, but not surprised. It was all so heartbreakingly familiar.

In the summer a law was passed allowing Parisians to claim a rebate on the rent they had paid during the Siege and the Commune. Frédérick duly applied to his local tribunal, but met with opposition from his landlord.[4]

'Monsieur Frédérick Lemaître', said the latter's counsel, 'is a very rich man. He has thirty thousand francs in penny-pieces hidden in his cellar, and he never goes out without twenty thousand francs in his pocket . . .'

'In penny-pieces?' interrupted the actor ironically. 'Gentlemen, this man is a slanderer, and I am poor . . . yes, poor!'

The president of the tribunal recalled that Alexandre Dumas, who was thought like Frédérick to be extremely rich, had died a few months before in absolute poverty, and gave judgment in the actor's favour.

Frédérick had not exaggerated his plight. Already[5] he had been obliged to sell all his valuable ornaments and bric-à-brac; and now, at a time of life when most actors of his standing would be enjoying a comfortable retirement, he found himself forced to go on working. He could not even obtain engagements in Paris, but was reduced to playing for a pittance in tiny suburban theatres such as the Gobelins or the Belleville. Yet he had

lost none of the old magic. The actor Porel, who as a boy played
with him about this time, told a friend[6] years later:

> The audience sometimes became restive, but one gesture from him
> was enough to silence them. He was magnificent! The look in his
> eyes above all. A look that contained the whole human soul; eyes that
> threw out sparks, that expressed love, ambition, contempt, humi-
> lity, madness, bestiality, innocence, genius. If you never saw
> Frédérick's eyes you cannot know what the look of a truly great
> actor is like—and you will never know now!

In March 1872 Frédérick returned to the Boulevard to take
the leading role in a play at the Ambigu by Frantz Beauvallet
entitled *Le Portier du nº* 15.[7] As the aged concierge Feuillantin,
he played to appreciative audiences for over forty nights, but
his appearance in the *Portier* had two unfortunate consequences.
At one of the last performances a scene-shifter with a grudge
against the stage-setter aimed a heavy flat at him, and narrowly
missed hitting Frédérick, who was left badly shaken. Then, in
the summer, Dennery and Plouvier withdrew the offer they had
made him of the title role in their drama *Le Centenaire*,[8] on the
pretext that he had just played a septuagenarian and 'towards
the end of life a few years do not make much difference to a man's
appearance'. Frédérick was wounded by the implication that he
was incapable of establishing a distinction between a man of
seventy and a centenarian, but there was nothing he could do.

As the letters from his creditors became more and more
menacing,[9] he sold his last precious possessions: his silverware,
his books, and finally the letters he had received from Hugo,
Balzac, Lamartine, Gautier, Gérard de Nerval and George
Sand.[10] And when, in February 1873, he appeared at the Ambigu
in his last creation, the title role in an absurd melodrama called
Un Lâche,[11] he remarked bitterly to his young friend and
biographer Henry Lecomte: 'You have to be hungry to play a
part like this!'

It was Henry Lecomte who came to his rescue a year later,
when he was threatened with utter destitution.[12] Calling at the
actor's flat one Sunday, Lecomte was told that his landlord was

going to sell his furniture that week. The young author went straight to the offices of the *Événement* and asked one of his friends on the staff to publish the following announcement the next day:

> Unbelievable, shameful, dreadful news!
> On Wednesday morning Frédérick Lemaître's furniture is going to be sold at No. 37 Boulevard Magenta. The great actor has been reduced to abject poverty. It should be added that he has been unable to find a theatre willing to put on a 'retirement benefit' which would have saved him.

Thanks to Lecomte's intervention, a committee was set up which organized a benefit performance at the Opéra featuring every sort of attraction from Coquelin *aîné* in *Les Précieuses ridicules* to the chorus of the Folies-Dramatiques in an extract from *La Fille de Mme Angot*. But a series of grotesque incidents put an end to Frédérick's hopes. First, outraged by the proposed desecration of the Opéra by a paltry operetta, a pompous music critic protested to the Minister, the programme was cut, and the organizers cancelled the benefit. Then, offended by the slight on his operetta, the manager of the Folies-Dramatiques announced that he was going to stage a benefit for Frédérick starring the famous tenor Tamberlick, whom he described as 'equal to the whole Academy of Music put together'. Finally Tamberlick himself, taking offence at this alleged insult to his fellow musicians, withdrew his support. And in the flurry of charges and counter-charges the original cause of all this activity was completely forgotten. On 9 August 1873 Frédérick's furniture was sold after all.

His chief source of comfort at this time was a young woman whom his friends knew as Mlle Annette and whose real name was Anna Linder.[13] She was to Frédérick in his last years what Louise Read was to the aged Barbey d'Aurevilly: a devoted companion, secretary and nurse. It may be that she first came to him as a pupil, for he gave occasional private lessons; but we cannot be sure. It has so far proved impossible to find any trace of her outside the memoirs of Frédérick's friends and his own correspondence. But we can obtain some idea of the relationship between Frédérick and Annette from the affectionate letters he sent her in the summer of 1873, when, according to Henry Lecomte, she had 'left him temporarily out of an over-scrupulous regard for convention'. In the last of these letters, dated 24 August, he wrote:

> You must have been surprised and upset, my dear, not to have had a letter from me yesterday. I meant to go and see you, hoping to have finished moving in here. But the man did not come on Friday after all, and only left here last night at seven!
>
> I am most anxious not to draw people's attention to us at this time, but tomorrow is my name-day, and I should dearly love to spend it with you. Till tomorrow then. Think of me, saddened by all these delays. I kiss you as I love you, that is to say with all the tenderness of a father, a brother and a friend.

The flat into which he had just moved, and where Annette soon joined him, was at No. 15 Rue de Bondy (now Rue René Boulanger), next to the stage-door of the rebuilt Porte-Saint-Martin. The new managers of the theatre, Ritt and Larochelle, had announced that they intended to maintain the literary traditions of the Porte-Saint-Martin, and for their opening production in September 1873 they chose Hugo's *Marie Tudor*.[14] They also engaged Frédérick, as the last surviving representative of the Romantic theatre, to play the part of the old Jew. It was only a minor role, but the actor Silvain, who was present on the first night, remembered Frédérick's rendering of it all his life, particularly the superb gesture with which he accompanied his ironical plea for alms. Fifty years later, the *doyen* of the Comédie-Française wrote: 'Dumaine, Taillade and other famous players were acting with him: I have forgotten them. He had only to cross the stage to leave a brilliant trail which half a century has been unable to efface.'

Marie Tudor was less successful than had been hoped, with the result that the managers of the Porte-Saint-Martin—still maintaining the theatre's traditions as established by Harel—decided to abandon literary drama in favour of spectacular shows.

They accordingly commissioned Adolphe Dennery to adapt *Round the World in Eighty Days* for the stage, using special scenic effects, performing animals and dancing-girls. The old Romantic actor they had taken on in September was dismissed.

In January 1874 he reappeared in *Le Crime de Faverne* at the little Théâtre de Cluny, where he hurt his head badly one night during the madness scene. He opened in another run of the same play at the Théâtre des Arts on Christmas Eve that year. And on 22 January 1875, suffering from an affection of the mouth which made it difficult for him to speak, he gave his last performance as Maître Séraphin, and left the stage, never to return.[15]

His doctors diagnosed his trouble as aphthae caused by acidity, and prescribed a variety of remedies ranging from potassium to hemlock.[16] 'I am poisoning myself every day', Frédérick told his eldest son,[17] 'in order to go on living.' He pretended that there was nothing seriously wrong with him,[18] blaming the aphthae on an *homard à l'américaine* he had eaten, and telling his friends: 'I am not ill but injured, and you recover from injuries.'

He was injured in a different sense in November, when the Italian actor Ernesto Rossi opened at the Ventadour in Dumas's *Kean*, playing the role Frédérick had created so brilliantly nearly forty years before. There were indignant protests in the Press at this affront to the sick actor, and the *Sifflet*[19] came out with a black-edged issue declaring:

> Oh, Master, fear nothing!
> Your genius soars at too great a height for the black crows ever to reach it. Your name is carved in indestructible rock. Your glory is immortal. You shall not die.
> Oh, Master, fear nothing!
> They have tried to compare him with you. They have attempted to efface your memory. They have dared even that!
> They are fools or mercenaries!

Rossi himself was either very thick-skinned or genuinely good-hearted, for he took no notice of these attacks and went out of his way to do honour to the old French actor. A few hours before his opening performance he wrote to assure Frédérick that he would be thinking of him all the time he was on the stage,[20] adding: 'If by some happy chance you feel well enough, come: every door will open to Kean.' And a month later he called on the sick man and offered to organize a benefit for him at the Ventadour. Frédérick accepted.

It proved harder to recruit a sufficient number of eminent artists than Rossi had imagined: the 1873 fiasco had not been forgotten. Originally advertised for 9 January 1876, the benefit had to be postponed for a week and was then put off till the 30th. In the meantime Frédérick's condition had grown worse.[21]

His doctors now realized that he was suffering from a cancer of the tongue, but decided that he was too weak to withstand an operation. On the 23rd he took to his bed, where he lay for three days, gazing dully ahead and occasionally talking indistinctly to himself. Towards midday on the 26th, while posters advertising his benefit were going up all over Paris, he beckoned Annette, his sons and his daughter to come nearer, and gave them his blessing. Unable to speak, he mimed his love for them and his sorrow at leaving them in a last, expressive performance. At three o'clock he became delirious; at eight in the evening he died.

The body was embalmed the next day, and friends and colleagues flocked to the Rue de Bondy to pay their last respects to the dead man. His face was calm now, his eyes half-open, his hair spread in a grey halo over the pillow. Marie Laurent brought a wreath of immortelles and laid it on the bed.[22] There was a card attached bearing the names of Frédérick's greatest roles: Kean, Robert Macaire, Ruy Blas, Don César de Bazan and Richard Darlington.

On the 29th, the day of the funeral, crowds were massed in the Rue de Bondy from an early hour.[23] At midday the hearse set off on its journey to the church of Saint-Martin-des-Marais, where a Requiem Mass was celebrated, and then on to the Montmartre Cemetery. The streets were lined with people, and

Q

several thousand followed the funeral procession. The speeches at the graveside lasted for over an hour. Hugo bade a moving farewell to his old comrade and his greatest interpreter. Mounet-Sully recited a poem by Richepin, tore the manuscript into shreds and scattered them on the coffin. It was a splendid occasion.

But memories are short, the public fickle. Of the thousands who had applauded Frédérick on the stage, only one man, the faithful Henry Lecomte, troubled to go to the sale of his effects at the Hôtel Drouot three months later. And the actor's private papers, Robert Macaire's snuff-box, Ruy Blas's cloak and Don César's sword were knocked down by a contemptuous auctioneer for a few francs.

CONCLUSION

IT is often maintained that an actor is a mere interpreter, a sounding-board for the dramatist and a plaything for the public, of no importance except as an instrument of entertainment or instruction. That may be true in most instances, but it cannot be said of Frédérick Lemaître, for his achievement and significance transcend the limits of the stage and reach into the realms of history and literature.

In history, he has his place as the author and creator of *Robert Macaire*, the *Mariage de Figaro* of the nineteenth century, which did more than any other work to bring about the downfall of Louis-Philippe. But he was also the supreme personification of the Romantic spirit, embodying its fervent passion in Edgard de Ravenswood, its unbridled turbulence in Kean, its ambitious idealism in Ruy Blas. As Gautier rightly remarked,[1] he and Marie Dorval were 'the actors of an age which was passionate to the point of delirium, and they expressed all the turmoil, all the fever, all the fire of those times'.

In literature, he has left his mark on some of the most notable plays of the period. He collaborated with Balzac, Hugo and Lamartine in the writing or rewriting of several of their works, from *Mercadet* to *Toussaint Louverture*. Plays such as *Vautrin* and *Kean* were specially made to his measure. And as a perceptive historian of the Romantic theatre has pointed out,[2] if so many of the great Romantic heroes bear a strong family resemblance to one another, the responsibility is chiefly Frédérick's: consciously or unconsciously, the authors wrote their parts with him in view.

As an actor, he was generally considered to be superior to all his contemporaries in the theatre. Silvain, who saw Coquelin *aîné*, Salvini, Irving and Mounet-Sully playing the classics in their prime, judged them less impressive than the seventy-four-year old actor he had seen in the last revival of *Le Crime de Faverne*.[3] In England as well as in France he was regarded for years as the supreme exemplar of his profession; and Frank Archer has recorded[4] how, after the first performance of *The Bells*, Irving's American manager, Colonel Bateman, 'swore excitedly and fiercely that the acting was equal to Lemaître's'. Among earlier players, Kean was undoubtedly the closest in spirit and technique to Frédérick, but he lacked the Frenchman's comic gifts. As for Talma, whom the traditionalists set above Frédérick, just as in England they set Kemble above Kean, Hugo once compared him with the great Romantic actor in a surprisingly fair estimate of their respective merits.[5] He told Jules Claretie:

> Talma was possessed of classical beauty; Frédérick's beauty was entirely modern. Talma looked like a Greek or Roman statue; Frédérick looked like a man. Talma had no faults and completely dominated the crowds who listened to him; Frédérick was full of faults. Talma had a deep, sonorous, sepulchral voice; Frédérick had a hoarse, abominable voice, and also—the expression is one he used himself—a jaw that weighed a ton. Talma was successful straight away and died successful. On the other hand, one might say of Frédérick that in spite of all his triumphs he never achieved the great, undisputed success he deserved. Well, of those two men, Talma seemed the more comprehensive, and Frédérick was the greater. Talma was perfect, Frédérick was uneven. Talma always pleased, Frédérick sometimes shocked. But Frédérick had movements, words, cries which shook audiences to their very depths, and astonishing flashes of brilliance which completely transfigured him and revealed him in all the dazzling splendour of absolute greatness. In a word, Talma had the more talent and Frédérick had the more genius.

Apart from the fire and passion of his delivery, what Frédérick's contemporaries most admired about his acting was its immense range. Balzac paid an implicit tribute to it when he wrote *Vautrin*, which required Frédérick to change both his costume and his character in every act. Hugo, in his funeral oration at Frédérick's graveside,[6] declared: 'Aristophanes is complementary to Æschylus, and what really moves an audience is terror joined with laughter. Frédérick Lemaître had this double gift, and that is why he was the first of all the dramatic artists of his time.' And Gautier, who never tired of praising Frédérick's many-sided genius,[7] once wrote:

> A great actor must be able to laugh and to cry, to render all the aspects of the human soul, all the emotions of life: that was Garrick's distinctive ability, and it is Frédérick's too. He is awe-inspiring and ludicrous; he terrifies you and amuses you; he is afraid of nothing, not even triviality, for he knows that in a moment he can be sublime if he wishes. In fact, it is by playing the most widely different roles, from Robert Macaire to Ruy Blas, by covering the whole gamut of dramatic effects from top to bottom, that he has brought his art to its present perfection.

There is a story[8] that one day Marie Dorval reproached Frédérick with his wild excesses, and he replied: 'Bah! If I didn't live like that, I shouldn't be able to act like this!' He expounded the same idea in Dumas's *Kean*, where he had to say: 'I know that I'm killing myself with this life of drink and debauchery—but what else can I do? An actor has to experience all the passions of humanity to be able to express them. I study them in myself, and that way I get them off by heart.' His private life was certainly just as disorderly and tempestuous as Kean's, and both actors had ample opportunity to 'study the passions of humanity in themselves'. But that is not to say that Frédérick, any more than Kean, gave free rein to those passions on the stage. 'Study' is the operative word; and Frédérick's surviving scripts show that in fact he pored over every line of his parts, rehearsed every intonation, practised every entrance and exit. Only when he had mastered a part intellectually did he bring his emotions into play, first thinking and then feeling himself into his role, so that he became to all intents and purposes one with the character he was representing. Where Mounet-Sully used to talk of inspiration as 'a god descending on the actor', Frédérick defined it more crudely[9] as 'a happy disposition of the stomach, the equilibrium of the digestive faculties'. In his career

the god often descended, the stomach was often in a happy disposition. And then Ruy Blas shed genuine tears, Paillasse broke
out into a sweat of horror, and Richard Darlington put the fear
of death into the actress who played his wife.

In his own time Frédérick was regarded as a naturalistic
actor, who rejected the artificial conventions of the Comédie-
Française and the Boulevard du Crime in favour of a realistic
representation of human life. It is certain that he went to enormous pains to make his performances appear true-to-life in
every respect. He would go through his part before a play was
put into rehearsal, altering speeches and situations which struck
him as improbable. He took care to see that his costume fitted
the character he was supposed to represent, unlike such players
as Mlle Mars, who outraged her authors by insisting on wearing
expensive dresses she had bought, however unsuitable they
might be. Above all, he excelled in devising little realistic
touches, such as the way the poverty-stricken Georges de Germany unfolded his handkerchief at table as if it had been a napkin. But despite all this, no one today would describe his acting
as naturalistic, and his impassioned delivery and flamboyant
gestures would probably arouse only laughter in twentieth-
century audiences accustomed to understatement and under-
playing.

Yet it would be absurd to judge him in accordance with present-day theatrical fashion, or to condemn him because he would
burst most modern plays open at the seams. He belonged to
an ardent, extravagant age, and he behaved on and off the stage
like the true Romantic hero he was. 'In an unaffected, spontaneous way', says Banville,[10] 'he walked along the ignoble pave-
ment as one would walk along a red carpet; and it was not his
fault if he bought a cigar at a tobacconist's shop with a gesture
worthy of Achilles.' He entered naturally and gladly into the
poetry and passion of Romantic drama, and he put the same
poetry and passion into the lesser works he often had to perform, raising shoddy melodramas to heights undreamt of by
their authors. As Louis Ulbach said of his performance in *Le*

Crime de Faverne,[11] 'he introduced Shakespeare into a play by MM. Théodore Barrière and Beauvallet . . .'

No actor ever gave himself more whole-heartedly to his art. Despite his robust appearance, he was often ill, but he made it a point of honour never to fail his public. One writer[12] has told how, during the original run of *Robert Macaire*, 'he staggered from the Porte Saint-Martin to the Folies-Dramatiques, dragging himself along and leaning against the walls; once he had arrived at the little theatre, he played the long farce with frantic agility and frenzied gaiety; then he went home as he had come, weak and tottering, and fools thought that he was drunk.' And Frédérick himself once wrote[13] to a friend: 'I sacrifice everything to the theatre—everything, do you hear?—even my dearest interests!'

In return, the theatre gave him brief moments of glory and long periods of fatigue and disappointment. Like a ruthless mistress, it treated him cruelly and despotically, and he regarded it with a mixture of love and hatred. There still exists a sheet of paper[14] on which he carefully copied out the great tirade on the theatre from Dumas's *Kean*, as expressing his own feelings to perfection:

> Once you have set your foot on the fatal path of the theatre, you must follow it to the end, exhaust its joys and its sorrows, drain its cup and its chalice, drink its honey and its lees; you must finish as you began and die as you have lived—die as Molière died, to the sound of clapping, hisses and cheers! But if there is still time for you not to take that road, if you have not yet opened the gate, then do not enter . . . believe me, on my honour, believe me.
>
> FRÉDÉRICK LEMAITRE.

In the whole history of the theatre, there is no more moving document than that poignant, bitter testament of suffering.

BIBLIOGRAPHY

THE following list is a selection of the most useful or interesting works and articles consulted in the preparation of this biography. Unless otherwise stated, the books cited below were published in Paris.

ABRAHAM (Émile): *Les Acteurs et les Actrices de Paris*, 1858.

ALLEM (Maurice): *La Vie quotidienne sous le Second Empire*, Hachette, 1948.

ALMÉRAS (Henri d'): *La Vie Parisienne sous le règne de Louis-Philippe*, Albin Michel, 1911.

ARAGO (Jacques): *Physiologie de tous les théâtres de Paris*, 1841.

ARCHER (Frank): *An Actor's Notebooks*, London, Paul, n.d.

AUBRY (J.-E.): *Passe-temps de l'Entr'acte*, Roger, 1863.

AUGUSTIN-THIERRY (A.): *Mlle George*, Albin Michel, 1936.

BANVILLE (Théodore de): *Les Pauvres Saltimbanques*, Lévy, 1853.

BEAULIEU (Henri): *Les Théâtres du Boulevard du Crime*, Daragon, 1905.

BERTAUT (Jules): *Le Boulevard*, Flammarion, 1924.

BILLY (André): *Vie de Balzac*, Flammarion, 1944.

BOULENGER (Jacques): *Les Dandys*, Calmann-Lévy, 1932.

BRAZIER (Nicolas): *Chroniques des petits théâtres de Paris*, Rouveyre et Blond, 1883.

BURNAND (Robert): *La Vie quotidienne en France en* 1830, Hachette, 1943.

CAIN (Georges): *Anciens théâtres de Paris*, Fasquelle, 1906.

CARR (Philip): *Days with the French Romantics*, London, Methuen, 1932.

CARSE (Adam): *The Life of Jullien*, Cambridge, Heffer, 1951.

CLARETIE (Jules): *Profils de théâtre*, Gaultier-Magnier, 1902.

CLAUDIN (Gustave): *Mes Souvenirs*, Calmann-Lévy, 1884.

CLÉMENT-JANIN (P.): *Drames et comédies romantiques*, Le Goupy, 1928.

CLOUARD (Henri): *Alexandre Dumas*, Albin Michel, 1955.

COPPÉE (François): 'Frédérick Lemaître', *Journal*, 23 Jan. 1896.

CUSTINE (Marquis de): *Souvenirs et portraits*, Monaco, Rocher, 1956.

DASH (Comtesse): *Mémoires des autres*, Librairie illustrée, 1896.

DELACROIX (Eugène): *Correspondance générale*, Plon, 1936–45.

DELÉCLUZE (Étienne-Jean): *Journal*, Grasset, 1948.

— *Souvenirs de soixante années*, Bibliothèque contemporaine, 1862.

DESCOTES (Maurice): *Le Drame romantique et ses grands créateurs*, Presses Universitaires, 1955.

DISHER (Maurice Willson): *Blood and Thunder*, London, Muller, 1949.

DONVILLE (François de): *Frédérick Lemaître*, Baur, 1876.

DORVAL (Marie): *Lettres à Alfred de Vigny*, Gallimard, 1942.

DRAPER (E. W. M.): *The Rise and Fall of the French Romantic Drama*, London, Constable, 1923.

DUMAS (Alexandre): *Mes Mémoires*, Cadot, 1852–4.

DUVAL (Georges): *Frédérick Lemaître et son temps*, Clichy, 1876.

EVANS (David-Owen): *Le Théâtre pendant la période romantique*, Presses Universitaires, 1925.

FEBVRE (Frédéric): *Le Journal d'un comédien*, Ollendorff, 1896.

FLAUBERT (Gustave): *Correspondance*, Paris, Conard, 1926.

FONTANEY (Antoine): *Journal intime*, Presses françaises, 1925.

FORSTER (John): *The Life of Charles Dickens*, London, Chapman and Hall, 1893.

FOUCHER (Paul): *Entre cour et jardin*, Amyot, 1867.

— *Les Coulisses du passé*, Dentu, 1873.

FOURNEL (Victor): *Le Vieux Paris*, Tours, Mame, 1887.

GAUTIER (Théophile): *Histoire de l'art dramatique en France depuis vingt-cinq ans*, Hetzel, 1858–9.

— *Histoire du Romantisme*, Charpentier, 1874.

— *Portraits contemporains*, Charpentier, 1874.

— *Souvenirs de théâtre, d'art et de critique*, Charpentier, 1883.

— *Souvenirs romantiques*, Garnier, 1929.

GINISTY (Paul): *Le Mélodrame*, Michaud, 1910.

— *Le Théâtre romantique*, Morancé, 1922.

— *Les Anciens Boulevards*, Hachette, 1925 .

— *Bocage*, Alcan, 1932.

GOT (Edmond): *Journal*, Plon, 1910.

GOZLAN (Léon): *Balzac intime*, Librairie illustrée, 1886.

HARTOG (W. G.): *Guilbert de Pixérécourt*, Champion, 1913.

HEINE (Heinrich): *Chroniques de la Gazette d'Augsbourg*, Delpeuch, 1927.

HERVEY (Charles): *The Theatres of Paris*, London, Mitchell, 1847.

HOLDEN (W. H.): *The Pearl from Plymouth*, London, B. T. & G. Press, 1950.

HOSTEIN (Hippolyte): *Historiettes et souvenirs d'un homme de théâtre*, Dentu, 1878.

HOUSSAYE (Arsène): *Les Confessions*, Dentu, 1885–91.

HUGO (Adèle Foucher, Mme Victor): *Victor Hugo raconté par un témoin de sa vie*, Brussels, Lacroix, 1863.

HUGO (Victor): *Choses vues*, Ollendorff, n.d.

JAMES (William): *The Naval History of Great Britain*, London, Macmillan, 1902.

JANIN (Jules): *Deburau*, Gosselin, 1832.

—*Histoire de la littérature dramatique*, Michel Lévy, 1853–8.

KRACAUER (S.): *Offenbach*, London, Constable, 1937.

LAFERRIÈRE (Adolphe): *Souvenirs d'un jeune premier*, Dentu, 1884.

LANDOY (Roger): 'Frédérick Lemaître à Bruxelles', *Éventail de Bruxelles*, 27 Sept. 1925.

LEBRETON (André): *Le Théâtre romantique*, Boivin, n.d.

LECOMTE (L.-Henry): *Un Comédien au XIXe siècle: Frédérick Lemaître*, Chez l'auteur, 1888.

LEGOUVÉ (Ernest): *Soixante ans de souvenirs*, Hetzel, 1886–7.

LEMAÎTRE (Frédérick): *Souvenirs de Frédérick Lemaître, publiés par son fils*, Ollendorff, 1880. (This work was in fact written by Frédérick Lemaître *fils* but was largely based on Frédérick's verbal reminiscences: it is therefore a valuable source if used with caution.)

LYONNET (Henry): *Dictionnaire des comédiens français*, Geneva, Revue Internationale, n.d.

MAURICE (Charles): *Histoire anecdotique du théâtre*, Plon, 1856.

MAUROIS (André): *Olympio*, Hachette, 1954.

— *Les Trois Dumas*, Hachette, 1957.

MILATCHITCH (Douchan Z.): *Le Théâtre de Balzac*, Hachette, 1930.

— *Le Théâtre inédit de Balzac*, Hachette, 1930.

MIRECOURT (Eugène de): *Frédérick Lemaître*, Havard, 1855.

— *Bocage*, Havard, 1856.

MONTORGUEIL (Georges): 'La Vieillesse de Frédérick Lemaître', *Temps*, 20 Jan. 1926.

MOREAU (Pierre): *Le Romantisme*, del Duca, 1957.

MOSER (Françoise): *Marie Dorval*, Plon, 1947.

NEBOUT (Pierre): *Le Drame romantique*, Lecène-Oudin, 1895.

NISARD (Désiré): *Essais sur l'école romantique*, Calmann-Lévy, 1891.

NOZIÈRE (Fernand): *Madame Dorval*, Alcan, 1926.

OLIVIER (Juste): *Paris en 1830*, Mercure de France, 1951.

PÉRICAUD (Louis): *Le Théâtre des Funambules*, Sapin, 1897.

PLAYFAIR (Giles): *Kean*, London, Reinhardt and Evans, 1950.

PLUNKETT (Jacques de): *Fantômes et souvenirs de la Porte-Saint-Martin*, Ariane, 1946.

PONTMARTIN (Armand de): *Mes Mémoires*, Calmann-Lévy, 1885–6.

RÉMY (Tristan): *Jean-Gaspard Deburau*, L'Arche, 1954.

RICHARDSON (Joanna): *Rachel*, London, Reinhardt, 1956.

SAND (George): *Histoire de ma Vie*, Michel Lévy, 1856.

— *Correspondance inédite avec Marie Dorval*, Gallimard, 1953.

SCHNEIDER (Louis): 'Deux Amours de Frédérick Lemaître', *Temps*, 16–17 Aug. 1930.

SÉCHAN (Charles): *Souvenirs d'un homme de théâtre*, Calmann-Lévy, 1883.

SELIGMAN (Janet): *Figures of Fun*, London, O.U.P., 1957.

SILVAIN (Eugène): *Frédérick Lemaître*, Alcan, 1930.

SOUCHON (Paul): *Autour de Ruy Blas*, Albin Michel, 1939.

SOULAINE (Pierre) et BOISSON (Marius): 'Le Roi du Boulevard du Crime', *Excelsior*, 15 Mar.–29 Apr. 1938.

STARKIE (Enid): *Petrus Borel*, London, Faber, 1954.

STEAD (Philip John): *Vidocq*, London, Staples, 1953.

STENDHAL: *Racine et Shakespeare*, Le Divan, 1928.

SULLY (Jeanne): 'Frédérick Lemaître', *Amateur* (*Bruxelles*), Nov.–Dec. 1956.

THACKERAY (William Makepeace): *The Paris Sketch Book*, London, Smith, 1885.

TRAILLES (P. de): 'Frédérick Lemaître', *Gaulois*, 29 Jan. 1876.

TREILLE (Marguerite): *Le Conflit dramatique en France*, Picard, 1929.

TREWIN (J. C.): *Mr. Macready*, London, Harrap, 1955.

TROLLOPE (Frances): *Paris and the Parisians in 1835*, London, Bentley, 1836.

VACQUERIE (Auguste): *Profils et Grimaces*, Michel Lévy, 1856.

VIGNY (Alfred de): *Correspondance*, Conard, 1933.

NOTES

CHAPTER ONE

THE YOUNG LION

1. Lecomte, I, pp. 307–8. FL's own copy of the civil record, dated 21 July 1874, is in the Author's Collection.
2. Lecomte, I, p. 308; II, p. 318.
3. Lecomte, II, p. 319. FL's father was born 11 May 1768, his mother 26 Aug. 1777. They were married 6 Vendémiaire, Year III.
4. Letter to Coussin of 13 Germinal, Year XI (Lecomte, II, p. 319).
5. Lecomte, I, pp. 3–4.
6. Lecomte, II, p. 318.
7. James, III, p. 227.
8. Lemaître, pp. 26–7; also FL's unpublished memoirs (Fonds Rondel).
9. Lemaître, p. 150.
10. Ibid., pp. 29–30. Entry dated 16 June 1809 in the Register of Deaths, Folio 45, Commune of Le Havre.
11. Letter of 16 June 1809 (Municipal Archives of Le Havre).
12. Lecomte, I, pp. 4–5; also FL's unpublished memoirs (Fonds Rondel).
13. Lecomte, I, pp. 5–6.
14. FL's unpublished memoirs (Fonds Rondel).
15. Lemaître, pp. 57–67; Lecomte, I, pp. 6–7.
16. Lecomte, I, p. 7.
17. Ibid., p. 8.
18. Ibid., pp. 8–10; Lemaître, pp. 71–3; FL's unpublished memoirs (Fonds Rondel).

CHAPTER TWO

PANTOMIME AND TRAGEDY

1. The following details of the Boulevard du Temple are taken from Beaulieu, pp. 5–9; Brazier, I, pp. 13–49; Cain, pp. 1–28; Fournel, pp. 131–43; Ginisty, *Les Anciens Boulevards*, pp. 13–25.
2. Beaulieu, p. 174.
3. Péricaud, pp. 36–41.
4. Beaulieu, p. 40. The manager was Sallé of the Théâtre Patriotique.
5. Lecomte, I, p. 12.
6. Ibid., p. 13.
7. Descotes, pp. 18–19.
8. Péricaud, pp. 14–17; Rémy, pp. 18–24.
9. Péricaud, pp. 21–3.
10. Rémy, p. 60.
11. Ibid., pp. 37–8.
12. Fonds Rondel.
13. Lecomte, I, p. 15; Péricaud, p. 17.
14. Lecomte, I, p. 16.
15. Beaulieu, pp. 101–4.
16. Lecomte, I, pp. 17–23.
17. Ibid., pp. 24–5. On Talma, cf. Treille, pp. 71–2, and Descotes, pp. 27–9.
18. Lecomte, I, pp. 25–6.
19. Ibid., pp. 27–43.
20. Laferrière, II, p. 79.
21. Lecomte, I, pp. 38–9.
22. Mirecourt, *F. Lemaître*, p. 56.
23. Letter of 22 Sept. 1822 (Lecomte, I, p. 40).
24. Letter of 29 Sept. 1822 (Ibid., p. 41).
25. *Journal des Théâtres*, 6 Mar. 1823.
26. Lecomte, I, pp. 43, 309.

CHAPTER THREE

THE BOULEVARD DU CRIME

1. Cain, pp. 29–36.
2. Cf. Lecomte, I, pp. 47–57.
3. Ibid., p. 58.
4. Playfair, p. 158.
5. Cf. Lecomte, pp. 62–8.
6. Letter of 19 Nov. 1824 (Ibid., pp. 70–1).
7. Ibid., p. 72.
8. 12 May 1825. *Cagliostro* was first performed 9 May.
9. Lecomte, I, p. 79.
10. Péricaud, pp. 23, 43, 58; Rémy, pp. 60–1.
11. Lecomte, I, pp. 79, 309–10.
12. *Pandore*, 24 Nov. 1825. Cf. also Lecomte, I, pp. 80–3.
13. Letter of 7 Feb. 1826 (Fonds Rondel).
14. Lecomte, I, pp. 86–90.
15. Lemaître, p. 91.
16. Lecomte, I, p. 91. Cf. also Lemaître, p. 90.
17. Undated letter (Lecomte, II, p. 320).
18. Lecomte, I, pp. 91–2.
19. Ibid., p. 91; Lemaître, pp. 91–2.

CHAPTER FOUR

MARIE DORVAL

1. Descotes, pp. 33–5; Lemaître, p. 93.
2. Gautier, *Hist. du Romantisme*, p. 2.
3. Carr, p. 31; Moreau, p. 69.
4. Draper, pp. 86–90.
5. Stendhal, p. 9.
6. Carr, p. 71.
7. Dumas, XI, p. 105.
8. Carr, p. 73; Clouard, p. 66; Draper, p. 96.

9. Carr, p. 84.
10. Delacroix, I, p. 197.
11. Trewin, pp. 81–2.
12. *Journal des Débats*, 18 June 1804.
13. Ibid., 4 Apr. 1807.
14. Moser, pp. 1–8; Nozière, pp. 1–20.
15. Sand, *Hist. de ma Vie*, IV, p. 206.
16. Gautier, *Hist. de l'art dram.*, VI, p. 104.
17. Disher, p. 169.
18. Legouvé, II, pp. 28–30.
19. Ibid., II, p. 32.
20. Lecomte, I, pp. 108–9.
21. Janin, *Hist. de la litt. dram.*, VI, p. 156.
22. 4 Mar. 1827.
23. Lecomte, I, pp. 111–13; Lemaître, pp. 103–9.
24. Lemaître, II, p. 328; Lemaître, p. 109.
25. Undated (Fonds Rondel).
26. Letter of 8 Oct. 1827 (Fonds Rondel).
27. Gautier, *Hist. de l'art dram.*, VI, p. 104.
28. M. Francis Ambrière, who has devoted twenty years to a study of Dorval's life, informs the present author that he has found no proof that she and FL were lovers, though he thinks it probable that they were.
29. 26 Mar. 1828.
30. 27 Mar. 1828.
31. 27 Mar. 1828.
32. Nozière, p. 36.
33. Lecomte, I, pp. 121–2.
34. Letter of 25 July 1828 (Fonds Rondel). Misquoted and misdated in Lecomte, II, pp. 321–2.
35. Fonds Rondel. Misquoted in Lecomte, I, p. 122, and II, p. 322.
36. Letter from Chedel of 25 Aug. 1828 (Lecomte, I, p. 123).
37. Fonds Rondel. Misquoted in Lecomte, I, p. 124.
38. Letter of 16 Sept. 1828 (Fonds Rondel).
39. Not 29 Oct., as stated in Lecomte, I, p. 123. Cf. Letter from Montgenet to FL of 27 Sept. 1828 inviting him to a dinner in the green-room after the first performance (Fonds Rondel).
40. Carr, p. 44; Maurois, *Les Trois Dumas*, p. 50.
41. Lecomte, I, pp. 125–7; Lemaître, p. 101.

42. Undated letter (Author's Collection).
43. Letter signed Berthier, Lenoir (Lecomte, I, pp. 127–8).
44. Descotes, pp. 85–92; Lecomte, I, p. 128.
45. *Revue du Théâtre* (1834), II, p. 317.

CHAPTER FIVE

ROMANTIC VICTORY

1. Dumas, XII, p. 129.
2. Descotes, pp. 67, 81–4.
3. Maurois, *Les Trois Dumas*, p. 112.
4. Dumas, XII, p. 200.
5. Ibid., XII, p. 221.
6. *Revue de Paris* (1829), I, p. 233.
7. Dumas, XII, pp. 297–320.
8. Letter of 23 May 1829 from FL to various editors (Lecomte, I, pp. 138–9).
9. Lecomte, I, pp. 134–8.
10. On 10 Sept. 1829 (ibid., pp. 144–8).
11. Lecomte, I, pp. 151–2.
12. Ibid., pp. 153–9.
13. 26–27 Oct. 1829.
14. Cf. Descotes, pp. 119–35; Draper, pp. 153–9; Maurois, *Olympio*, pp. 178–83; Starkie, pp. 30–41.
15. Gautier, *Hist. du Romantisme*, pp. 99–114; Pontmartin, I, p. 137.
16. Hostein, pp. 127–8; Lecomte, I, pp. 161–2; Silvain, pp. 45–6.
17. Augustin-Thierry, p. 40.
18. Dumas, XXIII, pp. 6–7.
19. Maurice, II, p. 113.
20. Gautier, *Hist. de l'art dram.*, I, p. 50.
21. Descotes, pp. 173–4; Draper, p. 162; Dumas, XIV, pp. 195–208.

R

CHAPTER SIX

THE JULY REVOLUTION

1. Olivier, pp. 174–6.
2. Carr, p. 103.
3. Dumas, XV, pp. 40–52.
4. Ibid., XV, pp. 61–77.
5. Ibid., XV, p. 91.
6. Ginisty, *Les Anciens Boulevards*, p. 34; Moser, p. 37.
7. Ginisty, *Bocage*, pp. 32–4; Carr, p. 107.
8. Olivier, pp. 267–8; Dumas, XV, p. 94; Carr, pp. 107–8.

CHAPTER SEVEN

MADEMOISELLE GEORGE

1. Contract of 5 July 1830 (Lecomte, I, pp. 312–13).
2. Augustin-Thierry, pp. 119–26; Dumas, XIV, pp. 120–41.
3. 14 Aug. 1830.
4. 17 Aug. 1830.
5. *Causerie*, 23 Jan. 1859.
6. 11 Oct. 1830. Cf. Dumas, XVIII, pp. 192–3; Lecomte, I, pp. 164–5.
7. 6 Nov. 1830. Cf. Lecomte, I, pp. 165–6.
8. Ancelot's *Le Roi fainéant* (Descotes, p. 175).
9. Dumas, XVII, pp. 162–3.
10. Ibid., XVIII, p. 203.
11. Cain, pp. 54–6.
12. Dumas, XVIII, p. 203.
13. *Courrier des Théâtres*, 12 Jan. 1831.
14. Clouard, p. 138; Descotes, pp. 176–8; Dumas, XX, pp. 20–22; Lecomte, I, pp. 167–8.
15. *Corsaire*, 2 Feb. 1831.
16. Ginisty, *Le Mélodrame*, pp. 210–11.
17. *Corsaire*, 27 Jan. 1831.
18. Lecomte, I, p. 108.

19. Mirecourt, *Bocage*, p. 60.
20. Gautier, *Hist. du Romantisme*, pp. 167–8.
21. Descotes, p. 205.
22. Maurois, *Les Trois Dumas*, p. 98.
23. Mirecourt, *Bocage*, p. 59.
24. Descotes, pp. 219–22.
25. Foucher, *Les Coulisses du passé*, p. 374.
26. 21 June 1831 (Lecomte, I, pp. 170–1).
27. Ibid., p. 174.
28. Descotes, pp. 227–30; Draper, pp. 184–5; Dumas, XXII, pp. 163–204, XXIII, pp. 154–66; Lecomte, I, pp. 175–9.
29. Legouvé, pp. 31–2.
30. *Courrier des Théâtres*, 30 Nov. 1831.
31. Cain, p. 210.
32. Dumas, XIV, pp. 123–4.
33. Ibid., XXIII, p. 158.
34. *Artiste* (1831), II, p. 212.
35. Dumas, XXIII, pp. 160–1.
36. Legouvé, p. 32.
37. Got, I, pp. 98–101.
38. *Courrier des Théâtres*, 15 Dec. 1831.

CHAPTER EIGHT

CARNIVAL, PLAGUE AND RIOT

1. Cain, pp. 57–9; Fournel, p. 146.
2. Carr, pp. 149–51; Claudin, pp. 30–1; Kracauer, pp. 26–7.
3. Carr, pp. 151–2; Kracauer, p. 26.
4. L. Rellstab (Kracauer, p. 29).
5. Ibid.
6. Letter from Harel of 5 Jan. 1832 (Maurice, II, p. 30).
7. Dash, III, p. 130; Foucher, *Entre cour et jardin*, p. 503; Lecomte, I, pp. 180–4.
8. Cain, p. 208; Dumas, XIV, pp. 124–5; Ginisty, *Les Anciens Boulevards*, pp. 36–7; Houssaye, I, p. 171; Rémy, pp. 96–7; Starkie, pp. 57–9.

9. Dumas, XIV, p. 124.
10. Ibid., XXV, pp. 306–8.
11. Lemaître, pp. 124–5.
12. Letter of 30 Apr. 1832 (Lecomte, I, p. 186).
13. Letter of 2 May 1832 (ibid.).
14. Letter from Bocage to FL of 3 May 1832 (ibid., pp. 186–7) in reply to letter from FL to Bocage of the same date (Fonds Rondel).
15. The details of the 1832 insurrection are taken from Dumas, XXVII, pp. 100–257.
16. Lemaître, pp. 137–44.

CHAPTER NINE

LUCRÈCE BORGIA

1. First perf. 21 July 1832. Cf. Lecomte, I, pp. 187–8.
2. Dumas, XXVII, p. 288.
3. Ibid., XXVIII, pp. 245–76; Lecomte, I, pp. 189–91.
4. Descotes, p. 238; Lecomte, I, p. 192.
5. *Courrier des Théâtres*, 16 Sept. 1832.
6. Descotes, p. 239.
7. 29 Dec. 1832 (Lecomte, I, pp. 314–15).
8. Descotes, pp. 241–6.
9. Ibid., pp. 231, 239.
10. Descotes, pp. 247–52; Draper, pp. 189–90; Adèle Hugo, II, pp. 337–52; Lecomte, I, pp. 192–202; Maurois, *Olympio*, pp. 221–224.
11. Cf. the comparison of the two plays in Descotes, p. 248.
12. *Courrier des Théâtres*, 4 Feb. 1833.
13. Dumas, XXIV, pp. 69–211.
14. On 25 Apr. 1833 (Lecomte, I, pp. 201–2).
15. Descotes, p. 252.
16. Mirecourt, *F. Lemaître*, p. 48.
17. Hervey, pp. 305–6.
18. Ibid., p. 306.
19. Mirecourt. *F. Lemaître*, pp. 44–8; *Entr'acte*, 11 Oct. 1868; Trailles.

20. Letter of 29 Aug. 1833 (Vigny, I, p. 355).
21. Custine, p. 37; Lecomte, I, pp. 202–7; Lemaître, pp. 174–8.
22. Letter to Harel, of 2 July 1833 (Fonds Rondel).

CHAPTER TEN

ROBERT MACAIRE

1. Letter from Colonel Mathieu of 13 June 1833 (Author's Collection).
2. Letter of 18 July 1833 (Lecomte, I, pp. 208–9).
3. Letter of 26 July 1833 (ibid., p. 209).
4. Letter of 26 July 1833 (Lecomte, II, p. 325).
5. Lecomte, II, p. 328; Lemaître, p. 180.
6. Letter of 5 Sept. 1833 (Dorval, p. 61).
7. Lecomte, I, p. 216.
8. *Garde Nationale de Marseille* (Lecomte, I, pp. 211–212).
9. Letter to Cobière, editor of the *Journal du Havre*, in a private collection.
10. Letter of 24 Oct. 1833 (Lecomte, *Marie Dorval au Gymnase*, Paris, 1900, pp. 33–5).
11. 5 Dec. 1833 (Lecomte, I, p. 218).
12. Lemaître, pp. 146–9, where the incident is misdated.
13. Letter of 11 Nov. 1833 (Lecomte, II, pp. 325–6).
14. First perf. 6 Nov. 1833. Cf. Descotes, pp. 252–8; Draper, pp. 191–4.
15. First perf. 28 Dec. 1833. Cf. Descotes, pp. 258–9; Draper, pp. 195–6.
16. On 19 Dec. 1833. FL's diary is reproduced in Lecomte, I, pp. 218–20. The original document is in the Jeanne Sully collection.
17. Cf. Letters of 7 and 8 Mar. 1834 from Victor Bertrand and Louis Jourdan (Author's Collection).
18. Diary entry for 20 Feb. 1834 (Lecomte, I, p. 219).
19. Letter to FL from M. Alhoy of 15 Feb. 1834 (Lecomte, I, pp. 220–2).
20. Lecomte, I, p. 222; Lemaître, pp. 189–91.
21. Heine, pp. 122–3.

22. Lecomte, I, pp. 223–36.
23. Houssaye, II, p. 253.
24. Banville, pp. 70–1.
25. Claretie, pp. 59–60.
26. Houssaye, II, p. 253.
27. Ibid., p. 254.
28. Gautier, *Hist. de l'art dram.*, V, pp. 260–1.
29. Lecomte, II, p. 2.
30. Houssaye, II, p. 268.
31. Kracauer, p. 34.
32. Cain, pp. 59–60; Rémy, p. 130.
33. Letter of 1 May 1845 (Flaubert, I, p. 169).

CHAPTER ELEVEN

THE FRENCH KEAN

1. No. 2 Rue Gloriette, Pierrefitte. Bought on 8 Oct. 1834. Cf. Lecomte, I, p. 238; Lemaître, pp. 200–4.
2. Lecomte, I, pp. 238–40; Lemaître, pp. 205–11.
3. Letter of 5 Feb. 1835 (Fonds Rondel).
4. First perf. 12 Feb. 1835. Cf. Descotes, pp. 276–83; Draper, pp. 197–9.
5. 28 Apr. 1834.
6. First perf. 28 Apr. 1835. Cf. Descotes, pp. 284–93; Draper, p. 199.
7. Contract of 18 July 1835 (Lecomte, I, pp. 315–16).
8. Lecomte, I, pp. 241–2.
9. Ibid., p. 243.
10. *Gazette des Tribunaux*, 1 Jan. 1836; Lecomte, I, pp. 244–50.
11. Contract of 14 Jan. 1836 (Lecomte, I, pp. 316–18).
12. Letters of 16 and 18 Jan. 1836 (Fonds Rondel). Misquoted by Lecomte, I, p. 252, and Descotes, p. 306.
13. Atala Beauchêne (Louise Beaudoin) was born at Orléans on 20 Oct. 1814 and died at Lyons on 29 Mar. 1894. Cf. Schneider.
14. *La Rampe et les Coulisses*, 1832, pp. 176–7.
15. Letter of 19 Oct. 1836 (Lecomte, II, p. 326).

16. Letter of 16 Oct. 1852 (ibid., p. 327).
17. Deburau was arrested on 22 Apr. and tried on 21 May 1836. Cf. Péricaud, pp. 154–62; Rémy, pp. 138–41.
18. *Courrier des Théâtres*, 24 July 1836.
19. Letter of 3 Aug. 1836 (Lecomte, I, p. 261).
20. Thackeray, pp. 294–5.
21. Gautier, *Hist. de l'art dram.*, II, pp. 249–50.
22. Letter of 31 Aug. 1836 (Lecomte, I, p. 266).
23. Heine, pp. 148–9.
24. Soulaine et Boisson, 13 Apr. 1938; *Gazette*, 28 Jan. 1876; Mirecourt, *F. Lemaître*, p. 56.
25. Péricaud, p. 187.
26. *Colombine*, 8 Oct. 1894.
27. Mirecourt, *F. Lemaître*, pp. 56–60.
28. Gautier, *Hist. de l'art dram.*, II, p. 250.

CHAPTER TWELVE

RUY BLAS

1. *Don Juan de Marana*, 30 Apr. 1836 (Descotes, pp. 303–4); *Caligula*, 26 Dec. 1837 (ibid., pp. 311–14).
2. Descotes, pp. 331–4; Richardson, pp. 19–24.
3. Carse, p. 31; Kracauer, pp. 36–40.
4. Gautier, *Hist. de l'art dram.*, I, p. 103.
5. *Revue de Paris* (1839), VIII, pp. 226–7.
6. Draper, p. 202.
7. Adèle Hugo, II, p. 393.
8. Letter from Dumanoir of 26 Sept. 1837 (Lecomte, I, pp. 274–5).
9. Contract of 14 May 1838 (Lecomte, I, pp. 320–1).
10. *Psyché*, 8 Sept. 1836.
11. Descotes, pp. 318–24; Lecomte, I, p. 279–95.
12. Letter of 15 Aug. 1838 (Souchon, p. 71).
13. Letter of 19 Aug. 1838 (ibid., pp. 76–7).
14. Letter of 4 Sept. 1838 (ibid., p. 96).
15. Adèle Hugo, II, pp. 395–6; Lecomte, I, pp. 280–1.
16. Clément-Janin, pp. 72–3; Descotes, pp. 321–2.

17. Gautier, *Hist. de l'art dram.*, I, p. 194.
18. Adèle Hugo, II, p. 399.
19. G. Planche, *Revue des Deux Mondes*, 15 Aug. 1838; J. Sandeau, *Revue de Paris* (1838), LIX, p. 197. For other notices of *Ruy Blas*, cf. Lecomte, I, pp. 290–2.
20. Undated letter (Bibliothèque Nationale).
21. Descotes, p. 324.
22. Lecomte, I, pp. 294–5.
23. Adèle Hugo, II, pp. 399–400; Lecomte, I, pp. 296–7.
24. Letter from FL to Joly of 14 Dec. 1838 (Fonds Rondel).
25. 10 Apr. 1839. Cf. Lecomte, I, pp. 298–303.
26. *Revue de Paris* (1839), IV, p. 136.
27. Lecomte, I, pp. 303–4; Schneider.
28. Fonds Rondel.
29. Letter of 24 June 1839 (Lecomte, I, p. 304).
30. Contract of 5 Dec. 1839 (ibid., pp. 321–2).

CHAPTER THIRTEEN

BALZAC

1. Billy, II, pp. 12–13.
2. Gautier, *Souvenirs romantiques*, pp. 176–7.
3. Milatchitch, *Le Théâtre de Balzac*, p. 78.
4. Billy, II, pp. 32–3.
5. Milatchitch, *Le Théâtre de Balzac*, p. 76.
6. Ibid., p. 104.
7. Fonds Rondel. Cf. also Stead, p. 170.
8. Lemaître, pp. 245–6.
9. E. Arago, *Avenir national*, 5 Apr. 1869.
10. Gozlan, p. 51.
11. Milatchitch, *Le Théâtre de Balzac*, p. 84.
12. Lemaître, pp. 247–8.
13. Gozlan, p. 55.
14. *Journal des Débats*, 16 Mar. 1840.
15. *Presse*, 18 Mar. 1840.
16. Lecomte, II, p. 11.

17. Schneider.
18. Billy, II, p. 36.
19. Lecomte, II, pp. 10–11.
20. Lemaître, pp. 251–2.
21. Ibid., pp. 242–3.
22. *Moniteur universel,* 26 Oct. 1868.
23. Billy, II, pp. 10–11; Lemaître, pp. 238–9.
24. Milatchitch, *Le Théâtre inédit de Balzac,* p. 116.
25. Lecomte, II, pp. 15–16.
26. Letter of 11 June 1840 (Author's Collection).
27. Undated letter of July 1840 (Fonds Rondel).

CHAPTER FOURTEEN

TO ENGLAND

1. Lecomte, II, p. 17.
2. First perf. 3 Apr. 1841. Cf. Lecomte, II, pp. 19–29.
3. Gautier, *Hist. de l'art dram.,* II, p. 112.
4. Contract of 23 Mar. 1841 (Lecomte, II, pp. 352–4).
5. Lecomte, II, p. 33.
6. Really Clarisse Midroy. Cf. Hostein, pp. 166–7; Lecomte II, pp. 32–3, 330–3; Schneider.
7. Gautier, *Hist. de l'art dram.,* II, p. 99.
8. Letter to FL of 22 July 1842 (Lecomte, II, p. 38).
9. Richardson, p. 58.
10. Lecomte, II, pp. 44–5.
11. Descotes, pp. 324, 337.
12. Lecomte, II, pp. 45–50; Legouvé, pp. 33–5.
13. Lecomte, II, p. 48; Milatchitch, *Le Théâtre de Balzac,* pp. 232–3.
14. Lecomte, II, pp. 49–50.
15. Ibid., p. 49.
16. Gautier, *Hist. de l'art dram.,* III, pp. 244–5.
17. Ibid., p. 245
18. Lecomte, II, pp. 58–60.
19. *Gazette,* 28 Jan. 1876.
20. Mirecourt, *F. Lemaître,* pp. 81–4.

21. Duval, pp. 217–20.
22. Trewin, pp. 205–6.
23. Contract with John Mitchell of 21 Dec. 1844 to give 12 performances at the St. James's from 17 Feb. to 15 Mar. 1845 (Lecomte, II, pp. 354–5).
24. *Illustrated London News*, 15 Feb. 1845.
25. Ibid., 22 Feb. 1845. ·
26. Ibid., 1 Mar. 1845.
27. Queen Victoria's diary for 24 Feb. 1845 (Royal Library, Windsor).
28. Ibid., 3 Mar. 1845. Cf. also *I.L.N.* of 8 Mar. 1845.
29. Lecomte, II, p. 61.
30. *I.L.N.*, 15 Mar. 1845.
31. Queen Victoria's diary for 10 Mar. 1845 (Royal Library, Windsor).
32. *I.L.N.*, 22 Feb. 1845.
33. Letter from Adelbert Gaules (Author's Collection).
34. Letter of 10 Oct. 1845 (Lecomte, II, p. 64).

CHAPTER FIFTEEN

ROMANTIC DECLINE

1. FL played his first season in Brussels from Sept. to Oct. 1842, his second from Mar. to Apr. 1845. On his visits to Belgium cf. Landoy.
2. Letter of 7 June 1845 to Fleury, manager of the Lyons theatres (Lecomte, II, pp. 62–3).
3. Lecomte, II, p. 63.
4. Moser, p. 220.
5. Ibid.
6. Gautier,*Hist. de l'art dram.*, IV, p. 149; Nozière, p. 114.
7. Hervey, p. 321.
8. Cutting in the Fonds Rondel.
9. First perf. 7 Mar. 1846. Cf. Lecomte, II, pp. 67–71.
10. First perf. 25 July 1846. Cf. Lecomte, II, pp. 73–6.
11. *Illustrated London News*, 23 Jan. 1847.
12. Queen Victoria's diary for 12 Feb. 1847 (Royal Library, Windsor).

13. Ibid., 18 Feb. 1847.
14. 6 Feb. 1847.
15. Alméras, pp. 32–3; Lecomte, II, p. 79.
16. Gautier, *Hist. de l'art dram.*, V, pp. 83–4.
17. Cf. Disher, pp. 170–1.
18. Lecomte, II, p. 89.
19. Ibid., pp. 99–100.
20. First perf. 25 July 1848. Cf. Lecomte, II, pp. 103–15.
21. Letter to Mme Hanska (Maurois, *Olympio*, p. 351).
22. Silvain, pp. 85–7; Vacquerie, pp. 300–18.
23. Lecomte, II, pp. 101–3, 116–21.
24. Péricaud, pp. 285–7; Rémy, pp. 197–203.
25. Lecomte, II, p. 73.
26. Hugo, I, p. 237.
27. Ibid., pp. 43–4.
28. Claretie, pp. 240–1.
29. Hugo, I, p. 237.
30. Nozière, p. 122.
31. Moser, p. 232.
32. Descotes, p. 337; Moser, pp. 232–8.
33. Silvain, p. 87.

CHAPTER SIXTEEN

DEATH OF THE BOULEVARD

1. Lecomte, II, pp. 126–45.
2. Houssaye, II, pp. 371–2.
3. Lecomte, II, pp. 147–53.
4. FL performed in Brussels from 17 May to 5 June (Landoy).
5. From 14 Jan. to 15 Feb. 1852 (ibid.).
6. Queen Victoria's diary for 22 Mar. 1852 (Royal Library, Windsor).
7. *Illustrated London News*, 20 Mar. 1852.
8. Queen Victoria's diary for 2 Apr. 1852 (Royal Library, Windsor).
9. Lecomte, II, pp. 155–6.

10. Ibid., p. 163. On *Taconnet*, by Béraud and Clairville.
11. First perf. 9 May 1853. Cf. Lecomte, II, pp. 173–8.
12. Gautier, *Hist. de l'art dram.*, IV, p. 306 (article of 3 Aug. 1846).
13. First perf. 21 Apr. 1854. Cf. Lecomte, II, pp. 179–82.
14. Hervey, p. 321.
15. Letter of Jan. 1852 (Fonds Rondel).
16. Lecomte, II, pp. 182–3; Schneider.
17. 10 Oct. 1854. Cf. Lecomte, II, p. 328; Soulaine et Boisson, 23 Apr. 1938; FL's accounts in the Fonds Rondel.
18. Lecomte, II, p. 183.
19. Archer, p. 303.
20. Forster, pp. 468–9.
21. Augustin-Thierry, p. 181.
22. Letter of 17 Feb. 1856 in a private collection.
23. Laferrière, pp. 19–24; Lecomte, II, p. 186.
24. First perf. 30 Apr. 1857. Cf. Lecomte, II, pp. 187–92.
25. Lecomte, II, p. 193.
26. First perf. 10 Mar. 1859. Cf. Lecomte, II, pp. 198–205.
27. First perf. 28 Dec. 1859. Cf. Lecomte, II, pp. 205–7.
28. Febvre, I, pp. 75–7.
29. Letter of 6 Apr. 1861 (Author's Collection).
30. Lecomte, II, pp. 196–7.
31. Died 9 May 1860 (ibid., p. 208).
32. Allem, pp. 16–17; Cain, pp. 148–53; Péricaud, pp. 490–7.

CHAPTER SEVENTEEN

THE OLD LION

1. First perf. 16 Aug. 1862. Cf. Lecomte, II, pp. 211–13.
2. Letter to FL from Walewski of 24 Feb. 1863 (Lecomte, II, p. 213).
3. Fonds Rondel.
4. First perf. 6 Apr. 1864. Cf. Lecomte, II, pp. 217–22.
5. *Journal*, 23 Jan. 1896.
6. Lecomte, II, pp. 178–9.
7. Undated letter from L. Léger (Author's Collection).

8. Letter of 26 Aug. 1864 (Lecomte, II, p. 223).
9. Lecomte, II, p. 222.
10. Febvre, I, pp. 74–5.
11. Fonds Rondel.
12. Augustin-Thierry, p. 187.
13. Holden, pp. 89–93.
14. Kracauer, pp. 257–65.
15. First perf. 13 June 1867. Cf. Lecomte, II, pp. 225–33.
16. Foucher, *Entre cour et jardin*, p. 509.
17. Letter in the Author's Collection.
18. *Lune*, 16 June 1867.
19. Lecomte, II, pp. 344–5.
20. First perf. 6 Feb. 1868. Cf. Lecomte, II, pp. 233–9.
21. Cain, p. 172.
22. Letter of 14 Feb. 1868 (Lecomte, II, p. 330).
23. First perf. 28 Sept. 1868. Cf. Lecomte, II, p. 240; also undated note from FL to manager (Fonds Rondel).
24. Undated letter (Fonds Rondel).
25. Lecomte, II, pp. 240–1.
26. Ibid., pp. 241–2.
27. On 1 Apr. 1869. Cf. Lecomte, II, pp. 243–4; Milatchitch, *Le Théâtre de Balzac*, pp. 96–8.
28. Lecomte, II, pp. 248–9.
29. First perf. 24 Feb. 1870. Cf. Lecomte, II, pp. 251–5.
30. Lecomte, II, pp. 255–7.
31. Ibid., p. 333; Schneider.

CHAPTER EIGHTEEN

LAST YEARS

1. Lecomte, II, p. 258.
2. Ibid., pp. 259–60.
3. Letter of 14 Dec. 1870 (Fonds Rondel).
4. Lecomte, II, p. 262.
5. Cf. Letter from the valuer Dhios of 9 June 1870 (Author's Collection).

6. Nozière, *Avenir*, 22 Jan. 1926.
7. First perf. 30 Mar. 1872. Cf. Lecomte, II, pp. 264–7.
8. Letter from Plouvier of 16 July 1872 (Lecomte, II, p. 268).
9. Cf. the threatening letters to FL from the Nat. Johnston firm of wine-merchants at Bordeaux (Author's Collection).
10. To Étienne Charavay, who paid him a total of 450 francs. Cf. Charavay's letters to FL of Dec. 1872 (Fonds Rondel).
11. First perf. 28 Feb. 1873. Cf. Lecomte, II, pp. 270–1.
12. Lecomte, II, pp. 272–9.
13. Ibid., pp. 280–4.
14. First perf. 27 Sept. 1873. Cf. Lecomte, II, p. 287; Silvain, p. 4.
15. Lecomte, II, p. 288.
16. Letters from FL to FL *fils* of 31 July, 30 Sept., 4 Oct. 1875 (Fonds Rondel). The long 'letter' published by FL *fils* in Lemaître, pp. 10–13, is an amalgam of these and other letters.
17. Letter of 31 July 1875 (Fonds Rondel).
18. Duplessis, *Gazette*, 28 Jan. 1876.
19. Leader signed: Raoul Dral (*Sifflet*, 21 Nov. 1875).
20. Letter of 9 Nov. 1875 (Lecomte, II, p. 289).
21. Duval, *Événement*, 29 Jan. 1876; Lecomte, II, p. 293; Punch, *Événement*, 28 Jan. 1876.
22. *Liberté*, 29 Jan. 1876.
23. Archer, pp. 305–6; Dossier 126861 : 6059 at the Préfecture de Police; *Gazette*, 30 Jan. 1876; *Rappel*, 31 Jan. 1876; Lecomte, II, pp. 295–303.

CONCLUSION

1. Silvain, p. 101.
2. Descotes, p. 346.
3. Silvain, p. 4.
4. Archer, p. 291.
5. Claretie, pp. 50–1.
6. Lecomte, II, p. 296.
7. Gautier, *Hist. de l'art dram.*, III, p. 229.
8. *Gaulois*, 12 Dec. 1897.
9. Febvre, p. 81.

10. Banville, *Mes Souvenirs*, Charpentier, 1882, p. 200.
11. Silvain, p. 105.
12. Banville, *Mes Souvenirs*, p. 200.
13. Letter to A. Joly of 19 Oct. 1843 (Lecomte, II, pp. 305–6).
14. Fonds Rondel.

INDEX

Académie Française, 206
Adélaïde d'Orléans, 82
Adieux du Boulevard du Temple, Les, 222
Æschylus, 245
Aguado, Alexandre, 154
Alexander I, Emperor of Russia, 72
Alexander II, Emperor of Russia, 228
Alexandre, Charles, 211
Alhoy, Maurice, 123, 137
Almanach des Spectacles, L', 36
Ambigu-Comique, Théâtre de l', Paris, 23, 34, 36, 46, 54, 66, 98, 102, 121, 133, 186; FL at, 35, 37–45, 67–8, 184, 217–18, 221, 225, 227, 230–2, 235, 237
Angèle (Dumas, Anicet-Bourgeois), 134–5
Angelo, tyran de Padoue (Hugo), 148, 161, 171
Angoulême, Louis-Antoine de Bourbon, Duc d', 75
Anicet-Bourgeois, Auguste, 113, 134, 198
Annales, Les, 57
Anthony of Padua, St., 85
Antier, Benjamin, 37, 38, 40, 67, 123, 137
Antony (Dumas), 91–3, 147
Apollon, Café d', Paris, 24
Arago, Étienne, 79, 80, 108
Archbishopric of Paris, 81
Archer, Frank, 218, 244
Aristophanes, 244
Arsenal, Bibliothèque de l', Paris, 59, 113
Arts, Théâtre des, Paris, 240
Astley, Philip, 30
Auber, Daniel-François, 47
Audinot (manager), 35

Audinot, Nicolas-Médard, 23, 24
Augier, Émile, 210
Auxerre, FL at, 145
Avare, L' (Molière), 182

Balzac, Honoré de, 147, 173, 174–83, 198, 203, 211, 237, 243, 244; on FL, 177, 180, 188, 204; FL on, 181, 183, 232
Banquet d'Anacréon (Paris restaurant), 125
Banville, Théodore de, 139, 246
Baptiste (Paul-Eustache Anselme), 59
Barba, Gustave, 151–2
Barber of Seville, The (Rossini), 196
Barbey d'Aurevilly, Jules, 229, 232, 238
Baron (Fay), 39
Barrière, Théodore, 230, 247
Barye, Antoine-Louis, 122
Bassano, Hugues-Bernard Maret, Duc de, 91
Ba-ta-clan (Offenbach, Halévy), 220
Bateman, Hezekiah Linthicum, 244
Baude, Jean-Jacques, 78
Bayonne, FL at, 135
Beauchêne, Atala (Louise Beaudoin), 153–5, 164, 166, 167–8, 172, 190
Beauharnais, Hortense de, Queen of Holland, 111
Beaumarchais, Pierre-Augustin Caron de, 137, 140, 171
Beaumarchais, Théâtre, Paris, 200
Beauvallet, Frantz, 237
Beauvallet, Léon, 230, 247
Beauvallet, Pierre-François, 187
Beauvoir, Roger de (Roger de Bully), 154, 169
Beethoven, Ludwig van, 49, 104
Belleville, Théâtre de, Paris, 236
Bellevue, FL at, 220

S

Belloy, Auguste, Marquis de, 176
Bells, The (Lewis), 244
Béranger, Pierre-Jean de, 76
Béraud, Antony, 59
Berline de l'émigré, La, 150
Berlioz, Hector, 50
Berry, Marie-Caroline des Deux-Siciles, Duchesse de, 111–12
Bertram (Mathurin), 60
Bertrand, Nicolas-Michel, 24, 27, 28, 29, 44, 156, 206; on FL, 30
Besançon, FL at, 129
Beudin, Jacques, 53, 94
Billion, Charles-Louis, 206
Bismarck-Schönhausen, Otto Eduard Leopold, Prince von, 228
Blanchard (mime), 28–9
Blanche, Dr. Émile, 231
Bocage (Pierre Touzé), 92–3, 107, 114, 122, 126, 135, 164; compared to FL, 92, 94, 115
Bonaparte, Prince Louis-Napoleon, 111, 146, 205, 206, 213, 234 (see also Napoleon III)
Bonaparte, General Napoleon, see Napoleon I
Bonnassieux, Jean-Marie, 195
Bordeaux, FL at, 135
Bordeaux, Henri-Charles-Ferdinand, Duc de, 83, 111
Borel, Petrus, 69, 122
Bosquet (Paris café-theatre), 24
Bouchardy, Joseph, 220
Bouffé, Hugues-Désiré, 45
Bouffes-Parisiens, Théâtre des, Paris, 220, 228
Boulanger, Clément, 122
Boulanger, Frédéric, 46
Boulanger, Julie, née Hallignier, 46
Boulanger, Louis, 122, 178
Boulet (National Guardsman), 81
Bourdais, Marie, 51
Bourmont, Louis de Ghaisnes, Comte de, 76, 78
Bourse, Paris, 79, 123
Bricard (café proprietor), 24
Bride of Woe, The, 193
Brussels, FL in, 196, 212, 213
Buloz, François, 195
Burgraves, Les (Hugo), 187
Byron, George Gordon, sixth Lord, 49

Cabet, Charles, 133–4
Cabinet des Gentilshommes (Paris café), 28
Cain, Georges, 230
Calais, FL at, 58, 59
Caligula (Dumas), 161
Callot, Jacques, 189
Carrel, Armand, 76
Cartouche (Louis-Dominique Bourguignon), 123
Caruel-Marido (manager), 66–7
Catherine II, Empress of Russia, 72
Cavaignac, General Louis-Eugène, 84, 142, 203
Cavé, Edmond-Ludovic-Auguste, 181, 182
Cazot, Nicolas-Joseph, 89
Célestins, Théâtre des, Lyons, 196
Cenci, Francesco, 126
Centenaire, Le (Dennery, Plouvier), 237
Cent et un Robert Macaire, Les (Daumier), 141
Châlons, FL at, 145
Champfleury (Jules Husson), 141, 205
Chant du départ, Le, 202
Charivari, Le, 142
Charles X, King of France, 60, 64, 65, 75–8, 82–3, 88, 201
Chateaubriand, François-René, Vicomte de, 49, 140
Châtiments, Les (Hugo), 234
Chatterton (Vigny), 97, 147
Chaudes-Aigues, Jacques-Germain, 169
Chevet (caterer), 122
Chiarigny, Félix, 44
Chiffon-né de par ici, Le (Jouhaud, Dutertre, Robin), 200
Choiseul - Praslin, Altarice - Rosalba - Fanny, Duchesse de, 201
Christine (Dumas), 61, 71–4, 134
Ciceri, Pierre, 126
Cigale et la Fourmi, La (La Fontaine), 221
Cinna (Corneille), 162
Cirque-Olympique, Théâtre du, Paris, 30, 88, 223
Claretie, Jules, 140, 207, 244
Clarisse, Mlle, see Miroy
Clement VIII, Pope, 127
Clément (actor), 159
Cluny, Théâtre de, Paris, 240
Cogniard, Hippolyte, 185, 186, 190, 200, 202

Cogniard, Théodore, 185, 186, 190, 200, 202, 205
Coisy (correspondent), 45
Collins, Wilkie, 217–19, 232
Comédie-Française, 26, 48, 50, 63, 66, 67, 69, 72, 91, 115, 126, 135, 147–9, 161, 164, 208, 239; and FL, 61, 141, 150, 182–3, 186–7, 195, 210, 212, 246
Comte, Théâtre, Paris, 26
Conservatoire, Paris, 30, 31, 33, 37, 47, 51, 166
Constitutionnel, Le, 113, 114, 147, 212
Coppée, François, 225
Coquelin, Constant, 238, 243
Coraly (dancer), 60
Corneille, Pierre, 162, 169
Corsaire, Le, 42, 43, 87
Couder (manager), 102
Courcy, Frédéric de, 153
Courrier des Théâtres, Le, 42, 43, 95
Coussin *père* (decorator), 15, 17
Coussin *fils* (architect), 145, 149
Covent Garden, Theatre Royal, London, 26, 187
Cromwell, Preface to (Hugo), 50–1
Crosnier, François-Louis, 92, 94, 109
Curtius (Curtz), 24
Custine, Astolphe, Marquis de, 126–8
Cuvelier de Trye, Antoine, 31

Dante Alighieri, 122
Dartois, Armand, 101
Daumier, Honoré, 84, 137, 141, 142
David d'Angers, Pierre-Jean, 119
Deburau, Jean-Charles, 222
Deburau, Jean-Gaspard, *alias* Baptiste, 28, 29, 44, 155–6, 205–6, 214
Deburau, Philippe, 28
Decamps, Alexandre-Gabriel, 122
Deed of Horror, The, 193
Delacroix, Eugène, 49, 50, 122
Delafosse, Isidore, 95
Delaistre, Jean-Marie, 90, 136
Délassements-Comiques, Théâtre des, Paris, 223
Delaunay, Joseph-Charles, 51
Delavigne, Casimir, 65, 66, 86, 115
Dennery, Adolphe (Adolphe Philippe), 183, 189–90, 196, 212, 214, 237, 240
Deschamps, Émile, 61
Deslandes, Paulin, 228

Desnoyers, Charles, 217
Devéria, Eugène, 70
Dickens, Charles, 30, 217–19
Dijon, FL at, 145
Dik-Rajah, 116
Dinaux (Goubaux, Beudin), 53
Dôle, FL at, 145
Doligny, Alcide, 95
Don Juan (Molière), 187
Don Juan de Marana (Dumas), 161, 163
Dorval, Allan (Louis-Étienne Allan), 51
Dorval, Caroline, 51
Dorval, Gabrielle, 51
Dorval, Louise, 51
Dorval, Marie, *née* Delaunay, 71, 88, 92–3, 94, 95, 97, 147–9, 153, 161, 164; early life, 51; and FL, 52–4, 56–60, 65, 68, 126–8, 131–2, 134, 186–7, 196–7, 209, 243, 245; FL on, 132, 209; death, 205, 207–9
Drouet, Juliette (Julienne Gauvin), 118, 134, 153, 164, 165–6
Drouot, Hôtel, Paris, 242
Drury Lane, Theatre Royal, London, 26, 187
Ducange, Victor, 53, 56, 80
Ducis, Jean-François, 49, 87, 146, 192, 193
Dulong, Jules, 45
Dumaine, Louis-François, 239
Dumanoir (Philippe-François Pinel), 189–90, 214
Dumas, Adolphe, 131–3
Dumas, Alexandre, *père*, 50, 51, 59, 62–4, 68, 71–4, 80, 85–6, 88, 104–5, 108, 121–3, 134–5, 161, 163–4, 174, 187, 245, 247; on FL, 87, 91, 95–6, 106, 107, 158; and FL, 89–92, 94–7, 106–7, 113–15, 117, 122, 128, 153, 156–60, 171, 195, 203, 213, 236, 240; and Dorval, 92–3, 95, 126, 147, 197, 208
Dumas, Alexandre, *fils*, 210
Dumas, General Thomas-Alexandre, 88
Dupuis, Adèle, 36
Duval, Georges, 191

École des Ménages, L' (Balzac), 174–5
Edmond (actor), 89

Empis (Adolphe-Dominique Simonis), 87
Egypt, Pasha of, 49
Emilia Galotti (Lessing), 45
Épi-Scié, Café de l', Paris, 24
Eugénie Grandet (Balzac), 181
Eugénie-Marie de Montijo de Guzman, Empress of the French, 220, 222, 231
Événement, L', 238

Fabien (Jean Jacques), 24, 29
Faucit, Helen, 191–3
Febvre, Frédéric, 227
Fechter, Charles Albert, 231
Ferrier, Ida (Marguerite Ferrand), 135, 164, 165, 171
Feydeau, Théâtre, Paris, 59
Fieschi, Giuseppe, 143
Fifteen Years of a Drunkard's Life (Jerrold), 52
Figaro, Le, 54, 57, 87, 231
Fille de Mme Angot, La (Clairville, Lecocq), 238
Firmin (François Becquerelle), 48, 63, 64, 71, 91, 122, 195
Firmin (minor actor), 37–9
Flaubert, Gustave, 93, 144, 152, 177
Folies-Dramatiques, Théâtre des, Paris, 136, 139, 145, 149, 222–3, 228, 238, 247
Fonbonne, Joseph-Philippe, 124–5
Fontaney, Antoine, 104
Foucher, Paul, 228
Fourberies de Scapin, Les (Molière), 187
Fournier, Charles, 210
Fournier, Marc, 212
Foy, General Maximilien-Sébastien, 76
France Dramatique, La, 151
Franconi, Antonio, 30
Franconi, Henri, 30
Franconi, Laurent, 30, 32, 34, 35, 39
Fresnoy (Jean Audeville), 34, 36
Funambules, Théâtre des, Paris, 24, 159, 206, 222–3; FL at, 26–30, 214; Deburau at, 28–9, 44, 155–6, 205, 214

Gaillardet, Frédéric, 105–6
Gaîté, Café de la, Paris, 57
Gaîté, Théâtre de la, Paris, 23, 36, 88, 98, 185–6, 187, 190, 212, 215, 220, 222–3

Garrick, David, 169, 245
Gaudon (showman), 23
Gaule et France (Dumas), 121
Gaule poétique, La (Marchangy), 117
Gautier, Théophile, 48, 63, 70, 71, 72, 163, 168, 171, 175, 186; on Dorval, 52, 56, 92, 197, 243; on FL, 56, 141, 158, 160, 169, 179, 184, 189, 197, 199–200, 215, 243, 245; and FL, 182, 197, 203, 237
Geffroy, Edmond-Aimé-Florentin, 195
Gentil de Chavagnac, Adolphe-Michel, 34
Geoffroy, Julien-Louis, 51, 183
George, Mlle (Marguerite-Joséphine Weymer), 73, 104, 122, 134, 219; and Harel, 72, 85–90, 94, 107, 109, 116–17, 123, 127–8, 206; and FL, 85–90, 94, 106–7, 109, 114, 120–1, 128, 165; and Dorval, 94, 126–8, 207; and Rachel, 206–7; death, 228
Géricault, Théodore, 49
Gill, André, 230
Globe, Le, 57
Gobelins, Théâtre des, Paris, 236
Gobert (Mongobert), 89, 91
Goethe, Johann Wolfgang, 59
Got, Edmond, 96
Goubaux, Prosper, 52–3, 94, 188
Gozlan, Léon, 177, 178, 179
Grâce de Dieu, La (Dennery, Lemoine), 185–6
Grande Duchesse de Gérolstein, La (Offenbach, Meilhac, Halévy), 228
Grand-Théâtre, Strasbourg, 57
Grandville (Jean Gérard), 122
Granier de Cassagnac, Bernard-Adolphe, 134–5, 169
Gratry, Alphonse, 49
Grenoble, FL at, 129
Guise, Henri, Duc de, 64
Guizot, François, 163, 201
Gymnase, Théâtre du, Paris, 20, 164, 179, 183
Gymnase-Enfantin, Théâtre du, Paris, 186

Halévy, Ludovic, 210, 220
Hallignier, Julie, *see* Boulanger, Julie
Hallignier, Sophie, *see* Lemaître, Sophie
Hamelin, Admiral Jacques-Félix-Emmanuel, 17, 18

Hamlet (Shakespeare), 50, 87, 132
Hanska, Evelina, Countess Rzewuska, Mme, 177, 180, 188, 203
Hapdé, Augustin, 27
Harel, Charles-Jean, 71, 95, 102, 104, 239; and George, 72, 85–90, 94, 107, 108, 116–17, 123, 127–8, 206; and Dumas, 85, 88–90, 105–7, 108, 134, 163–4; and FL, 85, 87–90, 107, 113–15, 120, 123–8, 133, 136, 149–52, 173, 175–8, 180–1; and Hugo, 115–19, 123, 163–4; death, 206
Harel, Paul, 85, 95, 104, 105
Harel, Tom, 85, 86, 104
Haussmann, Georges-Eugène, Baron, 222, 227
Havre, Le, FL at, 14–17, 133, 134
Haymarket Theatre, London, 26
Hazlitt, William, 41
Heine, Heinrich, 136, 142, 158
Henri III, King of France, 64
Henri III et sa Cour (Dumas), 61, 62–5, 68, 72, 122, 220
Hernani (Hugo), 63, 69–71, 73, 135, 168, 204
Hertford, Marchioness of, 100
Hippodrome, Paris, 24
Holland, Louis Bonaparte, King of, 11
Homer, 215
Horace (Quintus Horatius Flaccus), 169
Horace (Corneille), 97, 162
Hôtel de Ville, Paris, 80, 82, 201
Hôtel-Dieu, Paris, 103
Houssaye, Arsène, 139, 140, 141, 212
Hugo, Adèle, *née* Foucher, 118, 148, 164, 165, 166, 167, 168
Hugo, Victor, 50, 51, 60, 63, 64, 68, 69–71, 73–4, 75, 94, 104, 115, 123, 135, 161, 163, 171, 178, 185, 189, 203, 213, 239; and Dorval, 93, 148–9, 164; and George, 116–17, 126, 134, 165, 206–7; and FL, 117–21, 164–70, 183, 187, 200, 204, 234–5, 237, 242, 243; on FL, 120, 165, 167, 169–70, 235, 242
Huguenots, Les (Meyerbeer), 162
Hussein, Dey of Algiers, 77

Iliad, The (Homer), 215
Illustrated London News, 193, 198
Irving, Sir Henry (John Henry Brodribb), 243, 244

Jadin, Louis-Godefroy, 122
James II, King of England, 77
Janin, Jules, 54, 85, 105, 155, 162, 179, 189, 197, 200, 212, 214
Jardin Turc (*or* Café Turc), Paris, 24, 25, 37, 55, 143, 162
Jeanne (insurgent), 110
Jenneval (Jean-Charles Lemoine), 216–17
Jerrold, Douglas, 52
Joanny (Jean-Bernard Brissebarre), 18, 21, 27, 33, 48, 63, 68, 71, 122
Johannot, Alfred, 122
Johannot, Tony, 122
Joly, Anténor, 163–6, 170–2, 174–5, 184–5
Journal des Débats, Le, 135, 162, 212
Journal des Théâtres, Le, 33
Jouslin de la Salle, Armand, 90, 147, 149
Jouy, Victor de, 87
Jullien, Louis-Antoine, 162

Kean, Edmund, 41, 50, 106, 152, 158–160, 169, 244, 245
Kemble, Charles, 50, 169
Kemble, John Philip, 244
Kock, Paul de, 80, 110

La Battut, Charles de, 100, 101
Labiche, Eugène, 148
La Bourdonnais, François-Régis de, 76
Lady Melvil (Grisar), 170–1
Lafarge, Charles, 190
Lafarge, Marie-Fortunée, *née* Cappelle, 190
Lafayette, Marie-Joseph, Marquis de, 82–3
Laferrière, Adolphe, 220, 222
Laffitte, Jacques, 110
Lafon (Pierre Rapenouille), 31, 32, 48, 51, 58
La Fontaine, Jean de, 221
Lalanne, Jean-Baptiste, 29
Lamarque, General Maximilien, 107, 108, 113
Lamartine, Alphonse de, 49, 178, 210–211, 237, 243
Larochelle (Henri-Julien Boullanger), 239
Lassailly, Charles, 174, 181
Laurent, Marie (Marie Luguet), 216, 232, 241

Laurent-Jan, 176

Lecomte, L.-Henry, 27, 46, 47, 224, 237–8, 239, 242

Lefebvre, Charles, 123

Legouvé, Ernest, 96, 188

Legrand, Paul, 206

Lekain (Henri-Louis Cain), 169

Lemaître, Antoine-Louis-Prosper, *alias* Frédérick, *passim. Plays*:

Abbesse des Ursulines, L' (Desnoyers, Mallian), 87–8

Alchimiste, L' (Dumas, Nerval), 171, 172

André Gérard (Séjour), 220

Andromaque (Racine), 187

Athalie (Racine), 35

Auberge des Adrets, L' (Antier, Saint-Amand, Polyanthe), 37–40, 41, 68, 102–3, 123–4, 136, 137, 138, 146, 150, 194, 198, 202, 214, 232

Barbier du roi d'Aragon, Le (Fontan, Dupeuty, Ader), 113

Béatrix Cenci (Custine), 126, 128

Bonne Aventure, La (Foucher, Dennery, Goubaux), 215–16

Cagliostro (Antony, Léopold), 43–4

Cardillac (Antony, Léopold), 41–2, 45

Chiffonnier de Paris, Le (Pyat), 198–200, 202, 214

Cocher de fiacre, Le (Benjamin, Ruben), 44

Comte de Saulles, Le (Plouvier), 225

Crime de Faverne, Le (Barrière, Beauvallet), 230, 240, 244

Dame de Saint-Tropez, La (Anicet-Bourgeois, Dennery), 190, 193, 198, 217

Docteur noir, Le (Anicet-Bourgeois, Dumanoir), 198

Don César de Bazan (Dumanoir, Dennery), 189–90, 191, 193–4, 217, 221

Faust (Béraud, Merle, Nodier), 59–60

Faux Ermite, Le, 29–30

Fiancée de Lamermoor, La (Ducange), 56

Fils de l'émigré, Le (Anicet-Bourgeois, Dumas), 113–14, 121, 135

Hamlet (Shakespeare), 87

Henri III et sa Cour (Dumas), 220

Homme à trois visages, L' (Pixérécourt), 35

Iphigénie en Aulide (Racine), 34, 87

Kean (Dumas), 128, 152–3, 156, 159, 161, 164, 191, 217, 240, 243, 245, 247

Lâche, Un (Touroude), 237

Lucrèce Borgia (Hugo), 116–21, 122, 123, 233

Maître d'école, Le (Meurice), 221

Malheur aux vaincus (Barrière), 232

Marchand de coco, Le (Dennery, Dugué), 221, 222

Maréchale d'Ancre, La (Vigny), 94

Marie Tudor (Hugo), 239

Marino Faliero (Delavigne), 65–7

Marquis de Brunoy, Le (Théaulon, Jaime, Dartois), 152, 153

Mère et la Fille, La (Empis, Mazères), 87, 88, 145, 186

Michel Brémond (Viennet), 198

More de Venise, Le (Cuvelier), 31

Mort de Kléber, La (Cuvelier), 31

Mystères de Paris, Les (Sue, Goubaux,) 187–9, 198

Naissance d'Arlequin, La (Hapdé), 27

Napoléon Bonaparte (Dumas), 89–91

Othello (Shakespeare), 87, 146, 149–150, 192–3

Ours et l'Enfant, L' (Cuvelier), 30

Paillasse (Dennery, Fournier), 212, 213, 217

Peblo (Saint-Amand, Dulong), 68

Père Gachette, Le (Deslandes), 228–229, 230

Portier du n° 15, Le (Beauvallet), 237

Prisonnier amateur, Le (Dartois, Decomberousse, Laloue), 45

Pyrame et Thisbé, 22

Richard Darlington (Dumas, Goubaux, Beudin), 94–7, 102, 106, 107, 132, 146, 212, 214, 222

Robert Macaire (Saint-Amand, Overnay, Antier, Alhoy, Lemaître), 123, 137–41, 144, 145, 146, 148, 149, 150, 151, 178, 181, 202, 204, 214, 243, 247

Ruy Blas (Hugo), 164–73, 184, 185, 186, 191, 194, 213, 214

Saltimbanques, Les (Dumersan, Varin), 224, 225

Sonneur de Saint-Paul, Le (Bouchardy), 220

Tour de Nesle, La (Dumas, Gaillardet), 105–7, 113, 114, 117, 122, 129, 146, 186

Toussaint Louverture (Lamartine), 210–11, 243

Tragaldabas (Vacquerie), 203

Trente ans (Goubaux, Beudin, Ducange), 43, 52–4, 58–9, 68, 94, 129, 132, 133, 186, 187, 194, 217, 218, 227, 231, 235

Trois derniers quarts d'heure, Les (Antier, Alhoy), 123

Vautrin (Balzac), 176–8, 180–1, 184, 232, 243, 244

Vêpres siciliennes, Les (Delavigne), 86

Vieil Artiste, Le (Lemaître, Chavanges, Decomberousse, Maillard), 45–6

Vieux Caporal, Le (Dumanoir, Dennery), 215

Voleurs et les Comédiens, Les (Dupeuty, Antier), 67

Zacharie (Rosier), 184, 189

Parts:

Achilles, 34

Adolphe, Comte, 29

Bazan, Don César de, 194, 241, 242

Bilboquet, 224

Buridan, Captain, 105–7, 115, 117

Cardillac, 42

Cenci, Francesco, 127

Darlington, Richard, 94–6, 132, 134, 241, 246

Faliero, Marino, 65–8

Ferrand, Jacques, 188–9, 198

Feuillantin, 237

Forestier, General, 232

Gachette, 229

Gennaro, 117–20, 123

Germany, Georges de, 53, 56, 58, 132, 231, 246

Guise, Henri, Duc de, 220

Jean, 198–200

Joseph, Père, 87

Kean, 156–60, 192, 241, 243

Macaire, Robert, 37, 39, 40, 56, 102, 110, 122, 123, 125, 136, 137–42, 144, 152, 165, 166, 169, 177, 181, 194, 201, 202, 224, 241, 242, 245

Mallorno, 31

Mephistopheles, 59–60, 141

Moravia, Duke of, 30

Napoleon I, 89–91, 129

Orestes, 187

Paillasse, 212, 246

Ravenswood, Edgard de, 56, 243

'Roule-Paris', 44

Ruy Blas, 165–6, 168–70, 189, 213, 241, 242, 243, 245, 246

Séraphin, Maître, 230, 240

Simon, Antoine, 215

Vautrin, 175, 177–80

Vivaldi, 35

Zacharie, 185

Lemaître, Antoine-Marie, 14–17

Lemaître, Caroline, *see* Thiébaut, Caroline

Lemaître, Charles, 130, 211, 220, 221, 231, 233

Lemaître, Frédérick, *see* Lemaître, Antoine-Louis-Prosper

Lemaître, Julien-Adolphe-Frédérick, 55

Lemaître, Louis-Napoléon, 131, 220, 221

Lemaître, Sophie, *née* Hallignier, 133, 173, 185; marries FL, 46–7; FL writes to, 46, 55–6, 57–9; writes to FL, 57, 130–1, 134, 154; parts from FL, 154; death, 231

Lemaître, Victor-Sophie, *née* Mehrscheidt, 14, 17, 20, 27–8

Le Poittevin, Alfred, 144

Lessing, Gotthold Ephraim, 45

Levesque, Mlle (actress), 36

Lévy, Michel, 210, 211

Liard (rag-picker), 199

Ligier, Pierre-Mathieu, 66, 67, 115

Linder, Anna, 238–9, 241

Lireux, Auguste, 212

Liszt, Franz, 104

Lockroy, Joseph-Philippe-Simon, 73, 90, 134, 135

London, FL in, 45, 58–9, 145–7, 193–4, 196, 198, 213; FL refuses to go to, 232

Louis XIII, King of France, 69

Louis XVI, King of France, 140

Louis XVIII, King of France, 18, 20, 64, 75, 82

Louis-Philippe, Duc d'Orléans, *later* King of the French, 62, 88, 108, 111, 121, 162; and Charles X, 64, 77, 82–3; crowned, 83; attempts on life of, 112, 116, 143; and FL, 140,

178–81, 225, 243; caricatured, 142, 178–80; dethroned, 201

Louvre, Palais du, Paris, 80, 81

Lowe, Sir Hudson, 90

Lucchesi-Palli, Countess, *see* Berry

Luguet, René (Dominique-Esprit Bénéfand), 208

Lune, La, 230

Lyceum Theatre, London, 145

Lyons, FL at, 129–30, 196, 205

Macready, William Charles, 50, 169, 191–3

Mademoiselle de Belle-Isle (Dumas), 171, 174

Maillard, Théodore, 54

Malibran, Maria-Garcia, 64

Marchangy, Louis-François de, 117

Marguerite de Bourgogne, Queen of France, 105

Mariage de Figaro, Le (Beaumarchais), 140, 243

Marie-Amélie, Duchesse d'Orléans, *later* Queen of the French, 65, 115

Marie-Jeanne (Dennery), 196, 207

Marie-Louise, Empress of the French, 17

Marie Tudor (Hugo), 134, 135, 207, 239

Marion de Lorme (Hugo), 69, 93, 121, 122

Marivaux, Pierre de, 63, 171

Marmont, Auguste - Frédéric - Louis-Viesse de, Duc de Raguse, 78–80

Marquis de Villemer, Le (Sand), 226

Mars, Mlle (Anne Boutet), 50, 63, 97, 126, 161, 246; and Dumas, 62, 72, 92, 122; and Dorval, 65, 71, 147–149; and Vigny, 68, 147; and Hugo, 69–71, 148–9

Marseillaise, La, 108, 202

Marseilles, FL at, 130, 135

Martignac, Jean-Baptiste Gay, Vicomte de, 76

Martin, Sir Theodore, 193

Marty, Jean-Baptiste, 36

Massacre de la Rue Transnonain, Le (Daumier), 137

Massacre de Scio, Le (Delacroix), 49

Matharel de Fiennes, Charles, 212

Mathurin, Rev. R. C., 60

Maurice, Charles (Charles-Maurice

Descombes), 33, 35, 39, 42, 72, 90 97, 115, 120, 156

Mauzin, Alexandre, 170

Mazères, Édouard-Joseph, 87

Méditations (Lamartine), 49

Mehrscheidt, Anne, *née* Baron, 27–8

Mehrscheidt, Frédérick-Charles, 14, 15

Mehrscheidt, Victor-Sophie, *see* Lemaître, Victor-Sophie

Meilhac, Henri, 210

Mélingue (Étienne Marin), 170

Mélingue, Mme, *née* Thiesset, *see* Théodorine, Mlle.

Mémoires de Pierrot, Les, 222

Menneval (secretary), 91

Menus-Plaisirs, Théâtre des, Paris, 232

Mercadet (Balzac), 181–3, 243

Mérimée, Prosper, 104

Merle, Jean-Toussaint, 44, 57, 58, 59

Méry, Joseph, 132

Meurice, Paul, 221, 235

Meyerbeer, Giacomo, 162

Michelangelo (Michelangelo Buonarroti), 215

Michelet, Jules, 221

Michelot, Théodore (Pierre-Marie-Nicolas Michelot), 30, 31, 48, 63, 70, 71

Mille Colonnes,Estaminet des,Paris,143

Milner, H. M., 52

Milton, John, 60

Mirecourt, Eugène de (Jean-Baptiste Jacquot), 93

Miroy, Clarisse (Clarisse Midroy), 197; becomes FL's mistress, 186; acts with FL, 187, 190, 194, 198, 213, 215; betrays FL, 216–17; last visit to FL, 233; death, 233

Misanthrope, Le (Molière), 97, 187

Moëssard, Simon-Pierre, 178, 202

Molière (Jean-Baptiste Poquelin), 32, 63, 65, 137, 181–2, 226, 247

Moltke, Helmuth Charles Bernard, Count von, 228

Monceaux, Château de, FL at, 211

Monde Dramatique, Le, 156

Moniteur, Le, 78, 180

Montgenet, Baron de, 57, 60, 66, 67

Montmartre Cemetery, Paris, 231, 233, 241

Montparnasse Cemetery, Paris, 208

Montpellier, FL at, 135

Montrond, Casimir, Comte de, 100
More de Venise, Le (Vigny), 68–9
Morey, Pierre, 143
Morgan, Lady, *née* Owenson, 49
Mortier, Marshal Adolphe, 143
Mounet-Sully (Jean-Sully Mounet), 242, 243, 245
Mourier, Jean-Joseph, 136
Musard, Napoléon, 102, 162
Musset, Alfred de, 13, 96, 122

Nain Jaune, Le, 229
Nanteuil, Célestin, 122
Napoleon I, Emperor of the French, 13, 19, 24, 76, 78, 82, 107, 111; and FL, 15, 17, 18, 89–91, 129; and Talma, 31; and Dumas, 62, 88–91; and George, 72, 90, 207, 228
Napoleon III, Emperor of the French, 217, 219, 222, 228, 234
Napoleon, Prince (Napoleon-Joseph-Charles-Paul Bonaparte), 228
Napoléon à Schoenbrunn, 109
Naptal, Mme (Gabrielle-Geneviève Planat), 220
National, Le, 76, 78
Nerval, Gérard de (Gérard Labrunie), 50, 69, 237
Nicolet, Jean-Baptiste, 23, 24
Nîmes, FL at, 135
Nisard, Désiré, 148
Noblet, Louise, 95–6
Noces de Pierrot, Les, 205
Nodier, Charles, 59, 60, 61, 113
Normanby, Constantine Henry Phipps, first Marquess of, 154
Notre-Dame de Paris, 77, 80
Nouveautés, Théâtre des, Paris, 79, 88

Odéon, Théâtre de l', Paris, 26, 37, 49, 50, 71, 72, 94, 116, 186, 226; FL at, 31–5, 46, 85, 87–91, 133, 150, 220
Odry, Jacques-Charles, 224
Odyssey, The (Homer), 215
Offenbach, Jacques, 220, 228
Ogresse Gorgia, L', 121
Oliver, Captain Robert Dudley, 16
Olivier, Mlle (actress), 36
Opéra, Paris, 49, 179, 235, 238
Opéra-Comique, Paris, 46, 164
Orléans, Ferdinand-Philippe, Duc d', 104, 163, 168, 179, 180

Orléans, Louis-Philippe, Duc d', *see* Louis-Philippe
Orléans, Marie-Amélie, Duchesse d', *see* Marie-Amélie
Orphée aux enfers (Offenbach, Crémieux), 228
Orsay, Alfred, Comte d', 146
Othello (Shakespeare), 31, 68, 87, 192
Ourliac, Édouard, 176

Palais-Royal, Paris, 33, 78
Palais-Royal, Théâtre du, Paris, 155, 224
Pandore, La, 44, 45
Panorama Dramatique, Théâtre du, Paris, 26
Paphos (Paris café), 25
Paradis des voleurs, Le (Lefebvre), 123
Paris, Commune de, 236
Paris, Congress of, 219
Paris, Louis-Philippe-Albert d'Orléans, Comte de, 201
Parlement, Le, 232
Patrie, La, 215
Pau, FL at, 135
Paulin, J.-B.-Alexandre, 182
Pearl, Cora (Eliza Emma Crouch), 228
Pélissier (manager), 145, 146
Pépin, P.-T.-F., 143
Père Goriot, Le (Balzac), 177
Père-Lachaise, Paris, 206
Périer, Casimir-Pierre, 104
Petit-Lazzari, Théâtre du, Paris, 223
Petits-Pères (Paris church), 46
Peuple constituant, Le, 204
Phèdre (Racine), 186
Philippe (Emmanuel-Philippe Lavillenie), 41
Piccini, Alexandre, 51, 60, 149
Pixérécourt, René-Charles Guilbert de, 36, 51, 53, 98
Planche, Gustave, 169
Plouvier, Édouard, 225, 237
Poilloüe de Saint-Mars, Anne-Gabrielle de Cisternes de Coutiras, Vicomtesse de, 103
Poisoners and the Victim, The, 193
Polignac, Prince Jules de, 76, 77, 78, 201
Polyanthe (dramatist), 37, 38
Pontmartin, Armand de, 70
Porel (Désiré-Paul Parfouru), 237

Porte-Saint-Martin, Théâtre de la, Paris, 41, 49, 68, 88, 92, 93, 108, 129, 134, 161, 163, 164, 184, 196, 222, 233, 236; FL at, 44, 51–7, 59–60, 65–7, 94–7, 102–3, 105–7, 113–21, 123–8, 149–51, 170, 173–181, 185–91, 199–205, 210–12, 215, 235, 239–40

Poulletier, Dr., 107

Précieuses ridicules, Les (Molière), 238

Prémaray, Jules de, 215

Presse, La, 169, 215, 221

Prince of Wales Hotel, London, 45

Provost, Jean-Baptiste-François, 104, 109, 195

Prudent (actor), 89

Pyat, Félix, 198–200, 202

Rachel, Mlle (Élisa Félix), 97, 162, 171, 186, 195, 200, 206–7, 208

Racine, Jean, 32, 34, 35, 65, 87, 162, 169, 187

Racine et Shakespeare (Stendhal), 49

Radeau de la Méduse, Le (Géricault), 49

Raphael (Raffaello Santi), 182

Raucourt, Achille, 124

Raucourt, Françoise, 28

Read, Louise, 238

Régnier de la Brière, François, 195

Reichstadt, Joseph-Charles, Duc de, 111

Rémusat, François - Marie - Charles, Comte de, 178

Renaissance, Théâtre de la, Paris, 164, 166, 170, 171, 172, 184–5

René (Chateaubriand), 49

Revue de Rouen, La, 131

Richard Coeur-d'Éponge (Balzac), 181, 182

Richepin, Jean, 242

Rigoletto (Verdi), 115

Ritt, Jean-Eugène, 239

Rochefoucauld, Vicomte Sosthène de la, 49

Rodogune (Corneille), 207

Roi s'amuse, Le (Hugo), 115–16, 119, 121

Roméo et Juliette (Deschamps, Vigny), 61

Rosa, Salvator, 189

Rosier, Joseph-Bernard, 184

Rossi, Ernesto, 240–1

Rossini, Gioacchino, 122

Rouen, FL at, 18, 131

Round the World in Eighty Days (Verne), 240

Rowlandson, Thomas, 95

Sacre de Charles le Simple, Le (Béranger), 76

Saint-Amand, Lacoste, 37, 38, 137, 151

Sainte-Beuve, Charles-Augustin, 148

Sainte-Élisabeth (Paris church), 206

Saint-Firmin, Ferré, 168

Saint - Germain - l'Auxerrois (Paris church), 221

St. James's Theatre, London, 193–4, 198, 213, 214

Saint-Joseph (Paris church), 217

Saint-Laurent (Paris church), 233

Saint-Mandé, FL at, 107

Saint-Marcel, Théâtre, Paris, 207

Saint - Martin - des - Marais (Paris church), 241

Saint-Merry, Cloître, Paris, 110–11, 113

Saint-Victor, Paul de, 221

Saint-Victor, Pension, Paris, 52

Salvini, Tommaso, 243

Samson, Joseph-Isidore, 65, 162, 195, 208, 226

Sand, George (Aurore Dupin, Baronne Dudevant), 52, 197, 200, 203, 226, 237

Sandeau, Jules, 169

Saqui, Mme, née Lalanne, 24, 28, 29, 44

Sarcey, Francisque, 229

Schneider, Hortense, 228

Scott, Sir Walter, 49, 56, 94

Scribe, Eugène, 153, 179

Séjour, Victor, 220

Senépart (manager), 35

Sens, FL at, 129

Serres (actor), 102, 103, 109, 136, 150

Serres (manager), 44

Sery, Guillaume-Antoine, 17

Seveste, Edmond, 208

Seymour, Lord Henry, 99–100

Shakespeare, William, 31, 49, 50, 61, 146, 230, 247

Siècle, Le, 212

Sifflet, Le, 240

Silvain, Eugène, 239, 243

Smithson, Harriet, 50

Société des Droits de l'Homme, 142

Soulié, Frédéric, 73
Souvenir de la nuit du 4 décembre (Hugo), 234
Souvenirs de Frédérick Lemaître (FL fils), 106
Stendhal (Henri Beyle), 49, 72, 139
Strasbourg, FL at, 57
Sue, Eugène, 122, 187, 188, 215
Surgeon's Daughter, The (Scott), 94
Sylla (Jouy), 87

Tabatière, La (Lemaître, Maillard), 54, 55
Tacitus, Cornelius, 211
Taillade (Paul Tailliade), 239
Talleyrand-Périgord, Charles-Maurice de, 18, 76, 82, 141
Talma, François-Joseph, 28; votes for FL, 31–2; compared to FL, 31, 37, 44, 57, 59, 87, 91, 132, 169, 211, 244; death, 47–8
Tamberlick, Enrico, 238
Tartuffe (Molière), 161, 181, 187, 212
Tattet, Alfred, 154
Tautin, Jean-Baptiste, 36
Taylor, Baron Isidore-Justin-Séverin, 60, 61
Temps, Le, 78
Teste, Jean-Baptiste, 201
Thackeray, William Makepeace, 156
Théâtre-Français, Paris, 26, 37, 48, 162, 172, 226; and FL, 61, 183, 195, 212; Dumas at, 62–5, 174; Vigny at, 68, 147–8; Hugo at, 69–71, 73, 115–16, 148–9, 187; and Dorval, 126, 147–9, 208
Théâtre-Historique, Paris, 206
Théâtre-Lyrique, Paris, 223
Théâtre-National, Paris, 212
Théaulon, Emmanuel-Guillaume, 152–153
Théodorine, Mlle (Rosalie-Théodorine Thiesset), *later* Mme Mélingue, 125, 187
Thiébaut, Caroline, *née* Lemaître, 59, 217, 220, 231
Thiébaut, Élie, 217, 231
Thierry, Édouard, 179
Thiers, Adolphe, 76, 78, 81, 82, 83, 141, 201, 236
Thirty Years of a Gambler's Life (Milner), 52, 218

Tigresse-Mort-aux-Rats, 121
Tissot, Pierre-François, 122
Toulouse, FL at, 130, 135
Tournemine, Pierre, 66, 68
Toussaint Louverture, 211
Troyes, FL at, 145
Tuileries, Palais des, Paris, 17, 104, 108, 121, 180
Turpin, Dick, 123

Ulbach, Louis, 230, 246
Univers, L', 68

Vacquerie, Auguste, 203–4, 211
Vampire, Le (Nodier), 59
Variétés, Théâtre des, Paris, 79, 101–2, 121; FL at, 152–3, 156–60, 164, 214–15, 224
Variétés-Amusantes, Théâtre des, Paris, 21–2, 24, 27
Vaudeville, Théâtre du, Paris, 79, 80, 153
Ventadour, Théâtre, Paris, 164, 192, 240, 241
Verdi, Giuseppe, 115
Véron, Louis-Désiré, 114
Vert-Vert, 163
Victimes cloîtrées, Les (Monvel), 88
Victoria, Queen of England, 194, 198, 213–14
Vidocq, Eugène-François, 123, 177, 178
Vielin, Nicolas-Florent, 155
Viennet, Jean-Pons-Guillaume, 198
Vigny, Alfred de, 50, 51, 60, 61, 63, 64, 68, 73, 74, 94, 161; and Dorval, 93, 126, 131, 147, 187
Villeneuve, Fernand de, 163, 170, 171
Voltaire (François-Marie Arouet), 26, 32, 206

Waldor, Mélanie, 91
Wales, Albert Edward, Prince of, 228
Wellington, Arthur Wellesley, Duke of, 49
West London Theatre, 58
William III, King of England, 77
Woman in White, The (Collins), 232
Worth, Charles Frederick, 219

Zaïre (Voltaire), 26